Corporate Governance and Disclosure in GCC Banks

EMERALD STUDIES IN ISLAMIC ECONOMY AND FINANCE

Series Editors

Muhammad Ismail
University of Veterinary and Animal Sciences (UVAS), Swat, Khyber Pakhtunkhwa, Pakistan

Ahmet Faruk Aysan
Hamad Bin Khalifa University, College of Islamic Studies, Qatar

In an era where the global economic landscape is constantly evolving, *Emerald Studies in Islamic Economy and Finance* contributes significantly to the academic discourse surrounding Islamic economy and finance, building on the rich heritage of Islamic economic thought while embracing contemporary perspectives and challenges. The series is also committed to fostering rigorous academic inquiry, promoting scholarly collaboration, and ultimately enriching the understanding of Islamic economics and finance in the global context.

Forthcoming titles

Islamic Finance and Ethical Entrepreneurship in Action: Pedagogical Case Studies *Edited By Omer Rafique*

Islamic Transformation of Conventional Finance and Economy: Navigating Opportunities, Overcoming Challenges, and Implementing Solutions *By Imam Uddin and Muhammad Zeeshan Farrukh*

Human Capital and the Economics of Talent in Islamic Finance: Theory, Ethics and Practice *Edited by Muhammad Bilal Zafar, Hussain Mohi-ud-Din Qadri, and Hassinan Ali*

Corporate Governance and Disclosure in GCC Banks: Islamic Perspectives, Empirical Insights and Policy Implications

BY

ABDULLAHI AWEIS ABU

Lusail University, Qatar

AND

HABIB AHMED

Durham University, UK

emerald PUBLISHING

United Kingdom – North America – Japan – India – Malaysia – China

Emerald Publishing Limited
Emerald Publishing, Floor 5, Northspring, 21-23 Wellington Street, Leeds LS1 4DL.

First edition 2026

British Library Cataloguing in Publication Data
A catalog record for this book is available from the British Library

ISBN: 978-1-80686-280-1 (Print)
ISBN: 978-1-80686-279-5 (Online)
ISBN: 978-1-80686-281-8 (Epub)

Printed and bound by CPI Group (UK) Ltd, Croydon, CR0 4YY

INVESTOR IN PEOPLE

To my dear parents, wife, and my children:
To all of you, I dedicate this book and thank you for all your love, support, and supplications.

Contents

List of Abbreviations

AAOIFI	Accounting and Auditing Organization for Islamic Financial Institutions
AC	Audit Committee
BCBS	Basel Committee on Banking Supervision
CEO	Chief Executive Officer
CIBAFI	The General Council for Islamic Banks and Financial Institutions
CSR	Corporate social responsibility
ESG	Environment, social, and governance
GCC	Gulf Cooperation Council
IAF	Internal audit function
IAH	Investment account holder
IFSB	Islamic Financial Services Board
IIFM	International Islamic Financial Markets
MENA	Middle East and North Africa
OECD	Organization for Economic Co-operation and Development
OLS	Ordinary least squares
PLS-SEM	Partial least squares structural equation modeling
R&D	Research & development
SSB	Shariah Supervisory Board

Chapter One

Introduction

Abstract

This chapter serves as an introduction to the book by offering a broad overview of corporate governance and disclosure. The chapter then discusses the research motivation and states the research aim and objectives. The chapter also presents the research questions and the research methodology adopted for the study. The chapter concludes by discussing the research limitations and outlining the structure of the remaining chapters in the book.

Keywords: Corporate governance; disclosure; Islamic banks; Shariah governance; Shariah Supervisory Board

1.1. Background

Effective corporate governance is a critical pillar of current business practices and the market environment (Ahmed & Chapra, 2002), providing a structure through which a company's objectives are set, the means to attain them, and the means to monitor performance (Smith, 2009). Additionally, disclosure and transparency are fundamental to the effective functioning of capital markets (Healy & Palepu, 2001). Disclosure helps propel economic growth, enhances investor confidence in the market, and improves overall firm value (Bushman et al., 2004; Cheung et al., 2007). This book provides empirical insights into the effect of corporate governance on the extent of disclosure by Islamic and conventional banks in the Gulf Cooperation Council (GCC) markets.

Research on corporate governance has received considerable attention over the last two decades (Al-Hussain, 2009; Baydoun et al., 2013; CIBAFI, 2017; Husted & Sousa-Filho, 2019; Ridwan & Mayapada, 2020). The corporate accounting scandals in the last two decades and the 2008 financial crisis have brought the issue of corporate governance to the forefront. During the late 1990s and early 2000s, the world witnessed a series of corporate accounting scandals,

Corporate Governance and Disclosure in GCC Banks:
Islamic Perspectives, Empirical Insights and Policy Implications, 1–9

doi:10.1108/978-1-80686-279-520261001

including Enron and WorldCom (Jizi et al., 2014; Okaily et al., 2019). As a result, investors all over the world experienced more than $7 trillion in stock and investor losses (Al-Hussain, 2009). The accounting scandals and the 2008 financial crisis seem to have shaken investor confidence in the markets and have generated significant research interest in corporate governance and transparency issues, especially in developed countries.

Besides research interest from the academic community, governments, regulatory agencies, and standard setters in many parts of the world have taken a keen interest in introducing new regulations and standards designed to enhance corporate governance and the level of disclosure in financial institutions, restore investor confidence, strengthen the financial institutions, and enact measures to prevent future financial crises. Many countries have introduced regulations requiring firms to enhance board and audit committee independence and to separate the roles of CEO and board chairmanship. Industry standard setters have also issued guidelines and standards for effective corporate governance practices. For instance, in the United States, Congress passed the Sarbanes-Oxley Act of 2002, which introduced extensive regulations to enhance corporate governance practices and require greater transparency and disclosure.

On the other hand, the Basel Committee on Banking Supervision (BCBS) has issued corporate governance principles for the banking sector, providing guidelines on various aspects of bank governance, such as the board of directors, risk governance, and the role of internal audits (BCBS, 2015). Additionally, BCBS has issued Basel III, which sets out a global regulatory framework designed to enhance the quality of banks' capital to make them more resilient while, at the same time, introducing more robust risk governance, liquidity management, and disclosure requirements (BCBS, 2010).

More recently,[1] BCBS updated its Pillar 3 of Basel III, which deals with disclosure requirements aimed at enhancing transparency in financial institutions, especially in areas related to risk governance, capital quality, liquidity management, and loss-absorbing capacity. These new standards and regulatory requirements underscore the importance of effective corporate governance in restoring market confidence and enhancing transparency and disclosure levels in financial institutions. The General Council for Islamic Banks and Financial Institutions (CIBAFI) and the World Bank highlighted in their landmark corporate governance study the importance of corporate governance and transparency for the banking sector in general and for Islamic banks in particular (CIBAFI, 2017).

While the study of corporate governance has gained notable prominence in developed countries, it is still in its early stages in many emerging economies and developing countries, including those in the GCC (Al-Hadi et al., 2019; Al-Hussain, 2009). There is a notable weakness in the practice, awareness, and research

[1] It is worth noting BCBS's disclosure requirements, which were first issued as Basel part III in 2010, underwent a number of revisions, with the most recently revised document (Pillar 3 Disclosure requirements – consolidated and enhanced framework) being issued by BCBS in March 2017.

pertaining to corporate governance in these countries. Research indicates that corporate governance deficiencies negatively affect the overall market environment and result in poor transparency (Al-Hadi et al., 2019). For instance, Ahmed and Chapra (2002) assert that, because of the poor corporate governance in developing countries, information asymmetry is more severe, market participants are less experienced, and regulations are ineffective.

In addition to the prevailing weak corporate governance environment in developing countries, Islamic banks face additional governance challenges and risks, such as compliance with Sharia principles and Sharia governance requirements (AlQassar & Ahmed, 2021; CIBAFI, 2017; Hasan, 2011). In addition to being subject to general governance requirements, Islamic banks are required to adhere to Shariah rules and principles. Shariah (Islamic Law) requires that Islamic banks avoid any dealing that involves *riba* (interest), *gharar* (uncertainty), *maysir* (gambling) and engage only in *halal* (permissible) transactions (Ghayad, 2008; Haniffa & Hudaib, 2007). Furthermore, Shariah principles promote *adl* (justice), *qist* (equity), *ihsan* (benevolence), as well as accountability and transparency (Hassan & Harahap, 2010). Shariah teachings also promote social welfare, environmental conservation and protection, and sustainable development (Aribi & Gao, 2010). This puts on Islamic banks additional responsibilities to establish governance mechanisms designed to ensure that Shariah principles are achieved, and their rules are strictly followed.

One of the key governance mechanisms for ensuring strict adherence to Shariah rules and principles is the Shariah supervisory board (SSB). The SSB is an integral part of Islamic banks' governance systems (Ahmed & Chapra, 2002; AlQassar & Ahmed, 2021; Hasan, 2011; Istrefi, 2020; Nathan & Ribière, 2007) and is expected to advocate for greater transparency and disclosure. Transparency is deeply rooted in critical Islamic values such as honesty, truthfulness, and accountability in front of God (El-Halaby & Hussainey, 2015). This raises the community's expectation from Islamic bank management in general and the SSB in particular to commit to full disclosure and promote greater transparency. However, several studies seem to suggest that, despite the presence of SSBs, disclosure is generally weak in Islamic banks (Aribi & Gao, 2010; Haniffa & Hudaib, 2007). This underscores the need for empirical research examining corporate governance and the level of disclosure and transparency in Islamic banks.

1.2. Research Motivation and Statement of the Problem

Weak corporate governance, lack of transparency, and information asymmetry were among the chief issues that led to the 2008 financial crisis and the financial meltdown that ensued. This has generated significant research interest in examining the role of corporate governance in firms and its impact on various firm policies, including information disclosure. As a result, extensive research has been conducted in developed countries examining the impact of corporate governance characteristics on the extent of disclosure (Barros et al., 2013; Chen et al., 2010; Cohen et al., 2004; del Baldo, 2012; Dey, 2005; Forker, 1992; Healy & Palepu, 2001; Hermalin & Weisbach, 2012; Htay et al., 2012; Huafang & Jianguo, 2007;

Husted & Sousa-Filho, 2019; Jensen & Meckling, 1976; Khan et al., 2013; Natarajan, 2007; Sacconi, 2012).

While the study of corporate governance has gained notable prominence in developed countries, relatively little research has focused on developing countries (Al-Janadi et al., 2012; Al-Shammari & Al-Sultan, 2010; Al-Zuhair, 2008; Aribi et al., 2019; Hassan, 2013; Rizk et al., 2008). Research suggests that there is a notable weakness in practice, awareness and research on corporate governance in many developing countries, including those in the GCC. Chapra and Ahmed (2002) argue that corporate governance is considered generally weak in most developing countries. They assert that financial institutions (including Islamic banks) are most affected by weak corporate governance in developing countries, given their greater number of stakeholders and higher systemic risks.

In GCC markets, numerous studies highlight a general lack of awareness among companies regarding the role and importance of corporate governance. For example, a 2008 survey by Hawkamah found that more than 53% of banks and companies in the GCC market were unable to define corporate governance properly (Smith, 2009). In addition, Al-Hussain (2009) finds a similar lack of awareness and misunderstanding of corporate governance concepts in Saudi Arabia (the largest GCC country), not only by managers and directors, but also by legislators, stockholders, and the public. There is also a dearth of research within GCC countries on corporate governance practices and their effect on disclosure (Farook et al., 2011). In particular, there is a notable scarcity of empirical studies examining corporate governance in Islamic banks (Ahmed & Chapra, 2002). Islamic banks are financial institutions conducting their transactions in accordance with Shariah principles (Nathan & Ribière, 2007). To implement a *Riba*-free banking model, Islamic banks have developed several Islamic financial contracts, including sale-based financing instruments and profit-loss sharing investment instruments. These Islamic financial contracts include *Murabaha, Ijara, Musharaka, Mudaraba, Salam,* and *Istisna.*

The Islamic banking industry is a major player in financial markets and continues to grow significantly. According to the Islamic Financial Services Board, the industry is currently valued at $3.06 trillion (IFSB, 2022). Additionally, the Standard & Poor's Global Rating report states that Islamic banks were expected to grow at a rate of 10%–12% during 2021 and 2022 (Reuters, 2021). The GCC markets, including Saudi Arabia, Qatar, and the United Arab Emirates, play a crucial role in the global Islamic finance industry and are expected to continue growing in the coming years (IFSB, 2022). Islamic banks are expected to play a vital role in social development and welfare (Aribi & Gao, 2010), leading them to prioritize disclosure and transparency to enhance their overall performance and value. Nonetheless, disclosure practices in Islamic banks are notably behind (Aribi & Gao, 2010; Aribi et al., 2019; Farook et al., 2011; Haniffa & Hudaib, 2007). A detailed corporate governance study by CIBAFI reveals that Islamic banks exhibit significant weaknesses in their Shariah governance and fail to provide sufficient disclosures, particularly concerning Shariah compliance issues (CIBAFI, 2017). This highlights the need for research focusing on examining the impact of corporate governance mechanisms on the level of transparency of

Islamic and conventional banks (Hasan, 2011; Hassan & Harahap, 2010). This book aims to fill the gap highlighted above and contribute to the improvement of corporate governance mechanisms and disclosures by Islamic and conventional banks at both the policy and theory level. The main motivation behind this book is to examine the impact of corporate governance on the extent of disclosure by Islamic and conventional banks in GCC markets. This study helps shed light on how improvements to corporate governance and the level of transparency impacts Islamic banks' performance and overall value. Furthermore, this study paves the way for future research focusing on the link between corporate governance mechanisms and disclosure in GCC banks.

1.3. Research Aim and Objectives

The main aim of this research is to examine the impact of certain corporate governance mechanisms (e.g., board of directors, audit committee, and Shariah governance) on the extent of voluntary disclosure by Islamic and conventional banks and to fill the research gap highlighted above and contribute to the improvement of corporate governance mechanisms and disclosures by Islamic and conventional banks at both the theory and policy level. Furthermore, the study aims to pave the way for future research focusing on the link between corporate governance mechanisms and disclosure in GCC-listed Islamic and conventional banks. The research objectives include the following:

- Critically analyze the literature on corporate governance and disclosure, focusing on the research conducted to examine their causal relationships.
- Explore and analyze relevant theories and provide a theoretical framework for this book.
- Develop an index for board effectiveness and internal control strength to perform an analysis and examine their impact on the extent of disclosure.
- Investigate the impact of corporate governance characteristics (board effectiveness, internal control strength) on the extent of disclosure.
- Examine the impact of bank- and country-level factors such as size, profitability, leverage, and regulatory quality on the extent of disclosure.
- Develop a disclosure index to measure the extent of disclosure by both Islamic and conventional banks.
- Determine whether there is a significant difference in the extent of disclosure by Islamic and conventional banks.
- Develop a Shariah governance strength score to investigate its effect on the extent of disclosure by Islamic banks.

The motivation for this research is to make original contributions to the effect of corporate governance on disclosure levels in Islamic and conventional banks across the GCC countries. The GCC markets have been selected for this study because the GCC countries share similar socio-economic structures and institutional norms, thereby providing a control mechanism and allowing the researcher to make meaningful comparisons (Abdallah et al., 2015; Haniffa & Hudaib, 2007;

Musleh Al-Sartawi & Reyad, 2018). Moreover, the GCC market was chosen because it is a crucial market for the Islamic banking industry and highly liquid, with significant growth potential (Musleh Al-Sartawi & Reyad, 2018; Smith, 2009). The total assets of the Islamic banking industry in the GCC markets are estimated at USD 1.6 trillion as of the year ended 2021, representing 53.4% of global Islamic finance assets (ISFB, 2022). There is a great need for more research focused on the region, given the limited studies addressing governance issues facing the Islamic finance industry (Ahmed & Chapra, 2002; Grassa & Chakroun, 2016).

1.4. Research Questions

In line with the research objectives outlined above, the main question that this book aims to investigate is: How do corporate governance mechanisms (e.g., board of directors, audit committee, internal audit, etc.) affect the extent of disclosure by Islamic and conventional banks in the GCC markets? More specifically, the study investigates the following sub-questions in relation to the above main research question:

- How does the effectiveness of the board of directors impact the extent of disclosure?
- Does the strength of the internal control environment affect the extent of disclosure?
- How does the strength of Shariah governance affect the level of disclosure by Islamic banks?
- How do board characteristics such as independence, size, and frequency of meetings affect the extent of disclosure by Islamic and conventional banks?
- Is there an association between internal control characteristics (e.g., audit committee size, independence, meeting frequency, financial expertise, and internal audit independence) and the extent of disclosure?
- Do firm- and country-level characteristics affect the extent of disclosure?

1.5. Research Methodology

In line with the above research questions and objectives and consistent with prior studies, this book makes certain research philosophical assumptions. From an ontological perspective, the study adopts an objectivist position, and epistemologically, the study takes a postpositivist approach. Moreover, the study adopts a quantitative method and a deductive approach for the research inquiry.[2] Accordingly, the study starts with existing theories relevant to the research questions and develops a set of hypotheses which are then tested using observable data in order to confirm or reject the theories (Bryman, 2016; Saunders et al., 2012).

---

[2] For further details on the research philosophical assumptions adopted for this study, see the Research Methodology Chapter (Chapter Five).

In undertaking the research inquiry, the study adopts archival research, performs content analysis, and uses secondary data on banks and countries. Following the methods most commonly used by researchers in examining the impact of corporate governance on disclosure (Al-Shammari & Al-Sultan, 2010; Aribi & Gao, 2010; Barako et al., 2006; Barros et al., 2013; Chen & Jaggi, 2000; Eng & Mak, 2003; Haniffa & Cooke, 2002; Haniffa & Hudaib, 2007; Hassan & Harahap, 2010; Jizi et al., 2014; Milad & Bicer, 2020), the study performs content analysis for data collection, utilizing the annual reports of a sample of 52 Islamic and conventional banks listed in the GCC countries. Annual reports are chosen to perform the content analysis because they contain highly credible information, are widely distributed (Rizk et al., 2008), and are most often used by researchers (Gray et al., 2001). Jizi et al. (2014) argue that annual reports are read by a wide range of stakeholders, including shareholders, stakeholders, and financial intermediaries. Barros et al. (2013) conclude that annual reports are used by various stakeholders to assess company performance. Content analysis requires the use of a coding mechanism or a checklist (Aribi & Gao, 2010).

Consistent with prior studies (Haniffa & Hudaib, 2007; Meek et al., 1995), this study develops a voluntary disclosure checklist categorized by information type. The disclosure index comprises a total of 70 disclosure items that relate to six subcategories, namely: (1) strategy and background; (2) corporate governance; (3) risk governance; (4) sustainability, value creation, and social responsibility; (5) Shariah governance; and (6) financial information. Under each category, subcategories are developed, and the related voluntary disclosure items are listed (e.g., existence of an audit committee, under the corporate governance category) in line with prior studies and applicable guidelines of standard-setting bodies for Islamic banks, such as the Accounting and Auditing Organization for Islamic Financial Institutions (AAOIFI). For further details on the disclosure index, see Table AI in the Appendix.

To examine the impact of corporate governance mechanisms on disclosure, this study first develops two indices: board effectiveness and internal control strength. The study also develops an index of Shariah governance strength (specific to Islamic banks), comprising the SSB and other Shariah governance-related characteristics. These indices, along with the underlying individual characteristics, are used as determinants in examining the relationship between corporate governance and the extent of disclosure. Regression analysis is undertaken to examine the impact of the main corporate governance indexes and the individual variables on the extent of disclosure.

1.6. Research Contributions to Knowledge

Research indicates that corporate governance is of enormous importance to the economy and information disclosure plays an important role in markets (Healy & Palepu, 2001). Moreover, a lack of transparency and information asymmetry can lead to a breakdown in capital markets (Healy & Palepu, 2001). This underscores the importance of studying corporate governance and its impact on various firm policies, including information disclosure by firms (Hidalgo et al., 2011).

Research exploring the impact of corporate governance on disclosure by GCC banks will have significant importance for several reasons. First, this research will be of great relevance to Islamic and conventional banks in GCC and will help shed light on corporate governance and transparency issues which exist in this important region, which is central to the global financial industry. Islamic banks in the GCC markets are on the rise and are growing at a rate higher than conventional banks (King, 2018).

Despite their significant growth, Islamic banks in the GCC have received little research attention when it comes to research exploring the link between corporate governance and disclosure quality. Most prior studies examining the relationship between corporate governance and disclosure appear to focus on developed countries and cover financial and nonfinancial companies. Moreover, even those studies that examine developing countries, such as those in the GCC, often use samples of nonfinancial companies and do not comprehensively examine various types of disclosure, including governance, risk, financial, and Shariah governance. This book seeks to fill this gap by examining the impact of various corporate governance mechanisms, namely, characteristics of boards of directors, internal control, and Shariah governance on the extent of disclosure by GCC Islamic and conventional banks. This study develops a disclosure index that comprises a comprehensive set of disclosure items, including financial and nonfinancial information such as strategy, governance, risk, environmental, social, and governance, and Shariah governance. For further details on the disclosure index, see Table AI in the Appendix.

Second, the study fills the current research gap by using various corporate governance explanatory variables, including the board, audit committee, internal controls, and Shariah governance. Moreover, the study develops and uses a corporate governance quality index in three main dimensions of corporate governance, namely, board effectiveness, internal control strength, and Shariah governance strength, to comprehensively examine their impact on the extent of disclosure. The results of this comprehensive study will inform academics and researchers in the field and highlight future research in areas that have not received enough attention or problems that require further study. For instance, this study paves the way for future research focused on the role of internal controls in strengthening the corporate governance environment and in turn enhancing bank transparency and disclosure.

Third, the research plays an instrumental role in raising awareness and contributing to good corporate governance practices in Islamic and conventional banks. The research informs investors, policymakers, standard setters (e.g., AAOIFI, IFSB, etc.), and regulators and sheds light on ways in which corporate governance and disclosure practices in banks can be enhanced.

Finally, the research findings can be used by Islamic and conventional banks to lead the way in adopting best practices in corporate governance and information disclosure, thereby setting a good example not only for the Islamic finance industry but also for the entire banking sector in the GCC. It is also important to note that the GCC markets (e.g., United Arab Emirates, Bahrain, and Qatar) are positioning themselves to become key players in the global financial industry and a hub of Islamic finance and banking. Moreover, the majority of the world's Islamic banks are in the GCC (Rizkiningsih & Dewi, 2015). Thus, it can be expected that the outcome of this research will be timely to make significant contributions – at both the policy and theory level – to the improvement of corporate governance and disclosure practices of both Islamic and conventional banks.

1.7. Research Scope and Limitations

While this research will fill a current research gap that exists in the GCC region regarding the impact of corporate governance mechanisms on voluntary disclosure, the research outcome will have a few limitations. First, the specific nature of the research and its focus on Islamic banks in the GCC region will limit the applicability and use of the results to other regions, such as banks in Western global markets. This is because corporate governance mechanisms employed by Islamic and conventional banks in the GCC and the environment in which they operate are different than those in the Western global markets.

Second, the sample size is relatively small, as the study focuses on Islamic and conventional banks in the GCC countries, which are estimated to be about 50 Islamic banks. Third, the scope of the study examines specific areas of corporate governance (i.e., board characteristics) and their impact on voluntary disclosure. While these are important determinants of voluntary disclosure, there are other important governance mechanisms that could have an impact on voluntary disclosure. These limitations will provide an opportunity for future expanded research on the subject.

1.8. Research Structure and Outline

This book comprises eight chapters. The book starts with an introduction, followed by a survey of previous studies and pertinent literature. Chapter Two provides conceptual background on corporate governance and voluntary disclosure. Chapter Three presents the theories most commonly used for corporate governance and voluntary disclosure and proposes a theoretical framework for this book. Chapter Four surveys the relevant literature and critically analyzes prior studies in relation to the research questions and the study's hypotheses. Chapters Five, Six, and Seven present the research data and findings. Finally, Chapter Eight analyzes the results and provides a way forward with a summary and conclusion.

Chapter Two

Corporate Governance: Conceptual Overview

Abstract

Consistent with the research aim and objectives, this chapter provides a conceptual definition and an overview of corporate governance, discusses the main corporate governance approaches and systems worldwide, and presents an account of the Islamic perspective on corporate governance. The chapter provides an overview of the literature on voluntary disclosure in both developed and developing countries; critically analyzes the types of disclosure; and investigates its role, importance, and costs and benefits.

Keywords: Corporate governance; disclosure; information asymmetry; Shariah governance; Shariah Supervisory Board

2.1. Introduction

Corporate governance has become one of the most important research topics in the modern corporate environment (Van Greuning & Iqbal, 2008). The corporate scandals of the 1990s, such as Enron and WorldCom, and the 2008 financial crisis have shaken investor confidence and have generated significant interest in corporate governance and its role in firms (CIBAFI, 2017; Tessema, 2019; Tricker, 2015). In fact, research indicates that corporate governance failure was the chief reason behind these crises (CIBAFI, 2017; Tarraf, 2011). These events have shown that even the world's most developed economies such as the United States can be vulnerable due to gaps in their corporate governance structures (Millar et al., 2005). Corporate governance is crucial because it provides the structure and arrangements for how powers of decision-making are shared among the constituents of the organization and how control over the firm's assets is allocated (Hart, 1995). Shleifer and Vishny (1997) argue that corporate governance provides protection to shareholders and assures them that they will receive a return

Corporate Governance and Disclosure in GCC Banks:
Islamic Perspectives, Empirical Insights and Policy Implications, 11–37

Published under exclusive licence by Emerald Publishing Limited
doi:10.1108/978-1-80686-279-520261002

on their capital. CIBAFI (2017) asserts that corporate governance enables firms to have stronger performance, better access to finance, and maintain lower risk profiles. Moreover, it helps reduce economic instability and increases the potential for long-term growth.

2.2. Corporate Governance: An Overview

2.2.1. Definition

Because there is no single definition of corporate governance, I reproduce herein the most common definitions of corporate governance in the literature. The Oxford English Dictionary defines the word "corporate" as "relating to a large company or group" and the word "governance" as referring to the "action or manner of governing a state or organization." A corporation can be defined as a large company authorized to act as a single entity and recognized in the law as such (Calder, 2008). The Merriam-Webster Dictionary defines "governance" as "the way in which a company is controlled by the people who run it." In general, corporate governance describes the actions or manners of governing a large company or group. The Cadbury Committee (1992) defines corporate governance as the system by which companies are controlled and directed. This definition broadly describes corporate governance as a mechanism for controlling corporations but fails to capture the key stakeholders or highlight the value aspect of corporate governance. Shleifer and Vishny (1997) state that corporate governance deals with the ways in which suppliers of finance to corporations assure themselves of getting a return on their investments. This definition takes a narrow view of corporate governance, focusing on the protection of shareholder interests, without accounting for the interests of other stakeholders within the firm such as employees, and the community.

John and Senbet (1998) define corporate governance as the ways in which stakeholders control the firm in accordance with established legal and regulatory arrangements. Aoki (2001) defines corporate governance broadly as the structure of rights and responsibilities among the firm's stakeholders. This definition affirms that corporate governance should be concerned with not only the shareholders but also the rights and responsibilities of all stakeholders, including employees, customers, suppliers, creditors, and the community at large. Choudhury and Hoque (2006) define corporate governance as the legal and organizational structures that look after the internal integrity of a corporation. This definition emphasizes the legal aspects of corporate governance and underscores the importance of establishing integrity within the firm.

The Organization for Economic Co-operation and Development (OECD) defines corporate governance as

> a set of relationships between a company's management, its board, its shareholders and other stakeholders. Corporate governance also provides the structure by which the objectives of the company

are set, and the means of attaining those objectives and monitoring performance are determined. (OECD, 2004)

The OECD's definition goes beyond shareholders, taking the broader view of the entities with a stake in the firm, and who influence corporate governance (Tricker, 2015). This definition emphasizes the central role that corporate governance arrangements play in the firm's strategy and decision-making process.

A more value-oriented definition of corporate governance has been offered by J. Wolfensohn, President of the World Bank. In an article published in the Financial Times on June 21, 1999, Mr. Wolfensohn stated that "corporate governance is about promoting corporate fairness, transparency and accountability" (Ahmed & Chapra, 2002, p. 13). The values advocated for under this definition (fairness, transparency, and accountability) are considered important under Islamic law and are also more attuned to the social responsibility that corporations owe to the communities in which they do business. From this definition, we can infer that transparency and the disclosure of information to stakeholders are central to effective corporate governance; corporate mechanisms such as the board of directors and ownership structure are significant aspects of transparency and disclosure.

van Greuning and Iqbal (2008, p. 31) define corporate governance in banks as "a set of relationships between the bank's management, its board, its shareholders, and other stakeholders." This definition underscores the importance of relationships in corporate governance and the structures that govern such relationships. It also broadens the role of corporate governance to encompass not only the shareholders but also other stakeholders (e.g., employees, community).

Because this research focuses on GCC Islamic and conventional banks, the researcher has adopted the last two definitions. Throughout this study, corporate governance should be understood to mean the set of relationships between the bank's management, board, shareholders, and other stakeholders and the mechanisms that promote corporate fairness, integrity, transparency, and accountability.

2.2.2. The Role of Corporate Governance in the Firm

Corporate governance plays a significant role at both the market and firm levels, has great importance to the economy (Shleifer & Vishny, 1997), and is central to economic development and social well-being (Claessens & Yurtoglu, 2012). For the financial services industry in general and the banking sector in particular, corporate governance helps ensure efficient, viable, and sustainable growth (Dusuki, 2011). Hasan (2009a) argues that corporate governance's primary role in the financial and banking sector is to ensure fairness, accountability, and transparency not only to shareholders but also to all stakeholders who have an interest in the firm. Corporate governance is even more important for the Islamic banking industry as it helps Islamic banks to not only provide a fair return to stakeholders but also assure stakeholders of the bank's compliance with Shariah rules in all its products, transactions, and operational activities (Dusuki, 2011; El-Tiby & Grais, 2015).

The role of corporate governance in the firm becomes even more critical, given the divergence[1] between the goals of the agents and those of the firm's principals, coupled with the inability of owners to write complete contracts and monitor management's behaviors at zero cost (Cheng & Courtenay, 2006; Hart, 1995). Corporate governance mechanisms, such as the establishment of an effective board of directors, help firms minimize the problems arising from agency problems. Effective corporate governance allows owners to monitor management and to restrict them from shirking their duties or using the firm's resources to advance their own interests (Durnev, 2003). Hart (1995) argues that corporate governance provides the mechanisms by which owners establish checks and balances and monitor management's behavior to ensure consistency with the firm's goals and to protect against self-enriching behavior. While it is practically impossible to specify by contract all actions by management, the firm's owners rely on corporate governance mechanisms to allocate decision-making powers and monitor management's behavior (Hart, 1995).

2.2.3. Corporate Governance and Information Asymmetry

The separation of ownership and control gives rise to information asymmetry, whereby management has more information than the owners of the firm. This creates the need for internal corporate governance mechanisms such as a board of directors (John & Senbet, 1998) to reduce information asymmetry and contribute to greater transparency. Researchers have found a relationship between poor corporate governance and information asymmetry. For instance, according to Ahmed and Chapra (2002), weak corporate governance leads to poor or non-existent disclosure quality. Bonazzi and Islam (2007) also suggest that poor corporate governance leads to market failures, non-existent markets, moral hazards, asymmetric information, incomplete contracts, and adverse selection, among other problems.

Information asymmetry is generally present when one party has access to private information that could help another party to make better decisions (Connelly et al., 2011). Information asymmetry (also referred to in the literature as the "lemon" problem) arises when there is a difference in the level of information available to managers and to the firm's owners (Healy & Palepu, 2001), which can result in moral hazards and adverse selection. According to Eisenhardt (1989),

[1] The extant literature discusses the conflict of interest which exists between the principals (i.e., owners) and their agents (i.e., management), a matter known in the literature as an "agency problem." For example, Jensen and Meckling (1976) extensively discuss the agency problem between principals and agents, asserting that the agent will not always act in the best interest of the principal and, therefore, the principal needs to establish appropriate mechanisms (e.g., incentives and monitoring) to minimize the agent's deviation from the principal's goals. Other pioneering studies in agency problems include Alchian and Demsetz (1972), Ross (1973), Fama (1980), Fama and Jensen (1983), Eisenhardt (1989), and Hart (1995).

moral hazard refers to the agent's failure to put in the agreed-upon effort. Adverse selection occurs when the agent misrepresents his/her ability or skills, and the principal cannot verify these skills or abilities due to information asymmetry (Eisenhardt, 1989, p. 61). Moreover, when managers have insider information that is not made available to the owners, owners cannot accurately evaluate the performance of managers or the value of the firm (Barako et al., 2006). This underscores the importance of information disclosure and the critical role it can play in minimizing these issues.

Durnev (2003) suggests that firms with effective corporate governance are likely to have greater disclosure and be more transparent to outside investors. Hidalgo et al. (2011) argue that a fundamental objective of corporate governance is to enhance transparency and reduce the information asymmetry which arises from the separation of ownership and control in the firm. Rizkiningsih and Dewi (2015) suggest that information asymmetry can be greatly reduced and agency conflicts existing between managers and owners be addressed through effective disclosure of information. In their multinational study examining the impact of corporate governance on the extent of disclosure, Beekes et al. (2016) conclude that better corporate governance enhances the level of disclosure and transparency in the markets.

Healy and Palepu (2001) argue that information asymmetry and a lack of transparency by firms can lead to a breakdown of capital markets. In their study, Healy and Palepu propose several potential solutions to the problem, including writing optimal contracts between principals and their agents, enacting governmental regulations requiring managers to fully disclose their private information, and employing intermediaries such as analysts and rating agencies to gain access to private information held by managers. These measures underscore the central role that information disclosure plays in reducing agency problems and enhancing the overall corporate governance environment of the firm. However, as noted earlier, corporate governance means different things to different people, hence the importance of shedding light on various corporate governance models and approaches. These are discussed in further detail in the following sections.

2.2.4. Corporate Governance Models and Approaches

A review of the extant literature reveals that different models of corporate governance exist in different parts of the world. The model adopted depends on various factors, including decision-making style, historical and institutional differences, culture, and regulatory environment (Clarke & Dela Rama, 2008; Freeman & Reed, 1983; Iqbal & Mirakhor, 2004; Morck & Steier, 2005; Ungureanu, 2012). For example, the Anglo-American model of corporate governance (practiced in the USA and the UK) is driven by value maximization, in which firm managers are expected to maximize shareholder value (Ungureanu, 2012). In contrast, Continental Europe (e.g., Italy and Germany) takes a broader and more inclusive approach where the company serves the interests not only of the shareholders but also those of employees, unions, business partners, etc. (Ungureanu, 2012). The Japanese corporate governance model is characterized by concentrated ownership and a strong tendency toward corporate control. It emphasizes the need to harmonize the interests of various stakeholders (suppliers, customers, banks, social groups, etc.) and ensures that the firm maintains long-term business relationships with its stakeholders (Ungureanu, 2012). The corporate governance models cited here illustrate two main approaches: the Anglo-American shareholder model and the broader and more inclusive stakeholder model.

2.2.4.1. The Shareholder Model of Corporate Governance

The shareholder model is considered the most widely used model of corporate governance, especially in the United States and United Kingdom (Hasan, 2009a, 2009b). Under the shareholder approach, the primary goal of the firm is to maximize shareholder value (Jensen & Meckling, 1976), and managers are expected to serve the shareholders' interest only (Iqbal & Mirakhor, 2004). This is the premise on which Anglo-American corporate governance operates, associating corporate governance with mechanisms designed to preserve and maximize shareholder value (Cheffins, 2013), provide greater legal protection, and ensure that actions and decisions of the managers are congruent with those of the owners. Williamson (1984) argues that the firm's corporate governance structures, such as the board of directors, should be designed to safeguard the investments of the shareholders.

Despite the widespread acceptance of the shareholder approach among researchers and practitioners (Hasan, 2011; Sacconi, 2012), a growing number of researchers hold the view that this approach presents a narrow perspective of corporate governance (Filatotchev, 2008) and limits the responsibility of the managers of the firm to shareholders only (Abdel Karim & Archer, 2013; del Baldo, 2012; Sacconi, 2012). These researchers assert that the shareholder model fails to serve the interests of other important constituents of the firm, such as employees, customers, suppliers, and the community at large. Under the shareholder model, managers are not viewed as stewards who should be acting in the best interest of the principals of the firm, but rather as self-interested opportunistic agents who have to be constantly monitored and controlled (Lewis, 2005). Due to these shortcomings, the stakeholder model of corporate governance has been proposed as a viable alternative to the shareholder model, as discussed below.

2.2.4.2. The Stakeholder Model of Corporate Governance

Researchers advocate for the stakeholder approach as a broader, more inclusive model that serves the various interests of all those associated with the firm. According to Freeman and Reed (1983, p. 91), the word "stakeholders" refers to any identifiable group or individual on which the organization depends for its continued survival. Sacconi (2012) broadly defines stakeholders as individuals or groups who have an interest and stake in the firm. Freeman and Reed suggest that a list of stakeholders should include shareholders, employees, customers, suppliers, lenders, and society. Murphy and Topyan (2005) argue that a firm's key stakeholders comprise shareholders, creditors, suppliers, clients, employees, and other parties. Abdel Karim and Archer (2013) posit a similar view and argue that the stakeholder approach to corporate governance serves the interests of stakeholders and shareholders equally. Under this approach, firms have a responsibility to promote the interests of all stakeholders including employees, customers, communities, and the environment, as well as the interests of shareholders (Hasan, 2011). Moreover, the stakeholder model of corporate governance holds the view that managers have a fiduciary duty to serve the interests of a firm's stakeholders and that all stakeholders are considered to have the right to participate in firm decisions which affect their interests (Iqbal & Mirakhor, 2004).

It can be argued that the stakeholder model of corporate governance is more consistent with Shariah principles and is, therefore, more suitable to Islamic banks. This is because the stakeholder model of corporate governance is broader, takes into consideration the interest and welfare of all stakeholders who have influence over the firm, and is more aligned with the Islamic approach to property rights and contract frameworks (Bhatti & Bhatti, 2010; Iqbal & Mirakhor, 2004). The following section provides an overview of the Islamic perspective on corporate governance and discusses relevant issues which arise in Islamic banks.

2.2.5. The Islamic Perspective on Corporate Governance

Several studies explore and shed light on the Islamic perspective of corporate governance (Abu-Tapanjeh, 2009; Ahmed & Chapra, 2002; Alam et al., 2017; AlQassar & Ahmed, 2021; Bhatti & Bhatti, 2010; Choudhury & Hoque, 2006; Farooq & Farooq, 2011; Grais & Pellegrini, 2006; Grassa & Matoussi, 2014; Hasan, 2009a, 2009b; Hasan, 2011; Iqbal & Mirakhor, 2004; Lewis, 2005; Mansour & Bhatti, 2018; Sakti & Tareq, 2016). In general, these studies suggest that many of corporate governance mechanisms, such as a board of directors, are applicable to Islamic banks, similar to their conventional counterparts (Hasan, 2009a, 2009b). However, there are fundamental conceptual principles which shape the Islamic perspective on corporate governance that ought to be taken into account in the governance of Islamic banks (Mansour & Bhatti, 2018). These include the concept of *Towheed* and Shariah law (Choudhury & Hoque, 2006; Hasan, 2009b; Iqbal & Mirakhor, 2004; Lewis, 2005). To understand these fundamental principles of the Islamic model of corporate governance, it is crucial that we shed light on the Islamic faith and contextualize some of the key principles and teachings which influence corporate governance. In this context, it is important to note that the main purpose of Islamic corporate governance is to achieve the higher Shariah objectives. The means through which sound corporate governance is established must be in line with Shariah rules and principles (Bhatti & Bhatti, 2010). The Shariah provides its followers a complete way of life with guidelines and teachings that govern all aspects of life, including relationships among people, their financial dealings, and material needs (Presley & Sessions, 1994). Islam values human relations above material possessions and aims to strike a balance between the material and spiritual needs of human beings (Van Greuning & Iqbal, 2008).

It is essential that Islamic teachings and ways of life are viewed holistically and embraced in their totality. Islam is an integrated code of life whose goals encompass the individual and the community not only in this world but also in the hereafter as well (Abozaid & Dusuki, 2007). Islamic teachings emphasize the importance of justice and equity, two key themes that are built into all Shariah rules and principles (van Greuning & Iqbal, 2008) and that are essential to understanding the Islamic perspective on corporate governance.

2.2.5.1. The Concept of Towheed

Towheed, which means the unity and oneness of Allah (God), is undoubtedly a fundamental and overarching concept which provides the epistemological foundation for understanding the Islamic perspective on corporate governance. *Towheed*, which represents the foundational ontology of the Islamic faith (Alam Choudary & Nurul Alam, 2013), is the belief that God is the Creator of mankind and Owner of wealth. People are vicegerents of God, entrusted with this wealth to manage and use it in accordance with the principles and rules of Islamic law (Presley & Sessions, 1994). Though scant, there have been studies which attempt to shed light on the fundamental concepts underlying the Islamic corporate governance model (Abu-Tapanjeh, 2009; Alam Choudhury & Nurul Alam, 2013; Choudhury & Hoque, 2006; Grais & Pellegrini, 2006; Hasan, 2011; Htay & Salman, 2013; Iqbal & Mirakhor, 2004; Lewis, 2005; Maali et al., 2006; Mansour & Bhatti, 2018; Obid & Naysary, 2016; Presley & Sessions, 1994; van Greuning & Iqbal, 2008).

Choudhury and Hoque (2006) undertake an epistemological approach to explore the foundational concept of the Islamic corporate governance structure. Their study emphasizes that the overarching epistemological foundations of Islamic corporate governance are that of the oneness of God and the unity of knowledge. In a similar vein, Lewis (2005) argues that Islamic corporate governance is shaped by two important elements, namely, *Towheed* and Shariah law, and the two together provide a framework for understanding the Islamic perspective of corporate governance. Wilson (2006) asserts that *Towheed* is the key principle governing business philosophy in Islamic finance and consequently significantly influences the Islamic perspective on corporate governance. Hasan (2009a) argues that under the concept of *Towheed*, people are vicegerents (*khalifa*) of God who are entrusted with the responsibility to stand for justice and to uphold Shariah rules and principles. Moreover, according to the concept of *Towheed*, all resources (including wealth) belong to God and humans are merely entrusted with the responsibility to utilize and manage these resources in accordance with the Shariah (Hasan, 2009a). This means that all people are accountable to God and will be questioned on how they have used the resources with which they have been entrusted. From the aforementioned studies, it can be understood that the implications of *Towheed* are critical in adopting appropriate corporate governance approaches for Islamic banks.

2.2.5.2. The Role of Islamic Law (Shariah)

Along with the concept of *Towheed*, the Shariah is central to Islamic corporate governance. The word *Shariah* literally means, "the way to the source of life" and technically means the legal system that codifies behavior called for by the Holy

Quran and Sunnah (Lewis, 2005, p. 14). Shariah is pivotal to Islamic corporate governance because it governs all aspects of Muslim life, including financial dealings, and provides specific teachings and rules to which Muslims should adhere (Abu-Tapanjeh, 2009; Ahmed et al., 2015; Lewis, 2005). As Muslims believe that they are accountable to God for all their actions (Wilson, 2006), they view it as a religious duty to ensure that their financial and business transactions are conducted in accordance with their beliefs (Grais & Pellegrini, 2006; Lewis, 2005).

Arguably, compliance with Shariah law is the single most important defining issue of the Islamic bank's identity. Abdel Karim (1995, p. 287) ascertains that the Shariah forms the basic ground rules with which Islamic banks must comply in all their financial transactions. Wilson (2012) argues that it is the responsibility of the Islamic bank to provide assurance to its customers and stakeholders regarding the bank's compliance with Shariah principles and rules. In fact, Islamic banks' going concern and their long-term survival are directly linked to their ability to assure their customers and the community that they adhere to Shariah rules and principles. Shariah principles require that Islamic banks avoid any dealings that involve *riba* (interest), *gharar* (uncertainty), and *maysir* (gambling) and that they engage only in *halal* (permissible) transactions (Ghayad, 2008; Haniffa & Hudaib, 2007).

The term *riba* literally means excess, addition, and surplus (Dusuki, 2011; van Greuning & Iqbal, 2008). According to Kahf (2006, p. 5), *riba* is defined as "any contractual increment in a loan or debt due to the element of time." A broader definition is provided by Jalbani and Shaikh (2009), who define *riba* as "any excess benefit derived on a loan over and above the principal." van Greuning and Iqbal (2008) define *riba* as any unjustifiable increase of capital which can arise from loan or sale contracts. *Gharar* (uncertainty) is defined as any element of chance involving asymmetric information, uncertainty, risk, or even speculation (Archer et al., 2009). *Gharar*[2] arises in situations where there is uncertainty about the fulfillment of the subject of the contract (Ahmed et al., 2015), for example, where one party to a contract has information concerning the subject of the contract which is not made available to the other party, or there is a situation in which neither the seller nor the buyer has control over the subject of the contract (van Greuning & Iqbal, 2008). *Maysir* (gambling) is defined as "any activity which involves betting whereby the winner will take the entire bet and the loser will lose his bet" (Dusuki, 2011, p. 183). Clearly, *maysir* is a zero-sum game which creates no wealth. Instead, it creates risks for the sake of risk in the hope of high gains (Archer et al., 2009).

---

[2] The literature indicates that *gharar* in economic transactions can take different forms. For example, it can be due to the non-existence of exchanged counter-values or lack of control by the parties over the subject matter to be exchanged. It can also be due to inadequacy or inaccuracy of information arising from a failure to disclose material information of the subject matter (Dusuki, 2011). Ahmed et al. (2015) suggest that the prohibition against derivative products such as forwards, swaps, and options is a contemporary example of *gharar*.

Of all the Shariah prohibitions noted above, avoidance of *riba* is considered the most crucial issue that distinguishes Islamic banks from their conventional counterparts. The prohibition of *riba* is considered unequivocal (Kahf, 2006), and those dealing in *riba* have been warned in the strongest terms both in the Quran and in the tradition of Prophet Mohammed (Pbuh). The Quran (2:275) says, "But God has permitted sale and forbidden riba." In another verse, the Quran (2:278–279) says:

> Believers! Have fear of Allah and give up all outstanding interest if you do truly believe. But if you fail to do so, then be warned of war from Allah and His Messenger. If you repent even now, you have the right of the return of your capital; neither will you do wrong nor will you be wronged.[3]

In one of his sayings, Prophet Mohammed (Pbuh) says: "The Wrath of God is on the taker of *riba*, its giver, its writer and its two witnesses" (Kahf, 2006, p. 5). These verses and prophetic sayings establish beyond doubt that dealing with *riba* has grave consequences in Islam and, accordingly, it is the religious duty of Muslims to completely avoid any dealings that involve *riba*. While there are many reasons mentioned for the prohibition of *riba*, one of the main ones noted in the literature is that it leads to injustices (Kahf, 2006) since it allows the lender to increase his capital without any effort (Presley & Session, 1994). Siddiqi (2002) argues that interest results in an unfair dealing, inefficient allocation of society's resources and increases inequality in the distribution of income. van Greuning and Iqbal (2008) assert that the purpose of the *riba* prohibition in Islam is to achieve social justice and equality and preserve property rights. Therefore, it is arguable that by prohibiting interest, Islam ensures justice and fairness in financial transactions (Presley & Session, 1994), preserves property rights, and protects them from exploitation (van Greuning & Iqbal, 2008).

Shariah principles promote *adl* (justice), *qist* (equity), *ihsan* (benevolence) as well as accountability, transparency (El-Halaby & Hussainey, 2015; Hassan & Harahap, 2010; van Greuning & Iqbal, 2008), fairness, and the general welfare of society (Azid et al., 2007). Shariah teachings also promote environmental conservation and protection, as well as sustainable development (Aribi & Gao, 2010). This places additional responsibilities on Islamic banks to establish mechanisms that ensure Shariah principles are upheld, rules are strictly followed, and violations are adequately disclosed and reported.

Several previous studies (AlQassar & Ahmed, 2021; Bhatti & Bhatti, 2010; Choudhury & Hoque, 2006; Farook & Farooq, 2011; Grais & Pellegrini, 2006; Hasan, 2009a, 2009b; Hasan, 2011; Iqbal & Mirakhor, 2004; Lewis, 2005) explore

---

[3] Quran (2:278–279). Translation was obtained from Al-Mowdudi, Syed Abul Ala in his Tahfeem Al Quran, available at http://www.islamicstudies.info/tafheem.php?sura=2andverse=274andto=281. For further details on the meaning of these verses, refer therein.

the Islamic perspective on corporate governance and offer a conceptual framework for understanding the Islamic model, especially the mechanisms for allocating decision-making powers within the firm and monitoring management's behaviors. The framework generally rests on three key pillars: a *shuratic* decision-making process, the institution of *Hisbah*, and the Shariah supervision process and religious audit. These three pillars are discussed in more detail below.

2.2.5.3. The Shuratic Decision-making Process

The existing literature offers a conceptual framework for the *shuratic* decision-making process and its role within Islamic corporate governance. The term *shura* refers to the process of engaging in mutual consultation during decision-making to reach the best outcome (Bhatti & Bhatti, 2010; Ishak & Osman, 2016). Choudhury and Hoque (2006) argue that the *shuratic* process represents the most significant institutional model of Islamic corporate governance and the systematic application of its epistemological foundations. In the *shuratic* decision-making process, all participants contribute their knowledge truthfully and justly in a consultative manner to make the best decision (Bhatti & Bhatti, 2010). *Shura* is vital to Islamic corporate governance, bringing together the firm's senior management, board of directors, shareholders, employees, and other stakeholders to enable effective decision-making (Hasan, 2011, p. 58).

According to Lewis (2005), the shuratic process is based on seeking consensus with roots in the Holy Quran and the teachings of the Prophet (Pbuh). In several verses of the Quran, the shura principle is described as the decision-making model for the Muslim community. For example, in verse 38 of the chapter of Al-Shura, the Quran states, "who obey their Lord and establish Prayer; who conduct their affairs by consultation, and spend out of what We have bestowed upon them." In his commentary on this verse, Al-Mowdudi explains that consultation is a crucial pillar of Islamic life, and failing to conduct the affairs of the Muslim community in a consultative manner that includes all those whose interests are involved is a violation of the Shariah law prescribed by Allah. Abu-Tapanjeh (2009) argues that the Islamic approach to decision-making extends beyond shareholders, requiring that all those affected (such as employees, customers, and the community) participate in decision-making.

2.2.5.4. The Institution of Hisbah

The institution of *Hisbah* is considered one of the most important governance and oversight bodies established by the early Muslim community during the Caliphate of Omar Ibn Al Khattab (Pbuh). *Hisbah* can be described as the process of verifying adherence to Islamic principles within an economy (Bhatti & Bhatti, 2010). Broadly, *Hisbah* refers to the act of enjoining good and forbidding evil (Shan et al., 2015), which includes overseeing and monitoring market activities and enforcing compliance with Shariah rules and principles. Central to *Hisbah* are accountability, transparency, and fair dealings among market participants, which collectively strengthen and contribute to good governance and are key goals of

Islam (Bhatti & Bhatti, 2010). According to Wittmann (as cited in Hasan, 2011, pp. 75–76), the institution of *Hisbah* plays a crucial role in the market by regulating and supervising activities such as controlling scales and prices, protecting measurement standards, ensuring accurate valuation of coins used in the market, and preventing fraud. It is important to note that while the above studies discuss the historical role of *Hisbah*, they do not elaborate on practical mechanisms for its implementation in contemporary Islamic banks operating in today's markets.

2.2.5.5. Shariah Supervision and the Role of the Religious Auditor

Wilson (2012) argues that an Islamic bank has a responsibility to reassure customers and other stakeholders that it complies with Shariah principles and rules. To provide adequate assurance, appropriate mechanisms must be put in place. To do this, Islamic banks establish Shariah Supervisory Boards (SSBs) whose main role is to monitor, oversee, review, and report on the bank's compliance with Shariah principles and rules. These boards are supported by Shariah auditors who conduct audits to verify the bank's adherence to Shariah principles and rules and report any instances of noncompliance.

The SSB plays a vital role in Islamic banks. For the SSB to operate effectively, governance arrangements must ensure their independence, confidentiality, competence, consistency, and transparency (Askari et al., 2011). However, current research highlights notable gaps between the ideal role expected of the SSB and its actual practice. Many studies point out significant issues related to the SSB's role in Islamic banks and their capacity to properly monitor Shariah compliance, as well as to ensure adequate disclosure and transparency – not only regarding Shariah violations but also concerning the nature and rationale behind the *fatwas* issued by the SSB. Askari et al. (2011) express serious concerns about the state and practices of SSBs. For instance, they note the approval of questionable practices by Islamic banks, such as *tawarruq*, and criticize the lack of transparency and standardization in issuing fatwa rulings. Farook and Farooq (2011) contend that *fatwas* issued by the SSB are often not disclosed, and there is insufficient transparency regarding the basis, evidence, and reasoning behind these fatwas. Moreover, their findings indicate that errors or controversies related to SSB fatwas are not publicly acknowledged by the SSB, which hinders transparency.

There is an important question regarding the independence of Shariah board members. Of particular concern is the role that Islamic bank CEOs play in the appointment of these members. Research shows that CEOs have a crucial role in selecting board members (Hermalin & Weisbach, 1998; Vancil, 1987). Farinha (2003) argues that managers' dominance over boards may limit independent members' ability to effectively monitor management's performance. These studies highlight how management influence can threaten the SSB's independence, potentially hindering its capacity to objectively and effectively oversee compliance with Shariah rules and principles. Farook and Farooq (2011) contend that when management appoints SSB members, it significantly undermines their independence and raises questions about their ability to independently monitor and report on management's adherence to Shariah principles. The compensation of

SSB members by the bank also impacts their independence. Farook and Farooq (2011) find that SSB members often receive substantial pay for their services, with some Islamic banks paying basis points per funds managed, which may incentivize them to favor Shariah opinions that maximize profitability.

In summary, while the studies cited here offer valuable insights into key aspects of Islamic corporate governance, more work is necessary to develop a comprehensive framework and a clear understanding of its components. Although the conceptual framework for Islamic corporate governance is an important step, significant challenges still exist in implementing this framework and transforming it into an operational reality within Islamic financial institutions. The existing literature indicates that, for the most part, the Islamic corporate governance model has not been successfully adopted, and Islamic banks continue to operate under conventional corporate governance structures and arrangements (Bhatti & Bhatti, 2010). One notable exception is Malaysia, where the central bank (i.e., Bank Negara Malaysia) and the Malaysian government have made significant progress in establishing governance standards and structures for the Islamic finance industry. This book aims to add to the existing literature and address the gaps identified above by exploring the corporate governance framework of Islamic banks and examining its influence on transparency and disclosure levels.

2.2.6. Corporate Governance and Culture: Important Considerations

Hofstede (1984, p. 82) defines culture as "the collective programming of the mind which distinguishes members of one society from another." Culture can also be described as the learned, socially acquired traditions, lifestyles, and sets of beliefs of society's members, including how they think, feel, and act (Harris, 1987, p. 6; Hofstede, 1980, as cited in Baydoun & Millet, 2000; Haniffa & Cooke, 2002). Hofstede argues that culture significantly influences how firms are managed, and because people's values, beliefs, and expressions vary from one country to another, it is essential that a firm's governance style aligns with the country's cultural values.

Culture is arguably a key factor explaining different models of corporate governance, such as the Anglo-American, Continental European, and Japanese models found around the world. Clarke and Dela Rama (2008) note that in economies like Japan and other Asian countries, cultural and social norms play a crucial role in business dealings, and the corporate governance model reflects these norms. Millar et al. (2005) argue that cultural factors are vital for understanding business systems, organizational modes, and strategies, including corporate governance structures. For example, the relationship-based culture in countries like Indonesia and Thailand has led to ownership concentration and family-dominated boards in many firms and banks, significantly influencing their corporate governance and decision-making. Claessens and Yurtoglu (2012) contend that Western corporate governance approaches, including decision-making processes and the roles and responsibilities assigned in developed nations, may not be applicable to other countries due to cultural and social differences. To illustrate this, the authors cite Muslim countries, emphasizing that corporate governance there must align with Shariah law, given its central role in many aspects of Muslim life.

2.3. Information Disclosure: An Overview

2.3.1. Definition

Disclosure means revealing information or making something known (Rizkiningsih & Dewi, 2015). Disclosure of information and transparency play central roles in capital markets (Bushman & Smith, 2001; Gul & Leung, 2004; Healy & Palepu, 2001), contribute to economic growth (Bushman et al., 2004), greatly enhance shareholder protection (Cheung et al., 2007), and are often the purpose of many corporate governance reforms (Hermalin & Weisbach, 2012; Shehata, 2014). For the banking industry, one of the most comprehensive disclosure requirements was introduced in 2010 as part of Basel III in response to the 2008 financial crisis (BCBS, 2010). The Basel Committee has issued Pillar 3 Disclosure Requirements – Consolidated and Enhanced Framework with the purpose of restoring investor confidence, strengthening financial institutions, and putting measures in place to prevent future financial crises. For instance, in response to the financial crisis of 2008, the Basel Committee on Banking Supervision (BCBS) issued Basel III, which set out a global regulatory framework designed to enhance the quality of the bank's capital to make banks more resilient while at the same time introducing more robust risk governance, liquidity management, and disclosure requirements (BCBS, 2010).

More recently, BCBS updated its Pillar 3 of Basel III, which addresses disclosure requirements aimed at increasing transparency in financial institutions, particularly in areas related to the bank's risk governance, capital quality, liquidity management, and loss-absorbing capacity. These new standards and regulatory mandates emphasize the importance of strong corporate governance and transparency in rebuilding confidence in the markets and improving the value and overall performance of financial institutions.

Disclosure is generally divided into two main categories: mandatory and voluntary (Cheynel, 2013; Nugraheni & Anuar, 2014; Rizkiningsih & Dewi, 2015). Mandatory disclosure refers to information provided to meet legal requirements (Hassan & Marston, 2010, p. 7; Shehata, 2014) and includes a minimum set of details that must be disclosed in annual reports (Ousama & Fatima, 2010). For instance, mandatory disclosure might include information required by accounting standard-setting organizations, government agencies (e.g., Financial Services Authority in the UK), or capital market supervisory bodies (Rizkiningsih & Dewi, 2015). Conversely, voluntary disclosure involves the optional sharing of information that is considered relevant for the decision-making needs of users in annual reports (Meek et al., 1995; Verrecchia, 2001). This means that disclosed information – related to the firm's strategy, governance, or financial status – should be useful to stakeholders and users of the firm's annual report (Chau & Gray, 2002) and appropriately tailored to meet their informational needs (Hassan & Rohayem, 2009). Furthermore, voluntary disclosure includes information beyond what regulators and other oversight bodies require (Donnelly & Mulcahy, 2008; Popa et al., 2009). In essence, regarding voluntary disclosure, the firm has the discretion to decide whether or not to disclose certain information (Meek et al., 1995). This book considers both voluntary and mandatory disclosure and develops a disclosure index based on previous studies to evaluate the extent of disclosure by Islamic and conventional banks within the sample.

2.3.2. Overview of Disclosure Types

Voluntary disclosure can be either financial or nonfinancial in nature (Cotter et al., 2011) and may be historical, current, or forward-looking (Akhtaruddin & Rouf, 2012). Financial information includes foreign currency data and stock prices, while nonfinancial information may involve strategic, corporate governance, CSR, and other value-added details (Cotter et al., 2011). Strategic information might include acquisitions and disposals, research and development, and general corporate updates. Other nonfinancial disclosures include governance, risk management, environmental and social responsibility, and, for Islamic banks, compliance with Shariah rules and principles. Because of their significance and relevance to Islamic banks, disclosures related to CSR and Shariah governance are discussed in more detail next.

The study of CSR has gained increased attention over the last two decades due to growing global awareness of social and environmental issues. CSR is generally defined as "the continuing commitment by business to behave ethically and contribute to economic development while improving the quality of life of the workforce and their families as well as of the local community and society at large" (The World Business Council for Sustainable Development, 1999). CSR involves extending the accountability of organizations beyond the traditional role of providing financial accounting to the owners of capital to ensure that the firm fulfills its fiduciary duties toward all its stakeholders (Rizk, 2006; Sacconi, 2012). To demonstrate this, the firm has to make comprehensive disclosures about its CSR program, including its social and environmental activities (Hassan & Harahap, 2010) as well as employee and customer issues (Gray et al., 2001).

More recently, CSR has been expanded to include comprehensive environmental, social, and governance (ESG) factors in the overall assessment of the firm's commitment to social responsibility (Bassen & Kovacs, 2008). As a result, investors placed greater scrutiny on the firm's environmental impact, social responsibility, and corporate governance (Gillan et al., 2011). ESG initiatives demonstrate that a firm not only delivers on its social and environmental commitments but also adopts good governance. These practices are important indicators for stakeholders (e.g., investors) when assessing firms or making investment decisions. The assessment considers the factors, criteria, and principles[4] accepted globally

---

[4] ESG principles have been developed by international bodies such as the United Nations Principles for Responsible Investing (UN PRI), and more than 800 firms and fund managers have become signatories of the UN PRI (Gillan et al., 2011), generating significant interest in disclosure and reporting of information about the firm's ESG initiatives (Eccles et al., 2011; Kolk & Pinkse, 2010). These principles touch on a number of environmental, social, and governance areas, such as compliance with gas emission regulations, workplace health and safety issues, and board effectiveness.

as indicators of the firm's sustainability, and the extent to which it successfully adopts and incorporates them into its business operations.

ESG has gained greater importance[5] due to increased customer awareness and concern about ESG issues. These customers are increasingly demanding that firms adopt stronger ESG policies and demonstrate sustainable ways of doing business. In particular, financial institutions have witnessed significant demand from customers for adopting strong ESG initiatives and incorporating ESG into their investment decisions. To do this, financial institutions adopt various strategies, including ESG screening (positive or negative), integration of ESG goals into the traditional financial analysis, community investing, and shareholder engagement (Ahmed et al., 2015). Recent events such as social unrest in the United States due to police brutality against communities of color coupled with worsening climate change and the COVID-19 global pandemic brought the ESG issue to the forefront, creating more momentum for socially responsible investing. More than ever before, investors are gravitating toward investment choices that align with their principles and moral values, thus leaving no option for firms but to make ESG an integral part of their business model. A study done by PwC[6] finds that 82% of the participants in the study suggest that ESG is likely to play an important role in their operational or investment decisions.

In addition to allowing firms to discharge their social responsibility, sound ESG policies enhance profitability and operational efficiency. For instance, studies suggest that there is a correlation between a firm's profitability, share value, and its commitment to ESG initiatives (Bassen & Kovacs, 2008; Camilleri, 2015; Eccles et al., 2011; Gillan et al., 2011; Kolk & Pinkse, 2010). Firms with strong ESG policies are valued more than those with low ESG performance (Eccles et al., 2011) and are perceived as more efficient than those with low ESG performance (Gillan et al., 2011).

An important aspect of the ESG initiative is transparency and full disclosure, because in order to make informed decisions, investors and other stakeholders need access to relevant and timely information about the firm's ESG initiatives and related risks and opportunities. While some improvements have been noted, research indicates that there is still a need for more relevant and timely ESG disclosures.[7]

---

[5] The ESG market has grown significantly over the years, with the total ESG assets exceeding $22 trillion in 2016, and continues to grow at a double-digit rate (Global Sustainable Investment Alliance, 2017).

[6] For further details, refer to the PriceWaterhouseCoopers (PwC) study at: PwC and the Urban Land Institute: Emerging Trends in Real Estate® 2022. Washington, D.C.: PwC and the Urban Land Institute, 2021. https://www.pwc.com/gx/en/industries/financial-services/real-estate/emerging-trends-real-estate/global-outlook-2022.html

[7] For example, a study done by the CFA Institute found that 61% of the respondents indicated that companies need to provide an annual report with a cohesive set of ESG indicators. Similarly, the majority (69%) of respondents indicated that the ESG disclosures provided by companies should be subjected to some level of audit or information verification measures.

In summary, it can be argued that despite the notable progress made by conventional financial institutions, particularly those in Western countries, Islamic banks are lagging in adopting strong ESG initiatives (Ahmed et al., 2015; Sadiq & Mushtaq, 2015). Research indicates that although Shariah principles promote sustainability, Islamic banks have made little, if any, contribution to adopting sustainable ways of doing business and incorporating ESG initiatives into their operations (Ahmed et al., 2015). It appears that repeated calls made by various stakeholders (e.g., the academic community) for Islamic banks to adopt ESG factors have fallen on deaf ears, and management in Islamic banks have yet to realize the value that ESG presents to their firms (Sadiq & Mushtaq, 2015). Even in countries such as Malaysia where Islamic banks are well established, ESG is seen from a very narrow window of engaging in charitable activities or donating to certain community projects (Hasan, 2011).

2.3.3. Shariah Governance Disclosure

Islamic banks have certain additional specific disclosures in order to fully comply with Shariah principles and rules. Compliance with these rules and principles is the main feature distinguishing Islamic banks from conventional banks. For the Muslim customer, compliance with the Shariah is a matter of religious duty, as Muslims are not permitted to claim any revenue or income earned in a manner that violates Shariah rules and principles (Kasim, 2012).[8] Accordingly, disclosing information about Shariah compliance is extremely important for customers and other stakeholders of Islamic banks and represents a significant strategic imperative, thus requiring sound and effective disclosure policies.

Besides the above disclosure requirements, Islamic banks have certain accounting and financial information which should be reported in their annual reports to discharge their duty of being truthful and transparent with their stakeholders. For instance, Baydoun and Willet (2000) highlight certain accounting information which is specific to Islamic banks that should be included in their financial reporting, including the treatment of unrestricted *mudaraba*, details of the sources and uses of *zakat*, as well as *qard hassan*. Other disclosures noted in the literature include the role and activities of the SSB, unlawful transactions, and profit allocations for investment account holders (IAHs) (Aribi et al., 2019; Baydoun et al., 2018).

Despite its importance, the disclosure of information related to the Shariah rulings issued by the SSBs of Islamic banks is significantly lacking. Farook et al. (2011) state that *fatwas* (religious rulings) issued by the Shariah scholars are not disclosed, their rationale not provided, and any errors or controversies caused by the rules are never acknowledged publicly. Moreover, there is a lack of transparency

---

[8] Shariah rules specify that such income has to be excluded from the bank's revenues, and the Shariah Supervisory Board must ensure that the income is donated to a charity (Kasim, 2012).

as to how Shariah scholars sitting on Shariah boards derive their religious rulings, and there is no consistent framework for issuing these rulings (Farook et al., 2011).

2.3.4. Disclosure in Developed Countries

The study of corporate voluntary disclosure has interested researchers for several decades, and numerous studies have been conducted in developed countries examining the extent of disclosure in annual reports (e.g., Alchian & Demsetz, 1972; Barrett, 1977; Belkaoui & Karpik, 1989; Buzby, 1975; Cerf, 1961; Cooke, 1989; Firth, 1979; Meek et al., 1995; Singhvi & Desai, 1971; Wallace et al., 1994).

Cerf (1961), one of the very early pioneers in the field of corporate disclosure, examines the characteristics of companies in the United States and the extent of their corporate disclosure as reported in their annual reports. In his seminal study, Cerf concludes that company characteristics such as size, profitability, and number of shareholders are positively associated with the extent of the firm's disclosure in their annual reports.

Barrett (1977) conducted one of the earliest cross-country studies on voluntary disclosure, comparing the disclosure levels of 15 firms located in each of the United States, Japan, the United Kingdom, France, Germany, and Sweden and 13 firms located in the Netherlands. The study reveals that of all seven developed nations examined, firms in the United States and the United Kingdom had the highest levels of disclosure. According to Barrett, this can be attributed to the more advanced level of disclosure requirements that exist in both the United States and the United Kingdom, compared to the other countries. Barrett also reports that France had the least amount of disclosure among all the countries examined, which the author attributes to the inefficiency of the French financial markets in the dissemination of complete and timely information.

Belkaoui and Karpik (1989) conducted an empirical study on a sample of U.S. firms and, using data for 1973, examined the association between corporate social disclosure and economic and social performance. Their study finds a significant positive relationship between social disclosure and social performance, suggesting that firms are eager to make disclosures and capitalize on social improvement programs in order to impress their shareholders. While the study finds a positive association between social disclosure and economic performance, this association appears to be insignificant.

Lang and Lundholm (1993) empirically investigate the determinants of a firm's chosen level of voluntary disclosure, sampling 732 U.S. firms using analysts' evaluations of disclosures as reported in the Financial Analysts Federation Corporate Information Committee Report. Their study finds a positive relationship between the level of disclosure and a firm's size and performance, suggesting that, overall, voluntary disclosures are higher for larger as well as better-performing firms. While their findings are consistent with the theories used in the study as well as those in prior studies, the study also reports that disclosure level decreases in relation to the standard deviation of the firm's return on equity.

Meek et al. (1995) study the impact of certain firm characteristics, namely, size, country/region of origin, industry, leverage, profitability, and international listing status on the extent of voluntary disclosure for a sample of 226 firms listed in the United States, the United Kingdom, and continental European (i.e., France, Germany, and the Netherlands) markets. The authors develop a comprehensive disclosure checklist consisting of 85 items of information, categorized into strategic, nonfinancial, and financial information. Using regression analysis, the authors find that company size, country/region of origin, and international listing status are associated with the extent of voluntary disclosure, but the influence of these factors differs by the type of information disclosed (i.e., strategic, financial, and nonfinancial). Based on their study, the authors conclude that overall, larger firms make significantly greater disclosures than smaller firms, and the extent of their disclosure is affected by country/region of origin as well as international listing status. For instance, the study finds that companies in oil, chemicals, and mining appear to provide greater voluntary disclosure of nonfinancial information (e.g., environmental-related information).

2.3.5. Disclosure in Developing Countries

While a significant amount of research has examined the disclosure practices of firms in developed countries as discussed in the previous section, similar research in developing countries is lagging, with a limited number of studies focusing on these countries (Ahmed & Nicholls, 1994; Akhtaruddin & Rouf, 2012; Alhazaimeh et al., 2014; Alnabsha et al., 2018; Chau & Gray, 2002; Chow & Wong-Boren, 1987; Milad & Bicer, 2020; Naser et al., 2002; Rouf, 2017; Singhvi, 1967; Uyar et al., 2013; Wallace, 1987).

Uyar et al. (2013) assert that disclosure practices in developing countries, including the GCC and Malaysia, are different from those in developed countries (e.g., North America and Europe) mainly because of cultural and regulatory factors. For example, the disclosure practices of companies in Asian countries are significantly influenced by the cultural environment in which they operate, which is characterized by collectivism and an aversion to uncertainty, resulting in less transparency and voluntary disclosure (Chau & Gray, 2002; Huafang & Jianguo, 2007). The regulatory environment in many developing countries is not well-developed (Uyar et al., 2013) and often lacks effective enforcement mechanisms (Ahmed & Nicholls, 1994). This has led some companies to fail to comply with mandatory disclosure requirements, let alone disclosing voluntary information (Ahmed & Nicholls, 1994; Uyar et al., 2013; Wallace, 1988). However, while voluntary disclosure in developing countries is weak when compared to that in developed countries, some studies do show a recent trend toward an increase in the level of disclosure due to improved corporate governance and regulatory environment.

Naser et al. (2002) conduct an empirical study using a sample of 84 companies listed in the Amman Stock Exchange for the year of 1998/1999 to examine the relationship between the extent of disclosure and firm characteristics. The variables used for this study include size, external auditor type (Big 4 vs non-Big 4), leverage, profit margin, and liquidity. Consistent with prior studies, the study finds a positive and significant relationship between firm size, auditor type, and profitability. However, the study also finds a significant negative association between liquidity and the extent of disclosure. A plausible explanation for this negative association is that firms with high liquidity ratios are not subject to information disclosure demands from banks and creditors, as their borrowing needs are fewer.

Haniffa and Cooke (2002) study the impact of corporate governance and culture on the extent of voluntary disclosure in Malaysian-listed companies. The corporate governance characteristics used in this study are non-executive board members, CEO duality, non-executive chairperson, cross-directorship, and domination of the board by family members. Ethnicity (Malay vs. non-Malay) and education (accounting or business-related degrees) are used as proxies for culture. The authors develop a disclosure checklist comprising 65 disclosure items and use content analysis to examine the annual reports of a sample of 167 Malaysian-listed firms for the year ended 1995. Their study finds that firms with a greater number of family board members tend to disclose less information, which is consistent with prior studies. The explanation is that there is less need for disclosure, as the family board members have access to information. The authors find significant negative associations between non-executive chairpersons and the extent of disclosure, indicating that firms with boards chaired by non-executive directors disclose less information. As the authors acknowledge, this is inconsistent with prior studies as well as agency theory predictions, which suggest that independent directors are in a better position to ensure checks and balances, monitor management, and promote greater disclosure effectively. The authors seem to suggest that the non-executive chairperson may be deriving greater benefit from the lack of disclosure; however, no convincing explanation is provided as to the nature of the benefits derived and to what extent this affects the non-executive chairperson's ability to promote greater disclosure.

Barako et al. (2006) investigate the extent of corporate disclosure in 43 companies listed on the Nairobi Stock Exchange. Their longitudinal examination considers three independent variables, namely, corporate governance attributes, ownership structure, and company characteristics (e.g., size, leverage, and profitability), in assessing the impact of these variables on corporate disclosure. Specifically, the study examines strategic, financial, forward-looking, social, and board of director-related issues, concluding that the independent variables influence the extent of corporate disclosure. These findings are generally consistent with those of similar studies conducted in developed countries. The conclusion drawn is that the variables that influence the extent of disclosure are the same in developed and developing countries.

In summary, it can be observed that disclosure in developing countries, including the GCC, is generally weak (Azid & Alnodel, 2019). The cultural environment in Asian countries tends toward secrecy and a lack of transparency (Millar et al., 2005), which accounts for some measure of that lack of disclosure. Moreover, incentives for transparency are lacking in comparison to their corporate counterparts in Western countries (Alhazaimeh et al., 2014).

Despite the prevailing weak disclosure environment in the GCC, some studies indicate an upward trend in the level of disclosure reported in annual reports. For example, Gul and Leung (2006), who study disclosure practices of a sample of 120 Chinese firms, find that disclosure among Chinese-listed firms is on the rise.

The authors attribute this to the changing cultural landscape, characterized by more openness to the information needs of Western investors. In a similar vein, Al-Shammari and Al-Sultan (2010) also report improvement in the extent of disclosure in the annual reports of Kuwaiti-listed companies, where their disclosure index has increased from 15% to 19% for the period between 2008 and 2010. Similar results are reported by Grassa and Chakroun (2016), who perform a study of GCC Islamic and conventional banks' corporate governance disclosure practices.

2.3.6. Importance and Benefits of Disclosure

A growing body of research emphasizes the importance and benefits of disclosure (Alhazaimeh et al., 2014; Allegrini & Greco, 2013; Barako et al., 2006; Botosan, 1997; Cheynel, 2013; Darmadi, 2013; Deegan, 2002; Diamond & Verrecchia, 1991; Forker, 1992; Gray et al., 2001; Hassan & Harahap, 2010; Healy & Palepu, 2001; Hermalin & Weisbach, 2012; Jensen & Meckling, 1976; Lang & Lundholm, 1996; Sengupta, 1998; Williamson, 1984). Disclosure is considered an important pillar of corporate governance (Shehata, 2014) and crucial to the effective functioning of financial markets (Healy & Palepu, 2001). A comprehensive corporate governance study done by the General Council for Islamic Banking and Financial Institutions (CIBAFI) and the World Bank finds that of all the corporate governance themes surveyed, transparency and disclosure has been ranked highest (74.5%), thus clearly underscoring the importance of disclosure for overall good governance of Islamic banks (CIBAFI, 2017).

Research indicates that disclosure can improve the firm's reputation, enhance its value, and bring economic benefits (Bushman et al., 2004; Gray et al., 2001; Hassan & Harahap, 2010). Firms with a well-designed disclosure policy are likely to have more analysts following (Healy & Palepu, 2001), enhanced liquidity (Darmadi, 2013), a lower cost for capital (Botosan, 1997; Sengupta, 1998), and reduced uncertainty and information asymmetry between management and owners, on the one hand, and management and the firm's various stakeholders (i.e., employees, customers, and community), on the other hand (Alhazaimeh et al., 2014; Allegrini & Greco, 2013; Lang & Lundholm, 1996). Lang and Lundholm (1996) suggest that firms with better disclosure practices attract analysts, improve the accuracy of market expectations, reduce information asymmetry, and limit market surprises. Information disclosures provide an important means through which managers can communicate to stakeholders, influence perceptions about their organization (Deegan, 2002), and enhance the firm's reputation and value in the market (Barako et al., 2006). Leuz and Wysocki (2006) suggest that voluntary disclosure improves market liquidity and enhances investment decision-making and the firm's overall corporate governance. Voluntary disclosure also helps reduce the cost of capital.

A number of prior studies (Botosan, 1997; Cheynel, 2013; Healy & Palepu, 2001; Lang & Lundholm, 1996; Sengupta, 1998) report a negative relationship between the amount and quality of disclosure and the cost of capital. For example, Sengupta (1998) investigates the link between a firm's disclosure quality and the cost of its debt capital, and the findings suggest that firms with overall greater disclosure are at lower risk of defaulting. The resultant reward is a lower cost of debt capital. Botosan (1997) examines the association between the firm's disclosure and its cost of equity capital and reports a similar negative association between disclosure levels and cost of capital.

Additionally, Popa et al. (2009) assert that voluntary disclosure enhances the owner's ability to effectively monitor management, reduces agency costs, restores investor confidence, and greatly reduces the information problem between owners and managers. Hermalin and Weisbach (2012) posit similar points, highlighting that increased disclosure reduces information asymmetry, which in turn reduces the firm's cost of capital.

Overall, these studies underscore the importance of disclosure and transparency in the market as well as the benefits realized by greater voluntary disclosure. In contrast, inadequate disclosure frequently leads to negative results. Forker (1992) argues that poor disclosure quality creates uncertainty and provides the potential for opportunistic behavior by management. Moreover, withholding information useful in decision-making leads to adverse selection problems, which in turn results in costs being incurred by the firm. Withholding or concealing information negatively affects the firm's value, as information users view the lack of information unfavorably, and accordingly discount the firm (Verrecchia, 2001).

2.3.7. Cost and Other Considerations in Disclosure

The extant literature indicates that cost is an important factor in management decisions regarding disclosure. Verrecchia (1983) describes the costs of disclosing information as the cost of preparing and disseminating information to the users, as well as the costs arising from the disclosure of proprietary information. Lang and Lundholm (1993) posit similar points and suggest that costs of voluntary disclosure arise from various sources, such as the direct costs of preparing and presenting the information, and the loss of proprietary information and any legal issues arising from possible litigation. Proprietary costs arise when information disclosed puts the firm at a competitive disadvantage, causes damage, or results in increased government regulations (Meek et al., 1995, p. 556). Meek et al. (1995) argue that of all the various types of costs considered by management (e.g., information processing and litigation costs), proprietary costs are most important to a firm's management.

Empirical studies suggest that the disclosure of proprietary information can cause significant damage to the firm, even in the case where the information disclosed is favorable (Verrecchia, 1983). For example, following the disclosure by the Chrysler Corporation's chairman about improvements in the company's value, the United Auto Workers responded by offering fewer concessions, thus harming the company despite the favorable information (Verrecchia, 1983, p. 182).

Due to the costs of providing voluntary disclosure, firm managers consider benefits in deciding whether to disclose information. Verrecchia (2001) argues that voluntary disclosure by firm managers is dependent on the associated costs and the effect on the current and future value of the firm. Accordingly, Verrecchia concludes that managers will choose to disclose information that enhances the firm's current and future value or market capitalization and withhold or delay disclosures that damage the firm or result in higher proprietary costs.

Besides cost considerations, cultural factors also influence firms' disclosure decisions. Chau and Gray (2002) argue that Asian firms are significantly influenced by the cultural environment in which they operate. Gibbins et al. (1990) argue that disclosure is affected by corporate culture and the attitudes of management. Using a sample of 20 disclosing firms, Gibbins et al. (1990) conduct interviews to examine the factors affecting the firm's decision process regarding disclosure. Their study reveals that in addition to external consultants and advisors, the firm's decision is influenced by internal and external factors, including corporate history, strategy, internal politics, and norms and attitudes. Gibbins et al. (1990) argue that the CEO's attitude toward disclosure has a significant impact on the position taken by others within the firm and, therefore, any change in CEO may result in changes in the firm's disclosure decisions.

2.3.8. Motivation for Disclosure

As noted by Meek et al. (1995), voluntary disclosure is the free choice of company management. This raises the following question: what motivates firms and managers of firms to make voluntary disclosures? Chow and Wong-Boren (1987) cite a number of studies (Holthausen & Leftwich, 1983; Watts & Zimmerman, 1986) which argue that one of the key motivations for firms to disclose information voluntarily is to manage and control the conflict of interests among the firm's various stakeholders, such as shareholders, debt holders, and management. Deegan (2002) argues that while there are many reasons why a firm may make voluntary disclosures (e.g., to gain competitive advantage, attract investors, win a particular award), the chief motivation is the desire to legitimize the firm's operations. Deegan (2002) and other studies which espouse the above view base their argument on legitimacy theory, which focuses on the role of information and disclosure in the relationship between organizations, the state, individuals, and groups (Gray et al., 1996). Deegan (2002) further argues that the very existence of an organization is tied to its legitimacy, which is enhanced by the organization's transparency and the disclosure of quality information to its stakeholders.

Previous research studies also indicate that strong financial performance creates the impetus for more transparency and the disclosure of more information (Belkaoui & Karpik, 1989). One explanation for such behavior is that during strong financial performance, management is keen to use voluntary disclosure as a way to enhance the value of the firm (Gibbins et al., 1990) and send a positive signal to investors, not only about the firm's current value but future potential as well. Ruland et al. (1990) posit a similar argument, noting that good news (i.e., strong performance) gives great impetus for managers to be more transparent and make more disclosures. Skinner (1994) argues that firm managers use voluntary disclosure (particularly when firms are performing well) as a competitive advantage to distinguish their firms from lesser performing others. Moreover, attracting investors and gaining access to funding, coupled with demands from the capital markets for greater transparency, provide additional incentives for firms to significantly increase voluntary disclosure (Meek et al., 1995). Graham et al. (2005) postulate that a firm's management is motivated to disclose information by the desire for greater clarity and better understanding of their firm. However, the authors also point out that the extent of voluntary disclosure is often hindered by concerns about revealing proprietary information and the inability to continue providing the same levels of disclosure.

While the motivating factors described here may be applicable to Islamic banks disclosing information to users, there are other important motivating factors specific to Islamic banks. Maali et al. (2006) argue that the main motive behind the Islamic banks' information disclosure is to demonstrate their compliance with Shariah rules and principles and to fulfill their accountability to God and the Muslim community. Maali et al. (2006) outline the three principles behind an Islamic bank's information disclosure:

1. To show compliance with Islamic principles, in particular dealing justly with different parties.
2. To show how the operations of the business have affected the well-being of the Islamic community.
3. To help Muslims perform their religious duties.

El-Halaby and Hussainey (2015) highlight the important role that the *taqwa* (God consciousness) dimension plays in motivating the Islamic bank's decision to disclose information. They assert that accountability to God, the desire to convey the truth, and fulfilling their religious obligations toward society give greater impetus for Islamic banks to disclose information.

2.3.9. Disclosure and Transparency: An Islamic Perspective

Transparency in Islam is rooted in key Islamic values such as honesty, truthfulness, and accountability to God, which Muslims are expected to adhere to as articulated in numerous verses in the Quran and in the prophetic tradition (Bhatti & Bhatti, 2010; Ishak & Osman, 2016). Lewis (2001) cites at least six verses in the Quran which emphasize the importance of full disclosure in a manner that is truthful, fair, and accurate. Choudhury and Hoque (2006) argue that the prevalence of transparency and business disclosure in Islamic financial institutions increases institutional effectiveness, enhances stakeholders' trust, and helps promote and expand their business. The AAOIFI states in its Financial Accounting Standard No. 1 that information disclosure and transparency play crucial roles in creating trust between the Islamic bank and its stakeholders and provide the investment community much-needed assurance about the Islamic bank's ability to achieve its objectives.

In order to understand the role of disclosure in Islam, it is important that we first shed some light on the relationship of the Islamic faith as a religion and its impact on Muslims. Unlike other religions, Islam does not recognize the separation between religious and worldly affairs (Abdel Karim, 1995; Lewis, 2005), and therefore, the main purpose of Islamic businesses (including Islamic banks) is to satisfy the will of God through their adherence to Shariah teachings and principles (Maali et al., 2006). Ousama and Fatima (2010) argue that Islam has a significant impact on the lives of Muslims, including business activities and disclosure of information. The authors further explain that transparency and disclosure of information are considered important higher purposes (*maqasid*) of the Shariah that are specific to financial transactions.

It is important to highlight that the types of disclosure made, the criteria used, and the extent of such disclosure are influenced by, and tend to be in harmony with, the philosophical and ethical principles of the society in which such disclosures take place (Baydoun & Willet, 2000). Abdel Karim (1995) asserts that Islam views commerce, including financial transactions, as a matter of morality and, therefore, subject to the principles and rules of the Shariah. Islam puts an emphasis on providing sufficient, truthful information and on making full disclosure of that information to allow market participants to make informed business decisions. Moreover, Islam encourages social accountability to the Muslim *Ummah*, whereby businesses and companies are obliged to be transparent and make full disclosure with regard to their business transactions in a manner that allows the community to make informed decisions while assisting management to fulfill their accountability to God and society (Ousama & Fatima, 2010).

Shariah teachings imply that Islamic banks make full disclosures about their business transactions and how these transactions are complying with Shariah rules and principles (Aribi & Gao, 2010; Baydoun & Willett, 1997; Farook et al., 2011; Haniffa & Hudaib, 2001; Maali et al., 2006; Ousama & Fatima, 2010). In line with these requirements, a number of standard-setting bodies for the Islamic finance industry have issued principles and standards concerning the disclosure of information by Islamic banks. These bodies include the Bahrain-based AAOIFI and the Malaysia-based Islamic Financial Services Board (IFSB). For instance, the AAOIFI requires that, generally, Islamic banks adequately disclose all material information necessary for users of the bank's annual reports to make informed business decisions (Abdul Raman & Bukair, 2013). The AAOIFI has issued financial accounting standards[9] which require Islamic banks to fully disclose, among other things, basic information about the bank (name, nature of business activities, financial products, and services), its financial information (e.g., assets, liabilities, revenues, expenditures, and financial ratios), and its compliance with Shariah rules and principles (e.g., gains from prohibited sources or methods, spending on prohibited activities, and ways in which illegal income is disposed).

2.3.10. Disclosure in Islamic Banks

Disclosure and transparency are of significant importance to Islamic banks. By being more transparent, the Islamic bank can gain the confidence of its

---

[9] For further details, refer to the AAOIFI's Statement of Financial Accounting No. 1: Objectives of Financial Accounting for Islamic Banks and Financial Institutions and the Statement of Financial Accounting No. 2: Concepts of Financial Accounting for Islamic Banks and Financial Institutions.

stakeholders, enhance its credibility, and earn greater acceptance from the community (Ariffin et al., 2007). Similar to conventional banks, Islamic banks have to comply with regulatory requirements and meet market expectations in order to remain competitive. However, in addition to that, Islamic banks have to comply with Shariah rules and principles, including the need for full disclosure and transparency. Therefore, it can be argued that Islamic banks have a greater responsibility in ensuring that they adopt effective disclosure policies. Moreover, the Islamic model of profit-sharing creates a greater need for the disclosure of information that will enable the bank's IAHs to monitor their risk exposures and make informed business decisions (Ariffin et al., 2007; CIBAFI, 2017).

Though limited in rigor, there is a growing body of studies found in the literature which examine information disclosure and transparency from an Islamic perspective (Abdallah et al., 2015; Abdul Raman & Bukair, 2013; Albassam & Ntim, 2017; Al-Shammari & Al-Sultan, 2010; Aribi et al., 2019; Ariffin et al., 2007; Baydoun & Willet, 1997; El-Halaby & Hussainey, 2015; Farook et al., 2011; Haniffa & Cooke, 2002; Haniffa & Hudaib, 2007; Hassan & Harahap, 2010; Maali et al., 2006; Meutia & Devi, 2017; Neifar & Jarboui, 2018; Rafay & Farid, 2018; Ridwan & Mayapada, 2020; Rizkiningsih & Dewi, 2015; Wan Abdullah et al., 2015; Zubairu et al., 2011). A review of these studies reveals overall that disclosure in Islamic banks is significantly lagging and, in some cases, very poor (Azid & Alnodel, 2019). Some of these studies are discussed next.

Haniffa and Hudaib (2007) conduct a longitudinal study to examine the ethical identity of Islamic banks and to determine whether there is a gap between the information communicated and the ideal ethical identity. Using a sample of seven Islamic banks in the GCC markets, they develop an ethical identify index and analyze the information communicated in the annual reports of the sample banks for the period from 2002 to 2004. The results indicate variations and inconsistencies between the information communicated and the ethical identities of Islamic banks. Furthermore, the researchers find that six of the seven Islamic banks examined scored below average on the ethical identity index, suggesting that Islamic banks are not disclosing sufficient vital information to support their compliance with Shariah principles or their commitment to social goals.

Aribi and Gao (2010) conduct a study to examine whether Islam influences the extent of CSR disclosures made by Islamic and non-Islamic financial institutions listed in GCC markets. While the authors find that Islam has an impact on the extent of CSR disclosure by Islamic banks since they disclose information about zakah, non-interest loans, etc., they also report that the extent of CSR disclosure by Islamic banks still falls short of fully discharging their accountability toward God and meeting their stakeholders' expectations.

Wan Abdallah et al. (2015) study the corporate risk disclosure practices of a sample of 424 Islamic and non-Islamic firms listed in the GCC markets. The study investigates the impact of certain firm-level determinants such as firm type (i.e., Islamic or non-Islamic) and quality of the corporate governance mechanism on the extent of corporate risk disclosure. Using content analysis and examining the annual reports of the sample firms, the authors find that Islamic banks make less corporate risk disclosure than their non-Islamic counterparts. The findings are consistent with previous studies (e.g., Ariffin et al., 2007; Farook et al., 2011; Maali et al., 2006), which also suggest that Islamic banks are lagging in their disclosure policies.

Wan Abdullah et al. (2015) study the determinants of voluntary corporate governance disclosure for a sample of 67 Islamic banks in Southeast Asian and GCC countries. Overall, their study reveals that the level of corporate governance disclosure in Islamic banks is below 40%, thus further confirming that voluntary disclosure in Islamic banks is significantly lagging.

Aribi et al. (2019) conduct a study to explore the extent of Shariah disclosures by Islamic banks and determine whether these disclosures are consistent with the expectations of Islamic bank stakeholders. Their study, which examines a sample of Islamic banks in the GCC and Malaysia, concludes that, overall, Islamic banks are lagging in their Shariah disclosures and fall short in fulfilling stakeholder expectations.

2.4. Conclusion

In summary, this chapter provides an overview of the main concepts, definitions, and existing literature on corporate governance and disclosure. Additionally, the chapter examines prior studies related to corporate governance and disclosure. With respect to corporate governance, the chapter presents an overview and examines the different models used in different countries while focusing on the two main approaches, namely, the shareholder and stakeholder models. The chapter also examines cultural and Islamic perspectives of corporate governance. In terms of information disclosure, the chapter explores different types of disclosure, cost and benefit considerations, the importance and motivation behind disclosure decisions, as well as the Islamic perspective on the importance of transparency and disclosure. The chapter concludes with a discussion of disclosure in Islamic banks and surveys some of the earlier studies which examine the extent of disclosure in Islamic banks.

Chapter Three

Corporate Governance: Theoretical Foundations

Abstract

Chapter Two discussed the main concepts, definitions, and existing literature on corporate governance and disclosure. The chapter analyzed the corporate governance models used in different countries and examined cultural and Islamic perspectives of corporate governance. The chapter also surveyed the different types of disclosure, cost and benefit considerations, the importance and motivation behind disclosure decisions, as well as the Islamic perspective on the importance of transparency and disclosure. The current chapter presents theories relevant to corporate governance and disclosure and develops an integrated theoretical framework based on the researcher's understanding of how corporate governance affects the extent of disclosure.

Keywords: Islamic finance; theoretical framework; agency theory; stakeholder theory; signaling theory; legitimacy theory; information asymmetry

3.1. Introduction

A theory can be defined as a set of ideas or related concepts which can be used to explain and understand an event, situation, or social phenomena (Matthews & Ross, 2010, p. 32). On the other hand, Bhattacherjee (2012) defines theory as systematic explanations of an underlying phenomenon or behavior. Neuman and Robson (2014, p. 56) posit a similar view and further illustrate that a theory is a system of interconnected ideas which provide the researcher insight, explanations, and directions for the research study.

Theories associated with corporate governance and disclosure are extensively discussed in the literature (An et al., 2011; Ayuso et al., 2007; Bonazzi & Islam, 2007; Clarke, 1998; Connelly et al., 2011; Cotter et al., 2011; Donaldson & Preston, 1995; Eisenhardt, 1989; Fama, 1980; Fama & Jensen, 1983; Filatotchev, 2008;

Corporate Governance and Disclosure in GCC Banks:
Islamic Perspectives, Empirical Insights and Policy Implications, 39–57

Published under exclusive licence by Emerald Publishing Limited
doi:10.1108/978-1-80686-279-520261003

Freeman, 2010; Hart, 1995; Hill & Jones, 1992; Hughes, 1986; Jensen, 2010; Jensen & Meckling, 1976; Kaler, 2006; Lazonick & O'Sullivan, 2000; Mansell, 2013; Mason & Simmons, 2014; Omran & El-Galfy, 2014; Ross, 1973; Safieddine, 2009; Sarker, 1999; Shehata, 2014; Trueman, 1986; Watts & Zimmerman, 1978). These theories are agency theory, signaling theory, stakeholder theory, legitimacy theory, political economy theory, resource dependence theory, and property rights theory (Cotter et al., 2011). While each of these theories sheds light on some aspects related to corporate governance and voluntary disclosure, the extant literature suggests that agency, stakeholder, legitimacy, and signaling theories are the theories upon which the study of corporate governance is predicated, thus providing a theoretical framework for understanding its impact on information disclosure (An et al., 2011). Accordingly, in line with prior studies and consistent with the research question, this research employs the four aforementioned theories to develop a comprehensive theoretical framework for understanding and explaining the impact of corporate governance on disclosure by Islamic and conventional banks. This study also considers the specific nature of Islamic banks and how these theories apply to such banks.

This chapter provides an overview of these theories and discusses in detail prior studies which have considered these theories while highlighting their applicability to this book. In the first section, the researcher defines and reviews agency theory, examines the separation of ownership and control, and analyzes the theory from an Islamic perspective. In the second section, the chapter looks at stakeholder theory and discusses its main themes as they apply to Islamic banks. The third section examines legitimacy theory and provides an account of earlier studies that have used this theory in relation to the research question. Finally, the chapter defines and reviews the key concepts underlying signaling theory while discussing relevant prior studies. The chapter concludes with a summary analysis of the theories and the theoretical framework adopted for this study.

3.2. Agency Theory

3.2.1. Definition and Overview of Agency Theory

Agency theory is the most widely accepted theoretical perspective applied to the study of corporate governance (Daily et al., 2003). It is used by scholars in various fields, including accounting, economics, finance, marketing, organizational behavior, and sociology (Eisenhardt, 1989). Agency theory provides a framework for understanding corporate governance issues which arise within the firm (Hart, 1995) and has been recommended for the study of corporate governance issues related to principal–agent relationships (Eisenhardt, 1989). In general, agency theory is concerned with the separation of ownership and control in firms (Bonazzi & Islam, 2007). In this theory, the firm is viewed as a nexus of contracts among individuals with conflicting objectives (Jensen & Meckling, 1976) where a framework of contractual relationships is created covering the way inputs are joined to create outputs and the way receipts from outputs are shared among inputs (Fama, 1980, p. 290). In agency theory, management acts as an agent of control for their stockholders (Al-Hussain, 2009), which creates an agency relationship between the management and the owners of the firm. Ross (1973) states that the agency relationship arises when one party, known as the agent, acts for or represents another party, known as the owner. Jensen and Meckling (1976) posit a similar definition, explaining that the agency relationship is contractual, in which one or more persons (the principal) engage another person (the agent) to manage the firm and make decisions on their behalf. Hence, managers have exclusive responsibility and the mandate to make decisions that maximize economic return for their principals (del Baldo, 2012). However, under agency theory, it is assumed that the managers and owners of the firm have different interests (Hill & Jones, 1992). Similarly, Healy and Palepu (2001) point to the divergent interests between principals and agents where agents engage in self-enriching activities such as shirking responsibilities or empire building (Barros et al., 2013). This conflict of interests creates an agency problem (Healy & Palepu, 2001). Besides the divergence of interests and goals, Eisenhardt (1989) suggests that there is also a divergence of attitudes toward risk, meaning that the principal and the agent may conflict over actions or business decisions due to their different risk preferences (Eisenhardt, 1989).

The separation of owners from managers within a firm may give rise to agency problems (Al-Hussain, 2009; Fama, 1980; Jensen & Meckling, 1976). Fama argues that a firm's principals are generally too diverse and are, therefore, unwilling to take any direct interest in managing the firm. Since the principals are not typically active in managing the firm, that role is left to managers (Healy & Palepu, 2001). As Shleifer and Vishny (1997) point out, a concern is whether managers direct the firm's finances properly or invest in unproductive projects, resulting in losses or misappropriations. In a similar vein, Hart (1995) suggests that in the absence of proper monitoring (e.g., by the board), managers may pursue their own goals at the expense of the owners of the firm, indulge in extravagant perks, engage in unprofitable investments, or undertake projects that are not aligned with the firm's values or goals. Additionally, Hart (1995) points out that without proper monitoring, managers may be reluctant to lay off poorly performing workers or perhaps assert themselves as the most effective persons to run the company when in reality they are not.

A number of remedies have been suggested by the literature in addressing or minimizing agency problems. For example, Jensen and Meckling (1976) suggest that in order to reduce agency problems, owners may introduce some incentives to managers and establish mechanisms for monitoring that limit any aberrations. Among the incentives noted in the literature are managerial ownership (Fama & Jensen, 1983), pressure from managerial labor markets (Fama, 1980), and optimal contracts (Healy & Palepu, 2001). Among the suggested ownership schemes are stock option grants, restricted stock grants, and long-term incentive payouts (Baker & Anderson, 2010). While these incentives may partially address the problem, they may not eliminate completely conflicts between managers and shareholders, especially if managerial ownership is insufficient or the cost of such schemes is greater than the wealth generated by managers (Baker & Anderson, 2010).

Eisenhardt (1989) elaborates on optimal contracts and classifies them into behavior-oriented contracts (e.g., salaries and hierarchical governance) and outcome-oriented contracts (e.g., commissions and transfer of property rights). With regard to monitoring mechanisms, the literature suggests that the board of directors[1] is the most important body entrusted with the responsibility for providing internal monitoring (Fama, 1980; Fama & Jensen, 1983; Jensen & Meckling, 1976). As part of their monitoring responsibilities, the board of directors oversees the hiring of executive management and often reviews and approves key firm actions and decisions, including disclosure policies. Accordingly, this study argues that an effective board of directors contributes to greater transparency and information disclosure. Other monitoring activities discussed in the literature include auditing, incentive plans, budget restrictions, and operating provisions (Boonyawat, 2013, p. 14). Regulatory authorities also influence firms and serve as a management monitoring mechanism through rules and regulations with which management must comply (Baker & Anderson, 2010).

Information asymmetry is another issue which arises from agency problems. Information asymmetry exists between two parties where one party (e.g., managers) has private information that is not available to the other who could potentially make better decisions if they had access to that information (Connelly et al., 2011). Managers in the firm are perceived to have more insider information about the firm and its activities than the owners (Htay & Salman, 2013). The private information available to managers creates the opportunity for them to abuse their power and pursue their own interests at the expense of the firm owners, thus resulting in moral hazards (Htay & Salman, 2013). Furthermore, information asymmetry can also lead to adverse decisions, such as hiring inexperienced managers or investing in unprofitable projects based on incomplete or misleading information (ibid.). Information disclosure is important for reducing information asymmetry between the owners and the firm's managers. With full disclosure of information, managers can demonstrate that they are working for the best interests of the firm's owners.

3.2.2. Agency Theory and Separation of Ownership and Control

The separation of ownership and control is at the center of the study of agency theory. The issues that arise from the modern diffuse corporate ownership structure are intimately associated with agency problems (Jensen & Meckling, 1976) and are the main reason why establishing corporate governance arrangements is necessary (John & Senbet, 1998). Hart (1995) argues that since it is impossible to write a complete and comprehensive contract between the owners and management, agency problems are bound to arise, thus necessitating governance structures to minimize problems. Hasan (2011) points out that agency problems have a long history in the literature, dating back to Marshall (1920), Berle and Means (1991), and Smith (2009).

[1]The oversight and monitoring roles of the board of directors are extensively discussed in Chapters Two and Four of this book.

In their seminal work, Berle and Means (1991) examine the separation of ownership and control in the firm. They argue that, because of the diffuse ownership in large corporations, control inevitably falls into the hands of management, who do not necessarily operate the firm in the best interest of its owners (Williamson, 1984). Berle and Means study 200 of the largest corporations in the United States and find that, due to the diffuse ownership, shareholders had no control, as the managers make all the important decisions in running the corporation. Popa et al. (2009) argue that dispersed ownership further complicates the agency problems that exist between owners and managers, as it becomes difficult and costly for the former to monitor the actions and decisions of the latter, whose motive is their own self-interest.

la Porta et al. (1999) note that Berle and Means' primary concern regarding the separation of ownership and control is widely shared in the research community and was further developed by the central studies done by Jensen and Meckling (1976). However, despite this acceptance, other research findings suggest that the diffuse ownership image of corporations given by Berle and Means applies chiefly to large public companies in the United States and may not be applicable universally. For example, la Porta et al. (1999) find that globally, concentrated ownership with controlling shareholders is the more common ownership structure than dispersed ownership with controlling management, particularly for medium-sized firms and for countries with poor shareholder protection. Bebchuk and Weisbach (2010) also report similar findings, which indicate that companies with controlling shareholders dominate publicly traded firms in most countries.

The conflicting implications from the above findings are important, given the focus of this study on banks in the GCC countries where concentrated ownership, especially by government or family, is common even among large firms. Clearly, one important implication is that such concentrated ownership results in agency conflicts not only between the managers and owners but also between controlling owners (e.g., government) and minority shareholders (Bebchuk & Weisbach, 2010). la Porta et al. (1999) raise an important question about how the agency conflict between controlling shareholders and minority shareholders can be reduced. They suggest a number of potential solutions, including improving the legal system to better protect minority shareholders. Greater disclosure is also cited as essential to resolving the agency conflicts noted above (la Porta et al., 1999).

Jensen and Meckling (1976) argue that agency problems arise because managers do not always act in the best interests of shareholders. Jensen (1993) posits that this conflict of interest results in costs that must be borne by both the agent and the principal. Jensen and Meckling argue that the agent and principal cannot ensure that the agent will make decisions that are in the best interests of the principal at zero cost. Jensen and Meckling (1976) identify three types of costs associated with agency problems:

1. monitoring expenditures,
2. bonding expenditures by the agent, and
3. the residual loss.

Barako et al. (2006) explain that monitoring expenses are those incurred by the principal in monitoring the agents. These include the cost of establishing the board of directors and setting up independent board members and committees such as the audit committee to monitor and oversee management. Bonding costs are expenditures incurred to ascertain that the agent does not act against the interests of the owners or to compensate for losses incurred from activities that are harmful to the principal's wealth (Boonyawat, 2013). Examples of bonding costs include resources expended by the principal in performing audits, establishing internal control systems, putting budget restrictions on management, and providing incentive compensation schemes to managers (Jensen & Meckling, 1976). Residual loss arises from the agent's sub-optimization of the welfare-maximization objective (Barako et al., 2006). Jensen (1994) argues that the costs associated with agency problems motivate both the principal and the agent to find ways to minimize these expenses. Implementing appropriate corporate governance mechanisms should reduce these costs (Al-Hussain, 2009).

Monitoring by the board is one of the most important aspects of corporate governance mechanisms (Bonazzi & Islam, 2007). Without effective monitoring, agents are likely to pursue actions that are not in the interest of the principals (Fama & Jensen, 1983). However, monitoring by the board (including independent board members, audit committees, and external auditors) can be costly, an important factor when addressing agency problems (Ahmed & Chapra, 2002). Accordingly, some researchers argue that an appropriate ownership structure is a less costly mechanism for reducing agency problems. For instance, Fama and Jensen (1983) argue that costs can be reduced by offering such incentives as managerial ownership to managers.

Fama (1980) suggests that the managerial labor market also provides a low-cost mechanism for disciplining management, thus reducing the problems that arise from the separation of ownership and control. Fama further argues that the past performance of managers should determine future wages and human capital potential, thus providing a market-based incentive to minimize deviation from their contract with the owners of the firm. For such market-based control mechanisms to operate effectively, it is crucial that firms and managers provide accurate information not only about the firm's financial performance but also about its management, employees, and strategic plans and goals. Thus, accurate information disclosure enables effective monitoring of management's performance while minimizing agency problems.

3.2.3. Agency Theory and Islamic Banks

Agency theory issues are generally applicable to Islamic banks. Islamic banks, like their conventional counterparts, have relationships which create problems that arise from the separation of ownership and control. The governance arrangements of Islamic banks resemble the modern corporate structure in which shareholders appoint a board of directors who are responsible for governance oversight and monitoring management, hence creating agency problems which are similar to their conventional counterparts. In addition to these general agency problems, Islamic banks have some specific additional problems, such as the rights of IAHs,[2] ensuring compliance with Shariah rules and principles and establishing an SSB to oversee Shariah compliance (CIBAFI, 2017; Safieddine, 2009).

Safieddine (2009) conducted one of the few studies that the researcher is aware of that examines how agency theory is different in the context of the Islamic banking industry. The study, which explores governance issues in Saudi Arabia, Kuwait, Qatar, Bahrain, and the United Arab Emirates, highlights issues that are unique to Islamic banks, which must comply with Shariah principles and rules. Safieddine (2009) finds that while Islamic banks recognize the importance of governance, they are weak in a number of crucial areas such as audit, control, and transparency.

Safieddine (2009) explains that the agency problems faced by Islamic banks are complicated by the nature and structure of Islamic banks, which necessitates particular examination. Two important issues are worthy of mention in this regard. First, unlike other banks where shareholder wealth maximization is the primary goal, Islamic bank management has a mandate to ensure compliance with Shariah principles and rules in all transactions. It can be argued that management may deviate from this mandate by engaging in noncompliant transactions in order to pursue their own interests. Second, since Shariah principles prohibit Islamic banks from dealing with *riba* (interest), a contractual relationship based on equity participation (*mudarabah* or *musharaka*) is created in which depositors do not receive interest payments but rather are entitled to a share of the Islamic bank's profits. Ahmed and Chapra (2002) argue that this equity participation structure makes the depositors in Islamic banks key principals and stakeholders in the bank.

Depositors in Islamic banks, known as IAHs, provide the largest portion of the bank's funds and hence have a significant interest at stake (Ahmed & Chapra, 2002). Understandably, IAHs are concerned about the bank's compliance with Shariah principles and rules; however, they have no control over management as they do not have voting rights or representation on the board. They are thus deprived of the monitoring rights afforded to the bank's shareholders. This results in unique agency problems where IAHs are exposed to risks without having control rights. Therefore, *mudarabah* IAHs are particularly vulnerable to significant agency problems when compared to their counterparts in conventional banks who enjoy a guaranteed return without risk (Alhammadi et al., 2018; Safieddine, 2009).

The contractual relationship between the IAHs and the bank is often based on a one-tier *mudarabah* contract, which is a partnership between a capital owner (*rabb al-mal*) and manager (*mudarib*) who manages the investment for the purpose of making a profit (Kahf, 2013, p. 151). Under the unrestricted *mudarabah*

---

[2] IAHs in Islamic banks are exposed to risks greater than those faced by normal depositors in conventional banks but do not enjoy the rights afforded to equity investors (e.g., voting rights). In an IAH arrangement, the customer deposits funds in a profit-sharing account, which gives the Islamic bank the freedom to invest the funds on behalf of the customer and share the profits with the customer based on pre-agreed ratios. However, losses are entirely born by the customer (Alhammadi et al., 2018).

contract arrangements, Islamic bank management acts as an agent for the IAH, with complete freedom to manage the investments. The profits are distributed based on a mutual agreement; however, the IAH is expected to bear all the losses. Under such contractual arrangements where the cash flows and control rights of IAHs are separate, Islamic bank management may exploit the opportunity by putting less effort into managing the investments, by reporting less profit, or by extracting personal benefits at the expense of the IAH (Safieddine, 2009). The agency problems between IAHs and the management of Islamic banks are compounded by the existence of information asymmetry whereby Islamic bank management has superior and private information about the bank's operations and activity that is not available to IAHs (Farook et al., 2011). These issues highlight the importance of information disclosure in Islamic banks in order to enable IAHs to effectively monitor bank management and exercise their rights to protect their interests (Belal et al., 2015; CIBAFI, 2017).

From this analysis, it can be argued that agency theory helps us understand the agency relationships within Islamic banks and identify unique agency problems (e.g., role of the IAH) that exist within Islamic banks and how additional governance mechanisms can be established to minimize these problems while addressing the concerns of the IAH. Safieddine (2009) and CIBAFI (2017) report several corporate governance mechanisms suggested by researchers, including board representation of the IAH, enhancements to the role of the Shariah supervisory board, and involving the IAH in the strategic management of the bank.

Though agency theory is one of the most important theories of corporate governance, it has been criticized for being too narrow and focused on the shareholders and on profit-maximizing goals. Clarke and Del Rama (2008) argue that agency theory is almost entirely focused on listed companies, which does not describe the majority of business organizations, as most businesses around the world are not listed in stock exchanges.

Market-based agency theory has also been criticized for not considering the interests of other stakeholders of the firm. These concerns gave rise to the call to adopt a corporate governance model based on stakeholder theory, which is discussed in the next section.

3.3. Stakeholder Theory

3.3.1. Definition

The Oxford English Dictionary defines "stakeholder" as "a person with an interest or concern in something, especially business." The literature provides numerous definitions with regard to the stakeholder concept. Freeman (1997) lists up to 55 different definitions for the term "stakeholder," found in academic literature in various fields. According to Freeman, the earliest definition of stakeholder, dating back to 1961, is attributed to the Stanford Research Institute, which defined stakeholders as "those groups without whose support the organization would cease to exist." The key concept is that stakeholders have a stake in the operation of the firm; they share a common risk as well as the potential benefits or losses which result from the firm's operations (du Plessis et al., 2010). Alkhafaji (1989) defines stakeholders as those groups who have a direct interest in the survival of the organization, and without whose support the organization would cease to exist. This definition limits stakeholders to those with a direct interest in the organization, which arguably excludes stakeholders with indirect interests in the organization, such as society. A more encompassing definition is offered by Freeman (1984, p. 91), who defines stakeholders as "any group or individual who can affect or is affected by the achievement of the organization objectives." This definition takes into account not only groups but also individuals as stakeholders in the firm. It goes beyond the limited goal of maximizing shareholder value to include other organizational objectives critical to the long-term success of the organization, such as looking after employees and giving back to the community where the organization is doing business.

3.3.2. Overview of Stakeholder Theory

Freeman (1984) suggests that the stakeholder concept can be traced back to Adam Smith (1795) and Berle and Means (1991). According to Clarke (1998), the history of stakeholder theory goes back to the origins of industrialism and its philosophical conceptions of cooperative movement and mutuality in the 19th century. However, the term "stakeholder theory" was first used in 1963. One of the most important contributions to stakeholder theory was made by R. Edward Freeman, a scholar of strategic management and business ethics. His groundbreaking book on stakeholder theory, titled "Strategic Management: A Stakeholder Approach" and published in 1984, is considered one of the most important works on the subject. Freeman explains that the stakeholder concept was introduced in the literature in an international memorandum by the Stanford Research Institute in 1963. The term was meant to refer to "those groups without whose support the organization would cease to exist." Stakeholders originally included shareholders, employees, customers, suppliers, lenders, and society (Freeman, 1984, p. 32; Hill & Jones, 1992). Hill and Jones state that each of the above stakeholders is a significant contributor to the firm's achievement of its objectives; in exchange, they expect the firm to serve their interests. Since then, scholars have published more than 100 articles about stakeholder theory, covering not only finance and economics but also other fields such as accounting, management, and business ethics.

More general and comprehensive than shareholder theory, which focuses on value maximization, stakeholder theory is held to be the main alternative to shareholder theory (Donaldson & Preston, 1995; Filatotchev, 2008). Stakeholder theory is viewed as more equitable and as creating value for the firm in the long term. While shareholder theory is solely concerned with profit maximization for shareholders, stakeholder theory advocates for profit maximization and long-term value for the firm that pursues the interests of other stakeholders such as customers, suppliers, employees, and the community. To illustrate this point, Freeman et al. (2010, p. 11) state:

> We believe that in order to maximize profits, companies need great products and services that customers want, solid relationships

> with suppliers that keep operations on the cutting edge, inspired employees who stand for the company mission and push the company to become better, and supportive communities that allow businesses to flourish.

Simply put, stakeholder theory is about how customers, suppliers, employees, financiers, communities, and managers come together to create value for the firm (Freeman et al., 2010). In the literature, stakeholders are divided into internal and external stakeholders. Internal stakeholders are classified as those who are directly connected to the company, such as employees, managers, and shareholders. External stakeholders are those who are not directly linked to the company but somehow have an interest in it, such as customers, suppliers, communities, and government entities (Htay & Salman, 2013).

One of the criticisms cited in the literature about stakeholder theory is the difficulty of aligning the goals of all stakeholder groups. However, research indicates that this can be done with a careful balancing act on the part of management to ensure that the interests of the various stakeholders are attended to. For instance, Donaldson and Preston (1995) argue that under the stakeholder approach, the corporation is seen as an organizational entity through which numerous and diverse participants accomplish multiple, and not always entirely congruent, purposes. Also, it is crucial that clearly established principles and values are put in place in order to ensure that the interests of all stakeholders are dealt with fairly. Phillips (2003) argues that stakeholder theory deals with organizational management and ethics, addressing morals and values explicitly. At the center of the discussion are key principles and values such as stakeholder fairness, which assert that firms engage in cooperative activities that generate benefits and fulfil obligations toward their stakeholders in recognition of the benefits generated by those stakeholders.

Kaler (2006) goes even further to suggest that corporations have obligations that go beyond their shareholders and, as such, should be run for the benefit of their stakeholders. The stakeholders have a morally legitimate claim to have their interests served by the corporation (ibid.). Omran and El-Galfy (2014) assert that to ensure their ongoing survival, organizations need to seek the support of their stakeholders and to adjust their corporate activities accordingly. Advocates for the stakeholder approach argue that equal priority should be given to all parties with legitimate interests in the firm (Donaldson & Preston, 1995). Hence, under the stakeholder approach, the interests of various stakeholders will gain prominence, and firms will be inclined toward greater transparency and better disclosure policy. Stakeholder theory is also more aligned with Islamic banks and the general objectives of Shariah (Hasan, 2011).

The analytical literature concerning stakeholder theory presents principles from four different aspects: descriptive, instrumental, managerial, and normative (Ayuso et al., 2007; Clarke, 1998; Deegan, 2002; Donaldson & Preston, 1995; Freeman & McVea, 2001; Phillips, 2003). According to Donaldson and Preston, the descriptive aspect of stakeholder theory sheds light on the nature of the firm and examines whether the observers and participants share that view of the firm. The instrumental aspect investigates the association (if any) between the practice of stakeholder management and a firm's performance. The managerial aspect of stakeholder theory is broader, offering recommendations with regard to attitudes, structures, and practices which can be adopted for the effective management of stakeholder interests (Donaldson & Preston, 1995, p. 70).

The normative aspect of stakeholder theory, which is fundamental to the theory, is chiefly concerned with the moral and philosophical guidelines for managing stakeholders. Under this aspect, the interests of stakeholders are viewed to be legitimate, with all stakeholders having intrinsic value. Managers are presumed to include all of these legitimate interests in their decision-making process (Donaldson & Preston, 1995). Deegan (2002) posits a similar point and emphasizes the responsibility of the organization to consider the interests of all its stakeholders. Under normative stakeholder theory, managers are accountable to all stakeholders, who have an equal right to be treated fairly (Fernando & Lawrence, 2014). Deegan (2002) notes that this theory is prescriptive only and does not directly predict managerial behavior. In contrast, the managerial aspect of stakeholder theory emphasizes the need to manage particular stakeholders who are critical to the survival of the organization (Deegan, 2002). The more powerful the stakeholders are, the greater the effort by management to meet their expectations (Fernando & Lawrence, 2014).

While stakeholder theory has received significant attention and much has been written in its favor, the theory is not without criticism. The theory has been criticized for being too broad, giving arbitrary powers to managers and encroaching on the rights of shareholders (Iqbal & Mirakhor, 2004). Jensen (2010) argues that the theory has been used to justify and provide an excuse for managerial opportunism. According to Kaler (2006), opponents of the stakeholder approach argue that companies are the properties of shareholders, and therefore requiring them to benefit other stakeholders violates property rights and constitutes a breach of trust toward shareholders. Iqbal and Mirakhor (2004) posit a similar argument, noting that proponents of stakeholder theory fail to provide convincing evidence for why a firm's management should look after the interest of all stakeholders and why stakeholders should participate in decision-making and control of the firm. Another claim against the stakeholder approach is that it opens loopholes which allow managers to advance their own interests. This argument asserts that stakeholder theory gives managers arbitrary power to decide what is of social interest or act in the public's best interests (Clarke, 1998).

3.3.3. Stakeholder Theory and Corporate Governance

Stakeholder theory helps us understand how corporations are governed and how corporate decision-making powers are shared among various stakeholders, including shareholders, employees, customers, and the community. As noted earlier, stakeholder theory asserts that, in addition to shareholders, organizations must take into account the interests of other stakeholders and develop effective strategies for managing those relationships whose interests may be different and sometimes irreconcilable (Islam & Kokubu, 2018). One of the key issues at the center of the stakeholder model is whether all stakeholders are regarded equally or whether some have higher rights and claims to the corporation than others. Jensen (2010) argues that it is unproductive to frame the discussion around groups of stakeholders. Rather, he suggests that the focus should be on corporate behavior, determining what behavior will result in the optimal use of society's limited resources with the least social waste.

3.3.4. Stakeholder Theory and Disclosure

Stakeholder theory maintains that firms are accountable to their stakeholders and are responsible for reporting their performance to these stakeholders. According to Alam (2006), stakeholder theory requires the firm to disclose social, environmental, and financial information to all stakeholders, keeping them well-informed about the firm's operation. Through voluntary disclosure, firms can attract investors, enhance employee retention, and gain access to new markets or customers (Fernando & Lawrence, 2014).

A substantial body of the literature suggests that stakeholder theory provides valuable insights into the disclosure practices of firms (Ayuso et al., 2007; Ching & Gerab, 2017; Chiu & Wang, 2015; Farook et al., 2011; Islam & Deegan, 2008). For instance, Chiu and Wang (2015) use stakeholder theory to study the determinants of social disclosure quality for a sample of 246 listed firms in Taiwan. In their study, the researchers tested stakeholder theory empirically to explain the quality of information disclosure in an emerging economy. Their results suggest that certain characteristics, such as the stakeholder's power, strategic position, and economic resources, influence the quality of information disclosure, thus lending support to the relevance of stakeholder theory to corporate governance and voluntary disclosure.

A question arises as to whether the firm should disclose and respond to the information needs of all stakeholders in the same manner. Some researchers hold the view that firms respond to different stakeholders differently. According to Islam and Deegan (2008), stakeholder theory suggests that firms give priority to responding to the demands of powerful stakeholders. Therefore, if powerful stakeholders demand particular disclosures, the firm would revise its policy in order to provide the requisite disclosures. In this case, the firm's disclosure is motivated not by a genuine desire to be transparent and provide information useful to end users but rather to satisfy the demands of powerful stakeholders. However, in the context of Islamic banks, it is crucial that they are genuinely motivated by the desire to fulfil Shariah principles and rules and to deliver on their responsibility toward all of their stakeholders, including shareholders, customers, employees, and the community at large.

3.3.5. Stakeholder Theory and Islamic Banks

Due to the narrow focus on agency theory and its emphasis on shareholder wealth maximization, some researchers have promoted stakeholder theory as an alternative for Islamic banks. Stakeholder theory, which emphasizes fairness and consideration for all stakeholders, appears to be more closely aligned with the Islamic model of corporate governance (Htay & Salman, 2013).

Van Greuning and Iqbal (2008) classify stakeholders within Islamic banks into three categories, namely, internal stakeholders, multilateral institutions, and regulatory, oversight, and monitoring entities. Internal stakeholders include the board of directors, SSB, executive management, IAH, shareholders, and employees. Multilateral institutions are entities such as the Islamic Development Bank, Accounting and Auditing Organizations for Islamic Financial Institutions, Islamic Financial Services Board, and International Islamic Financial Markets. Regulatory and oversight entities include government regulators and supervisors such as central banks.

In line with the principles of stakeholder theory, Islamic banks are accountable to their stakeholders and must give due consideration to their interests and needs, including the disclosure of information that demonstrates that the bank has discharged its responsibilities.

3.4. Legitimacy Theory

Legitimacy theory explains why firms make voluntary disclosures (Fernando & Lawrence, 2014; Kent & Stewart, 2008; Tilling, 2004). Deegan (2002) argues that firms choose to make voluntary disclosures in order to gain legitimacy, protect their reputation, and ensure the ongoing survival of their organization. This section provides an overview of legitimacy theory, discusses its main concepts, and analyzes its relevance to corporate governance and voluntary disclosure.

3.4.1. Definition

Legitimacy theory is a system-oriented theory with roots in political economy theory (Deegan, 2002). One of the principal corporate governance theories, legitimacy theory, is relevant to understanding the motivation behind the disclosure practices of firms (Kent & Zunker, 2013).

The Merriam-Webster English Dictionary[3] defines legitimacy as the state or condition of being legitimate, that is, what is allowed according to rules or laws, real, accepted, or reasonable. Lindblom (1994) defines legitimacy as the situation in which the firm's value system is in alignment with society's value system. A more comprehensive definition is provided by Suchman (1995, p. 574), who defines legitimacy as a generalized perception or assumption that the actions of an entity are desirable, proper, or appropriate within some socially constructed system of norms, values, beliefs, and definitions.

3.4.2. Overview of Legitimacy Theory

According to Islam and Deegan (2008), legitimacy theory holds that firms continually attempt to ensure that they are perceived as operating within bounds and

[3] Refer to the Merriam-Webster Dictionary, version 2016.

norms accepted by the societies in which they do business. It is important to note that what is acceptable, or considered within social bounds and norms, is subject to change and that which is perceived to be legitimate and appropriate in one society may not be appropriate in another (Islam & Deegan, 2008). Therefore, firms need to adopt and develop strategies for protecting their legitimacy and ensuring that they continue to be perceived as operating within the bounds and norms accepted by society (ibid.).

Under legitimacy theory, organizations do not have an inherent right to resources in society such as human capital, raw materials, and customers. An organization's survival will be jeopardized if it is perceived to be operating in a manner that is not acceptable or legitimate (Deegan, 2002; Lindblom, 1994). Legitimacy theory is based on the assumption that there is a social contract that exists between the organization and the society within which it operates (Kent & Stewart, 2008; Omran & El-Galfy, 2015). The social contract stipulates that the organization delivers socially desirable ends, provides benefits to society, and in return gets society's acceptance to operate and use its resources (Guthrie & Parker, 1989; Omran & El-Galfy, 2015). Legitimacy theory deals with society as a whole and does not differentiate between different organizational stakeholders. Organizations are expected to take into account not only the rights and interests of investors, or other powerful stakeholders, but also the rights of society as a whole (Yusoff & Alhaji, 2012). According to Suchman (1995), organizations seek legitimacy in order to gain the acceptance of their stakeholders, enhance organizational stability, and maintain credibility within society. By maintaining their legitimacy, organizations are able to ascertain access to key resources vital to the organization's survival such as human and financial capital and attract customers for their products and services (Tilling, 2004).

3.4.3. The Legitimacy Gap and the Legitimization Process

The literature indicates that in order to gain and maintain legitimacy, organizations engage in four legitimization stages, namely, establishing, maintaining, extending, and defending their legitimacy (Tilling, 2004; Umoren et al., 2015). Islam and Deegan (2008) argue that this process is continuous, with the organization engaged in one or more of the above stages at any given time. In each of these phases, disclosure is critical in enabling the organization to maintain its operational legitimacy. Regardless of these aforementioned phases, an organization may still experience threats to its legitimacy due to unexpected scandal or to an incident that negatively affects its reputation (Fernando & Lawrence, 2014).

The legitimacy gap can be described as the difference that exists between society's beliefs about how an organization should act and how the organization is perceived to have acted (Deegan, 2006). Omran and El-Galfy (2015) note that a legitimacy gap may arise due to an incongruence between the organization's values and those of society. A gap can also arise as a result of changes in society's expectations, though the organization has not changed the way it operates (Deegan, 2006). Social expectations evolve continuously, and values and norms may change over time (Fernando & Lawrence, 2014). Failure to adapt and address legitimacy gaps or threats may ultimately result in the forfeiture of the organization's right to exist (Tilling, 2004). As a result, managers strive to ensure that they operate within the boundaries of their social contract. This creates an incentive for greater voluntary disclosure and demonstrating adherence to the firm's social contract (Kent & Stewart, 2008). Disclosure provides an important avenue for social acceptance and an enhanced reputation (Deegan, 2002). By providing greater disclosure, a firm can reduce the legitimacy gap and safeguard its ability to operate and access society's resources (Deegan, 2006; Gray et al., 1995).

A number of prior studies suggest that firms voluntarily disclose information in order to gain and maintain legitimacy in the society in which they operate. For instance, Haniffa and Cooke (2005) conduct a longitudinal study to examine the impact of culture and corporate governance on the extent of social disclosure by a sample of 160 Malaysian-listed companies. Using legitimacy theory as the basis for their study, the authors find that companies provide social disclosures as part of their strategy to gain and maintain their legitimacy in society and influence in government circles.

Kent and Zunker (2013) examine the annual reports of a sample of 970 Australian-listed firms to determine whether the firms' disclosure practices are driven by efforts to seek legitimacy in society. Their study found that companies provide voluntary disclosure of employee information to gain and maintain legitimacy in society. Similarly, Ching and Gerab (2017) find that a sample of 46 Brazilian-listed firms for the period from 2008 to 2012 disclosed quality information to legitimize their firms in society.

Despite its wide acceptance, there has been some criticism raised against the effectiveness and usefulness of legitimacy theory. For instance, Guthrie and Parker (1989) examine the disclosure practice of a major Australian monopoly company, Broker Hill Proprietary Company Ltd, using the company's annual reports over a period of 100 years. Their study does not find strong evidence of legitimacy theory as a primary explanation for the disclosure practices of the company. Fernando and Lawrence (2014) point out that legitimacy theory has been criticized for its vagueness and limitations in explaining why organizations choose not to disclose information or why they disclose information selectively.

3.4.4. Legitimacy Theory and Islamic Banks

Notwithstanding the concerns noted above, legitimacy theory has important implications for Islamic banks, given the social expectation that they operate in accordance with Shariah rules and principles and uphold the higher objectives of Shariah (*maqasid al Shariah*). Farook et al. (2011) postulate that the need for Islamic banks to operate within the value system of Muslim society is vital to the survival of Islamic banks and to their ability to gain legitimacy. Islamic banks are accountable to society, and to discharge this responsibility and maintain their legitimacy, they need to demonstrate compliance with Shariah rules and principles through full disclosure (Farook et al., 2011). Failure to adhere to Shariah rules and principles is likely to erode society's confidence in Islamic banks and, over time, threaten their legitimacy to operate. Therefore, this book argues that

Islamic banks should give greater importance to disclosure and transparency to demonstrate to society in general and to the Muslim community in particular that they are operating within the boundaries and values of their community, including full adherence to Shariah rules and principles.

3.5. Signaling Theory

Signaling theory has gained significant attention in recent years as a means of shedding light on the voluntary disclosure practices of organizations and how that information is interpreted by the receiving party. Signaling theory, which is mainly concerned with how to reduce information asymmetry between two parties, has been used in various disciplines, including management, marketing, human resources, and accounting (Connelly et al., 2011). This section discusses how signaling theory helps explain important aspects surrounding the extent of information disclosure made by Islamic and conventional banks. Annual reports provide users with important information about the bank, its management, and its board. Accordingly, the current research uses signaling theory to help explain the determinants of voluntary disclosure in firms in general and the banking sector in particular.

3.5.1. Definition and Overview

Signaling theory is mainly concerned with information asymmetry problems in markets and helps explain how the asymmetry can be reduced (An et al., 2011; Morris, 1987). Signaling theory is used in the literature to gain an understanding of management's motivation to disclose information (Bae et al., 2018; Omran & El-Galfy, 2014). Generally, signaling theory assumes that the information disclosed conveys positive attributes and qualities about the firm which outsiders may find useful (Connelly et al., 2011). While signaling theory has its roots in the labor markets,[4] the theory can be applied wherever there are information asymmetry issues (Morris, 1987; Spence, 1973). Accordingly, the theory has been used in various disciplines, including management, human resources, marketing, and accounting, to explain information asymmetry (Bae et al., 2018; Connelly et al., 2011; Grossman, 1981; Hughes, 1986; Ross, 1977; Spence, 1973; Trueman, 1986; Zhang & Wiersema, 2009).

Connelly et al. (2011) explain that signaling theory's primary elements comprise the signaler, the receiver, and the signal itself. The signaler consists of insiders, such as executives or managers, who possess insider information about the organization or product (ibid.). Insiders, including managers, have access to a

---

[4] For instance, in his seminal work, Spence (1973) extensively discusses how signaling in job markets can help reduce information asymmetry between job applicants and potential employers and distinguish high-quality candidates from those of low quality. Spence explains that job applicants use their educational qualifications to signal their quality and productivity to potential employers.

wide range of information about the company which is not available to investors, such as the quality of a product, the soundness of new investment projects, the future profitability of the firm, as well as risks (An et al., 2011; Kent & Zunker, 2013). Managers can enhance their firm's value through useful voluntary disclosures that reduce investor uncertainty (Omran & El-Galfy, 2015). Voluntary disclosures provide an opportunity for the firm's management to disclose useful and credible information that will in turn enhance the firm's competitive positioning and its ability to attract investors, while reducing uncertainty in the market (Omran & El-Galfy, 2014).

Signaling theory assumes that managers tend to disclose positive information to enhance the firm's value and its reputation in the marketplace (Kent & Zunker, 2013). Accordingly, managers who choose to voluntarily disclose both positive and negative information are likely to be perceived by the market as providing superior information (ibid.). Besides disclosure, the quality of a firm's corporate governance may also enhance the firm's value in the market. Zhang and Wiersema (2009) argue that the quality of the corporate governance, including the prestige of the board of directors and the characteristics of senior management, provides a signal about the firm's quality to investors and in turn affects the stock price of the firm.

3.5.2. Prior Studies on Signaling Theory

An examination of the extant literature suggests that a significant number of studies in various disciplines have used signaling theory to explain information disclosure by companies. A selection of these studies is discussed below.

Hughes (1986) examines the information asymmetry found between managers with insider information and investors of the firm. Hughes uses a bivariate signaling model wherein an entrepreneur in a risky firm communicates insider information about the firm's value to investors. The study aims to establish whether the information is credible and can be relied upon by investors to make appropriate decisions. Based on the results of the study, Hughes concludes that the disclosure is credible because any false disclosures would result in significant detrimental penalties to the firm.

Zhang and Wiersema (2009) investigate the signaling role of the CEO to investors and the effect of signaling on the firm's quality. Building on studies that examine the impact of boards of directors and top management characteristics on an investor's valuation of the firm, the results, which are consistent with prior studies, indicate that the characteristics of the firm's board of directors and top management provide a signal to investors about the firm's quality, which in turn affects the firm's stock valuation.

Bae et al. (2018) conduct study to examine the determinants of sustainability reporting for a sample of Global Initiative Reports (GRI) from Bangladesh, India, and Pakistan for the period from 2009 to 2016 using signaling theory. The study analyzes the GRI reports to determine how the governance bodies of the companies examined use GRI reports to signal positive information to the market. The authors document that the governing bodies have strong effect on using these GRI reports as a signal to the market and shareholders.

3.6. Proposed Integrated Theoretical Framework

Based on the examination of the theories discussed within this chapter, this book puts forth a combination of agency, stakeholder, legitimacy, and signaling theories in order to understand the determinants of information disclosure and address the research question. This integrated approach is consistent with previous studies (An et al., 2011; Deegan, 2002; Fernando & Lawrence, 2014; Gray et al., 1995; Morris, 1987; Yusoff & Alhaji, 2012) that hold that the overlapping nature of these theories provides valuable insight, and therefore, it is incorrect to treat them as separate and distinct theories (Deegan, 2002).

For example, Gray et al. (1995) point out that there is a considerable overlap between legitimacy theory and stakeholder theory. Researchers suggest that these two theories are complementary rather than competing (Islam & Deegan, 2008). Similarly, Morris (1987) studies the relationship between signaling theory and agency theory and finds that both theories are consistent and have a considerable amount of overlap between them. An et al. (2011) argue that an integrated theoretical framework based on agency, stakeholder, legitimacy, and signaling theories provides a sound foundation for examining the determinants of intellectual capital disclosure. This book builds on this approach and makes further contributions to the literature by applying the integrated theoretical framework to explain the determinants of comprehensive categories of firm disclosure, including strategic, governance, risk, financial, and Shariah compliance information.

By adopting the integrated theory approach, the researcher seeks to better understand the nature of corporate governance, its role in the firm, and how it affects the extent of information disclosure and transparency. Agency theory provides us with insight to understand problems and conflicts between owners and management. Moreover, it helps us understand how conflicts and information asymmetry between owners and managers can be reduced through effective disclosure strategies (Donnelly & Mulcahy, 2008). With greater information disclosure, managers can reduce uncertainty and demonstrate to owners and other stakeholders that management is acting in their best interest. Stakeholder theory goes beyond the firm's owners and management, which is the main concern of agency theory, and helps us understand how the firm can discharge its responsibilities toward various stakeholders, such as shareholders, employees, customers, and the community. Stakeholder theory explains how information disclosure can help a firm demonstrate its commitment to meeting stakeholder expectations and enhance the relationship between the firm and its stakeholders. Legitimacy theory helps us explain the role of information disclosure in helping organizations gain legitimacy and acceptance in the society where they operate in order to sustain and preserve their existence. Moreover, it sheds light on how information disclosure enhances management's opportunities to maintain organizational legitimacy. Finally, signaling theory helps us understand how information disclosure provides organizations opportunity to enhance their value by signaling useful information to their stakeholders and society at large.

These four theories combined provide an integrated theoretical framework to comprehensively examine the determinants of information disclosure and

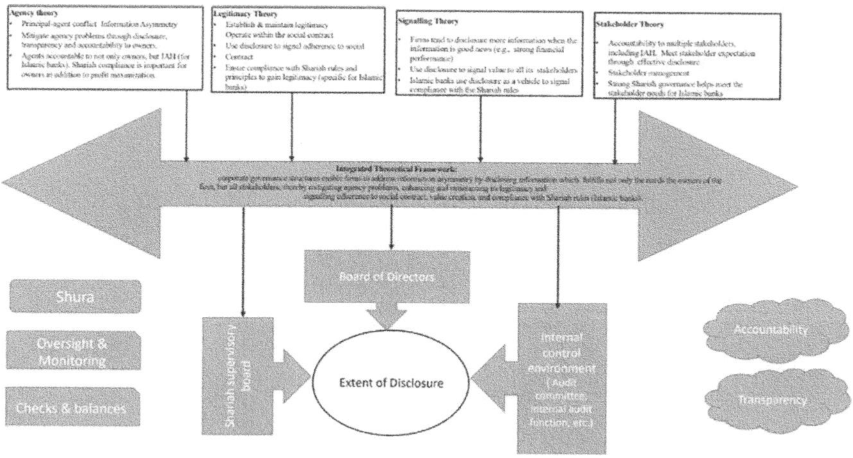

Fig. 3.1. Integrated Theoretical Framework. *Source*: Self-developed model in line with prior studies.

adequately address the research questions. The integrated framework explains how the governance system of the firm can promote disclosure and transparency policies aimed at reducing information asymmetry not only between the principal and the agent, but more importantly between the firm and its stakeholders and the society in which it operates. Furthermore, the integrated theoretical framework enables this book to understand how effective information disclosure policies can help firms meet stakeholder expectations, discharge accountability toward society, and maintain their legitimacy. Fig. 3.1 depicts the integrated theoretical framework adopted for this book.

3.7. Conclusion

In summary, this chapter presents an overview of the main theories of corporate governance and voluntary disclosure, namely, agency, stakeholder, legitimacy, and signaling theories. The chapter provides definitions and overviews of the main concepts of the above theories and how they relate to the study's research questions. This book aims to examine the impact of certain corporate governance mechanisms (board of directors, audit committee, etc.) on the extent of disclosure. Relevant prior studies are also discussed and critically examined. The chapter also analyzes these theories and proposes an integrated framework for this book in order to answer the main research question.

Chapter Four

Corporate Governance: Surveying the Literature

Abstract

Chapter Three discussed the theoretical framework for understanding and analyzing the relationship between corporate governance and voluntary disclosure. Using an integrated theoretical framework derived from the combination of agency, stakeholder, legitimacy, and signaling theories, this study investigates the impact of corporate governance mechanisms such as the board of directors and the audit committee on the extent of voluntary disclosure by Islamic and conventional banks. This chapter surveys the extant literature on the impact of corporate governance on the extent of disclosure by Islamic and conventional banks and examines prior studies relevant to the research questions. More specifically, the chapter focuses on the board characteristics and internal control elements that are the most studied aspects of corporate governance (Wan-Hussin, 2009). The chapter examines in detail their impact on the extent of disclosure. The chapter also discusses prior studies specific to Islamic banks and the role of Shariah governance in the extent of disclosure. The chapter then presents the hypotheses developed for this book in line with the relevant literature and the integrated theoretical framework discussed in Chapter Three. The chapter concludes with remarks on key points from the literature review.

Keywords: Corporate governance; Islamic finance; Shariah Supervisory Board; board of directors; audit committee; internal audit; external Shariah audit

4.1. Introduction

Research interest in studying the association between corporate governance and the extent of disclosure has been on the rise, especially in the conventional industry. Research indicates that corporate governance mechanisms such as boards

Corporate Governance and Disclosure in GCC Banks:
Islamic Perspectives, Empirical Insights and Policy Implications, 59–100

doi:10.1108/978-1-80686-279-520261004

of directors are important determinants for information disclosure because the board is responsible for overseeing key policies, including those related to disclosure (Gul & Leung, 2004). A survey of the literature reveals many studies that examine the relationship between corporate governance characteristics and the extent of disclosure by firms (Akhtaruddin & Rouf, 2012; Alhazaimeh et al., 2014; Appuhami & Tashakor, 2017; Barros et al., 2013; Cheng & Courtenay, 2006; Cohen et al., 2004; del Baldo, 2012; Dey, 2005; Durnev; 2003; Eng & Mak, 2003; Forker, 1992; Garas & ElMassah, 2018; Grassa et al., 2018; Healy & Palepu, 2001; Hermalin & Weisbach, 2011; Ho & Shun Wong, 2001; Htay et al., 2012; Huafang & Jianguo, 2007; Husted & Sousa-Filho, 2019; Jizi et al., 2014; Khan et al., 2013; Milad & Bicer, 2020; Natarajan, 2007; Neifar & Jarboui, 2018; Sacconi, 2012; Said et al., 2009; Tessema, 2019).

A closer examination of these studies suggests several determinants of disclosure, including the impact of corporate governance characteristics, such as board independence, size, meeting frequency, CEO duality, internal control, and Shariah governance strength on the extent of disclosure. The studies indicate the existence of a relationship between these corporate governance characteristics and the extent of disclosure (Khan et al., 2013). However, it is worth noting that most prior studies examining the relationship between corporate governance and disclosure focus on developed countries (Barako et al., 2006) and cover financial and nonfinancial companies. Studies which examine developing countries often use samples of nonfinancial companies and do not undertake comprehensive analysis of various types of disclosures, including strategy, corporate governance, risk governance, CSR, and Shariah governance (for Islamic banks). This study seeks to fill this gap by comprehensively examining the impact of corporate governance on the extent of disclosure by GCC Islamic and conventional banks.

4.2. Board of Directors and Disclosure

The board of directors is an integral part of corporate governance, providing crucial oversight and monitoring roles in firms (Abdelsalam et al., 2008; di Guida et al., 2022; Hart, 1995; John & Senbet, 1998). The board is responsible for deciding on the compensation, hiring and firing of senior management and provides valuable input into the firm's strategic planning process (Bushman & Smith, 2001). Overall, the board of directors has an oversight role in critical areas related to the firm, including strategy, governance, talent, integrity, and performance (Fucci & Cooper, 2019).

The board is the ultimate internal monitor, charged with scrutinizing the highest decision makers within the firm (Fama, 1980) and ensuring that management protects the firm's constituents (Williamson, 1984), particularly in firms where there is diffuse ownership whose stockholders cannot readily scrutinize management themselves (John & Senbet, 1998). Donnelly and Mulcahy (2008) posit similar points and further emphasize the need for the board to establish appropriate mechanisms to ascertain effective management of the firm and assess the performance of top executives toward achieving the firm's objectives. Prior studies have found a relationship between corporate failures and the absence or ineffectiveness of board monitoring. For instance, in examining the reasons behind the collapse of HealthSouth[1] in 2001, Larcker and Tayan (2011) report that the board's compensation committee and the audit committee met only once during the same year. The lack of effective monitoring by these two important board committees allowed management to overstate earnings and pay themselves hefty bonuses, which resulted in one of the most publicized corporate fraud cases in the United States.

On the other hand, having independent board members plays a critical role in enhancing board effectiveness. The role of independent board members in corporate governance has become increasingly important in recent decades. As a result, some countries have enacted laws stipulating the inclusion of independent board members. Bebchuk and Weisbach (2010) suggest that, following accounting scandals, one of the main corporate governance changes has been to strengthen the independence of boards of directors. For instance, the United States enacted the Sarbanes-Oxley Act of 2002, which requires that all members of the audit committees of listed companies be independent directors (Bebchuk & Weisbach, 2010; Wan-Hussin, 2009). Similar regulations have been adopted in other parts of the world, including Europe and Australia, requiring companies to appoint independent board members as a means of improving the corporate governance practices of their companies. Independent board members are widely accepted as an indicator of best practices for corporate governance and are required by most capital markets, especially for the banking industry (Hawkamah, 2017). The CIBAFI's study on corporate governance suggests that independent board members play a significant role in strengthening the overall effectiveness of corporate governance in Islamic banks and financial institutions (CIBAFI, 2017).

Research indicates that information disclosure and transparency are important parts of the board's monitoring and oversight roles (Allegrini & Greco, 2011; Barros et al., 2013; Gul & Leung, 2004). Cheng and Courtenay (2006) argue that, as part of its monitoring responsibilities, the board of directors helps establish internal mechanisms that ensure adequate information disclosure in line with the interests of shareholders. van Greuning and Iqbal (2008) suggest that the key responsibilities of the board are to maintain transparency, make accurate disclosures, and ensure the integrity of disclosed information. By doing so, the board helps minimize information asymmetry, strengthen its monitoring ability, and enhance management's business decision-making (Donnelly & Mulcahy, 2008). In addition to the research community, standard-setting bodies have also recognized the crucial role that the board of directors plays in the disclosure policy of Islamic financial institutions. For example, the IFSB has stressed in its disclosure

---

[1]HealthSouth was a Fortune 500 U.S. company providing healthcare services, headquartered in Alabama, USA. The company collapsed in 2001 following accusations of overstating earnings by $1.4 billion in order to meet market expectations and paying millions of dollars in bonuses to senior management (Larcker & Tayan, 2011).

standards[2] the need for the board of directors to establish disclosure policies that promote transparency.

Numerous studies, especially in Western countries, have investigated the effect of board characteristics on disclosure (Akhtaruddin & Rouf, 2012; Albassam & Ntim, 2017; Allegrini & Greco, 2013; Chen & Jaggi, 2000; Cheng & Courtenay, 2006; Grassa et al., 2018; Gul & Leung, 2004; Jizi et al., 2014; Lim et al., 2007; Sulub et al., 2020). These studies show that board characteristics are generally associated with the extent of disclosure by firms and that effective boards contribute to the enhancement of the firm's transparency and disclosure practices. The characteristics most frequently cited are board independence, size, meeting frequency, and CEO role duality. This book seeks to investigate this association and determine the impact that overall board effectiveness, as an important dimension of corporate governance, has on the extent of disclosure by Islamic and conventional banks in GCC markets. The relevant prior studies are discussed below in detail.

Eng and Mak (2003) conduct a study on a sample of 158 firms listed on the Singapore Stock Exchange. The authors examine the annual reports of the firms to determine the impact of corporate governance on voluntary disclosure. The authors consider board composition and ownership structure as proxies for corporate governance, along with several control variables including size, profitability, leverage, industry, and auditor type. The authors use OLS regression analysis to test the association between the extent of disclosure and the explanatory variables of interest. The results of the study indicate a negative association between independent board members and the extent of disclosure. The finding is inconsistent with most prior studies, which have found a positive association between board independence and disclosure. The authors suggest that the negative association between board independence and disclosure may be attributed to the nature of the independent directors' role in the Singapore market, where most of them represent the interest of the blockholders[3] who appoint them. In this capacity, they are given direct access to information, thus making them less inclined to put pressure on management to provide more disclosure. As for the control variables, the authors document that size is positively associated with the extent of disclosure, while leverage is negatively associated with the extent of disclosure. The findings, which are consistent with prior studies, suggest that larger firms provide greater disclosure while firms with higher levels of debt provide less information.

Gul and Leung (2004) study a sample of 385 Hong Kong-listed companies to investigate the effect of board characteristics on the extent of voluntary

---

[2]The IFSB's standard on disclosures, issued in 2007, details the disclosures recommended by the IFSB to promote transparency and market discipline. In particular, Section 2 of the standards details the general principles of the recommended disclosure policies for Islamic financial institutions.

[3] Eng and Mak (2003) define blockholders as the owners who hold substantial amount of the ordinary shares of the firm, usually estimated to be 5% or more of the ordinary shares.

disclosure. The board characteristics considered in this study are board independence, board experience, and CEO duality. The study also controls for firm characteristics such as size, leverage, profitability, audit firm size, listing status, and industry type. Using information obtained from the annual reports of the sample firms, the authors use content analysis to develop a disclosure index comprising 44 items, which relate to various categories such as background and financial and nonfinancial information. The results of the two-stage OLS regression analysis indicate that CEO role duality is strongly and negatively associated with the extent of disclosure. Moreover, the authors find that the proportion of expert independent board members has a significant negative association with the extent of disclosure. The authors note that expert independent directors substitute for the need for having greater disclosure given their expertise in monitoring managers to protect the interests of the owners. While the study makes interesting observations about the role of expert independent directors being a substitute for more disclosure, the result should be approached with caution, as the study suffers from the limitation of relying on rather old data with a limited number of corporate governance-related proxies. As for the control variables, the study finds that firm size, ratio of market to book value, and profitability have a significant relationship with the extent of disclosure.

Cheng and Courtenay (2006) study a sample of 104 firms listed on the Singapore Stock Exchange to examine the impact of several board-related characteristics on the extent of disclosure. The authors consider board size, independence, and CEO role duality. The result of OLS regression analysis reveals a significant positive association between board independence and level of disclosure. The findings suggest that firms with boards with a majority of independent members have a higher level of voluntary disclosure than firms with a minority of independent board members. The authors also find that the regulatory environment enhances the association between the proportion of independent board members and the extent of disclosure. However, the authors find that board size and CEO role duality are not associated with the extent of disclosure. Overall, the main finding of the study emphasizes the central role that independent board members play in monitoring management and encouraging greater disclosure to minimize information asymmetry between the firm's managers and the owners.

Akhtaruddin et al. (2009) investigate the impact of corporate governance on the extent of voluntary disclosure for a sample of 110 Malaysian-listed companies. The authors use board size, board independence, ownership structure, and proportion of the audit committee members to the total members of the board. Using a disclosure index consisting of 74 items of financial and nonfinancial information (e.g., strategy, risk governance), the authors examine the annual reports of the companies and find a significant positive association between board size and the extent of voluntary disclosure. The authors suggest that a larger board size is more effective in influencing management to disclose more information. Furthermore, the authors find a significant positive association between board independence and extent of disclosure. However, the authors find a negative association between ownership structure and disclosure, while they find no significant relationship between audit committee and the extent of disclosure.

Hidalgo et al. (2011) conduct a study with a sample of 100 Mexican-listed firms to examine the effect of corporate governance mechanisms on the extent of intellectual capital disclosures. The corporate governance mechanisms considered for the study are board and audit committee characteristics (board size, independence, audit committee independence, and CEO role duality) and ownership structure (e.g., family ownership, ownership concentration, and institutional shareholding). The study controls for firm size, profitability, and leverage. The authors develop an unweighted disclosure index of 58 disclosure items divided into 3 categories, namely, structural capital, human capital, and relational capital. Using multivariate regression analysis, they investigate the annual reports for the period from 2005 to 2007. The results of the regression analysis reveal that board size is significantly and positively associated with the extent of disclosure. On the other hand, the authors document that institutional shareholding has a negative significant association with intellectual capital disclosures, suggesting that an increase in institutional ownership results in a decreased level of intellectual capital disclosures.

Allegrini and Greco (2013) undertake a study to examine the impact of corporate governance on the extent of disclosure for a sample of 177 Italian-listed firms. Board size, independence, meeting frequency, and CEO role duality are proxies for corporate governance and used in the study as explanatory variables. The authors also consider board committee-related variables such as audit committee diligence and the existence of an independent compensation and nomination committee as proxies for corporate governance. Firm size, profitability, leverage, and listing status are used as control variables. The authors perform an OLS regression analysis to test the impact of corporate governance variables on the extent of disclosure. They find that board size has a positive and significant impact on the extent of disclosure. Moreover, the study finds that board meeting frequency is positively and significantly associated with the extent of disclosure. CEO role duality is found to have a marginally significant and negative association with the extent of disclosure, whereas board independence is found to have no impact on the extent of disclosure. On the other hand, the authors find that audit committee meeting frequency has a positive and significant impact on the extent of disclosure. As for the control variables, the authors report that only firm size is found to have a significant positive relationship with the extent of disclosure. Overall, the study supports the authors' conclusion that large and diligent boards of directors contribute to greater levels of disclosure.

Barros et al. (2013) study the effect of corporate governance practices on the extent of voluntary disclosure in France. With a sample of 206 listed firms, the authors analyze the annual reports of the firms for the years 2006–2009. The study considers certain board characteristics such as board independence, meeting frequency, and directors' participation in board meetings and investigates the impact of these variables on the extent of disclosure. Using content analysis, the authors develop a disclosure index comprising strategic, financial, and CSR-related items. The results of their empirical analysis show a significant and positive association between board independence and level of disclosure. They also find that board meeting frequency is significantly and positively associated with the level of disclosure, thus suggesting that boards which meet more often contribute to higher disclosure and promote greater transparency. The study, however, finds a negative association between the board members' participation in board meetings and extent of disclosure.

Jizi et al. (2014) study the effect of board characteristics on CSR disclosure with a sample of large U.S.-listed banks. Among the board characteristics considered for the study are board size, independence, and CEO role duality. Moreover, audit committee characteristics, board meeting frequency, size, profitability, and risk are used as control variables for the study. Using the annual reports of a sample of large U.S. banks for the period from 2009 to 2011, the authors perform regression analysis and find that both board size and independence have a positive and significant association with the extent of CSR disclosure. The authors note that firms with larger and more independent boards are more likely to provide greater disclosures. They also examine the impact of CEO role duality on the extent of CSR disclosure and find that it is positively and significantly associated with a bank's CSR disclosure. The authors suggest that the positive association provides evidence that powerful CEOs do encourage greater transparency of a bank's CSR activities for their own benefit and in an effort to appease their stakeholders. Regarding the control variables, the authors suggest that audit committee meeting frequency, audit committee financial expertise, board meeting frequency, return on average assets, and risk (beta) are all associated with the extent of disclosure. Size and leverage are not found to have an impact. The study concludes that effective boards (i.e., boards with large and more independent board members) play a significant role in enhancing transparency and disclosure. Moreover, the study concludes that audit committee and board diligence can be plausible explanatory variables since they are found to be associated with the extent of disclosure.

Uyar et al. (2015) study the annual reports of 25 Turkish banks for the period from 2008 to 2012 to examine the impact of certain board characteristics including board size, independence, and diversity on the extent of CRS disclosure. The categories of CSR disclosure analyzed in this study include environment, energy, employees, customers, and community involvement. Using a panel data analysis, the authors find a positive and significant relationship between board independence and the extent of CRS disclosure. The authors also report that board diversity is positively and significantly associated with the extent of CSR disclosure. The remaining variables are not found to have any significant impact on the extent of CRS disclosure.

Grassa and Chakroun (2016) conduct a study on a sample of 72 Islamic and conventional banks within GCC countries to examine the impact of ownership structure and board characteristics on the extent of corporate governance disclosure. The board characteristics considered explanatory variables are board size and independence and CEO duality. The study controls for variables that are most associated with the extent of disclosure, which are size, profitability, leverage, bank age, listing status, and country transparency index. Using content analysis, the authors develop a disclosure index as well as the three subindexes. The result of their inferential analysis reveals that board size is positively associated with the extent of corporate governance disclosure. The authors also find that board independence is positively and significantly associated with the extent of disclosure. CEO role duality is also reported to have a significant and positive association with the extent of disclosure. Regarding the control variables, the study finds that bank size and country transparency index have an impact on the extent of disclosure. No significant impact is reported for the remaining control variables.

Shehata (2017) undertakes a study to examine the effect of board characteristics and diversity on the extent of corporate governance disclosure for a sample of 270 nonfinancial firms listed in GCC markets. The board characteristics considered by the author are board size, independence, CEO role duality, and the proportion of family members on the board. The diversity variables considered for the study are the proportions of foreign board members, foreign members in the senior management group, as well as proportions of female members on the board and proportion of female members in the senior management group. Several control variables are used in the study, including size, company age, leverage, liquidity, profitability, auditor type, industry type, and ownership structure. The author develops an index comprising six categories of corporate governance disclosure, including board and management structure, ownership structure, and audit. The results of OLS regression analysis reveal that board independence has a significant positive association with the extent of corporate governance disclosure. The remaining board characteristics (board size, CEO duality, etc.) are not associated with the extent of corporate governance disclosure. The author also finds that two diversity variables, namely, the proportion of foreign board members and the proportion of foreign members on the senior management team, have a positive impact on the extent of corporate governance disclosure. Regarding the control variables, the study documents that both profitability and auditor type are positively related to the extent of corporate governance disclosure. The remaining control variables are not related to corporate governance disclosure.

Garas and ElMassah (2018) examine the impact of corporate governance on the extent of CSR disclosures for a sample of 147 firms in the GCC countries. The study, which covers the years from 2007 to 2012, considers several proxies of corporate governance, such as ownership structure (e.g., managerial ownership and ownership concentration), board effectiveness (board independence, CEO role duality, etc.), and audit committee independence. The study uses control variables such as firm size, leverage, age, and return on assets. The result of multiple linear regression analysis shows that both managerial ownership and ownership concentration have a significant positive impact on the extent of CSR disclosure. Moreover, board independence and CEO role duality are significantly and positively associated with the extent of CSR disclosure. Audit committee independence also has a significant positive association with the extent of CSR disclosure. Regarding the control variables, the study finds that firm size is positively associated with the extent of disclosure, while return on assets is negatively associated with the extent of CSR disclosure. No significant impact is reported for leverage and firm age. Overall, the findings of the study provide evidence that effective boards contribute to enhancing the transparency and level of CSR disclosure in firms that operate in the GCC environment. However, even though the study considers different proxies of corporate governance such as board of directors, ownership structure, and audit committee, the study focuses on CSR disclosure as the dependent variable and does not consider other types of disclosure, thus limiting the ability to be generalized.

Husted and Sousa-Filho (2019) perform a study to examine the impact of board characteristics on the extent of ESG disclosure for a sample of 176 firms listed in four Latin American countries (Brazil, Mexico, Columbia, and Chile). Board size, number of women on the board (board diversity), board independence, and CEO duality are used as explanatory variables and tested empirically to determine their impact on the extent of ESG disclosure. The study controls for several variables which are found in the literature to have a relationship with ESG disclosure. These are size, leverage, R&D investment, industry, and cross-listing. To perform the empirical testing, the authors use generalized least squares regression analysis. The results of the study reveal that board size and board independence have positive and significant effects on the level of ESG disclosure, thus indicating that larger and more independent boards are likely to provide greater ESG information. The authors also find that CEO duality is negatively and significantly associated with ESG disclosure. This finding, which is consistent with some studies, suggests that powerful CEOs tend to provide less ESG disclosure. However, unexpectedly, the study reports that the number of women on the board is negatively associated with the extent of disclosure. The authors provide a number of explanations, including the lack of an adequate number of women on the board (i.e., three or more women on the board) to have a positive impact on ESG disclosure, and the cultural setting of Latin American countries which are characterized by a greater degree of collectivism, thus diminishing the ability of individual women board members to positively influence the firm's ESG disclosure policies. Similar results to this study are reported by Muttakin et al. (2015), who find that the number of women on the board is negatively associated with the extent of CSR disclosure for a sample of nonfinancial firms in Bangladesh. With regard to control variables, the study finds that R&D investment, size, and cross-listing are associated with ESG disclosure.

Khandelwal et al. (2020) conduct a study of a sample of 205 nonfinancial Indian-listed firms to examine the impact of board characteristics on the extent of risk disclosure. The board characteristics considered for the study are board size, board independence, executive and non-executive directorship, multiple directorship, and number of women on the board (board diversity). The study controls for firm size, liquidity, growth, and the existence of an audit committee. To measure the dependent variable, the authors compute a risk disclosure trend using content analysis of the risk disclosures reported in the annual reports. The result of their generalized method of moment analysis finds that board diversity as well as non-executive and multiple directorships has a significant positive impact on the extent of risk disclosure. However, the study finds that board size, board independence, and executive directorship have no impact on the extent of risk disclosure.

In summary, from a review of the substantial body of literature, it can be understood that prior studies provide strong support for the impact of corporate governance mechanisms such as board of directors on the extent of disclosure. However, most of these studies are focused on specific types of disclosure rather than considering various strategic, financial, and nonfinancial disclosures, as is the case with this book. This gap demonstrates the need for further research to build on the prior literature and examine the impact of board characteristics on the extent of a comprehensive disclosure index which is comprised of various disclosure categories.

4.3. Internal Control and Disclosure

Internal control is essential to the establishment of strong corporate governance and significantly enhances information disclosure (Agyei-Mensah, 2016; BCBS, 2015; Chalmers et al., 2019). Internal control is defined as a set of structures and processes, which are affected by the organization's board, audit committee, management, and other personnel, designed to provide assurance about the achievement of objectives. Internal controls enable the organization to effectively govern its operations, ensure proper checks and balances, and establish appropriate processes to mitigate risk and support the achievement of organizational objectives (BCBS, 2015). Both the audit committee and the internal audit function (IAF) are key components of the internal control environment (Jiang et al., 2018). Together these bodies provide oversight, monitoring, and independent assurance regarding the control activities and processes established by management in support of the achievement of organizational objectives (Al-Zwyalif, 2015; Mihaela & Iulian, 2012). These components of the firm's internal control environment are discussed next.

4.3.1. Audit Committee Characteristics and Disclosure

The audit committee, which is charged with the responsibility of supporting the board in monitoring the integrity of the financial reporting process and the strength of the internal control environment of the firm, is one of the most important board committees (Akhtaruddin & Haron, 2010; Allegrini & Greco, 2013; Appuhami & Tashakor, 2017; Buallay & Al-Ajmi, 2020; Klein, 2002; Kusnadi et al., 2016; Li et al., 2012; Madi et al., 2014; Othman et al., 2014; Samaha et al., 2015). DeZoort et al. (2002, p. 41) define an audit committee as "qualified members with the authority and resources to protect stakeholder interests by ensuring reliable financial reporting, internal controls, and risk management through its diligent oversight efforts." To properly discharge their oversight responsibility, the audit committee must be given unfettered access to information and be empowered with the authority to act. It is also crucial that the audit committee members are independent and honest and have expertise in financial matters (BCBS, 2015; CIBAFI, 2017; DeZoort et al., 2002).

The crucial role of the audit committee has been brought to the forefront following high-profile corporate governance failures such as Enron and the 2008 financial crisis.

As a result, many countries around the world have introduced laws and regulations aimed at strengthening the corporate governance structure, including the requirement to establish an audit committee which is largely made up of independent members. The audit committee is instrumental in the governance of firms and supports the board's efforts to ensure effective monitoring of management.

The existence of an audit committee demonstrates the firm's commitment to sound corporate governance practices (BCBS, 2015; CIBAFI, 2017; Ho & Shun Wong, 2001; Kent & Stewart, 2008), greatly enhances transparency and disclosure, and significantly improves the quality of monitoring and financial reporting (Buallay & Al-Ajmi, 2020). For example, Ho and Shun Wong (2001) examine the impact of corporate governance on the extent of voluntary disclosure and find a significant positive relationship between the existence of an audit committee and the extent of disclosure.

Klein (2002) asserts that the primary role of the audit committee is to oversee and monitor the firm's financial reporting, auditing processes, and internal controls. Similarly, DeZoort et al. (2002) suggest three important responsibilities for audit committees: financial reporting, internal controls and risk management, and overseeing audit activities. Samaha et al. (2015) suggest that audit committees play a crucial role in promoting greater disclosure, clarity, and dissemination of accurate and useful information to investors and other stakeholders of the firm. More recently, the role of audit committees includes ascertaining the integrity of the firm's financial systems and controls, transparency, risk governance, compliance, and dealing with ethical issues.

An examination of the extant literature suggests that a strong and effective audit committee plays a crucial role in enhancing a firm's overall corporate governance environment (Akhtaruddin et al., 2009; Appuhami & Tashakor, 2017; Buallay & Al-Ajmi, 2020; DeZoort & Salterio, 2001). Moreover, an effective audit committee is one of the variables used to examine the impact of corporate governance on such aspects of the firm as performance (Kajola, 2008), earnings management (Klein, 2002), corporate fraud (Beasley, 1996), and financial reporting and disclosure (Akhtaruddin et al., 2009; Allegrini & Greco, 2013; Al-Shammari & Al-Sultan, 2010; Anderson et al., 2004; Appuhami & Tashakor, 2017; Barako et al., 2006; Buallay & Al-ajmi, 2020; Forker, 1992; Ho & Shun Wong, 2001; Kent & Stewart, 2008; Li et al., 2012; Samaha et al., 2015). Select prior studies related to the audit committee characteristics considered for this book are discussed next.

Ho and Shun Wong (2001) study a sample of Hong Kong-listed firms to examine the impact of board characteristics and audit committees on the extent of disclosure. Using content analysis, the authors develop a weighted relative disclosure index comprising various disclosure items obtained from annual reports. The results of their regression analysis reveal that the existence of an audit committee is strongly and positively associated with the extent of disclosure. The authors also report a significant negative relationship between the percentage of family board members and the extent of disclosure. The authors argue that the result of their study provides support regarding the need for regulatory bodies to require firms to have an audit committee, as this will likely enhance the transparency and information disclosure policies of firms.

Kent and Stewart (2008) examine the impact of corporate governance characteristics on the extent of disclosure for a sample of 965 Australian-listed companies for the year 2004. The authors consider several audit committee-related characteristics as proxies for corporate governance. These include audit committee existence, size, independence, meeting frequency, and financial expertise. Overall, the results of their regression analysis reveal a positive association between audit committee effectiveness and extent of disclosure. As for individual audit committee characteristics, the study finds that audit committee meeting frequency is significantly and positively associated with the extent of disclosure, postulating that an increase in the number of audit committee meetings is likely to enhance audit committee effectiveness and contribute to greater levels of disclosure by the firm. On the other hand, their study reveals that audit committee size and financial expertise are negatively associated with the extent of disclosure of information. No association is found between audit committee independence and the extent of disclosure.

Akhtaruddin and Haron (2010) conduct a study on a sample of 124 Malaysian-listed firms to examine the effect of corporate governance mechanisms, including audit committee effectiveness, on the extent of corporate voluntary disclosure. Audit committee independence and financial expertise are used as proxies for audit committee effectiveness. In line with prior studies, the study uses firm size, profitability, leverage, and auditor type as the control variables. To measure the extent of disclosure, the study develops a voluntary disclosure index comprising 64 items that are related to firm's background information, strategy, governance, financial, and CSR. The result of hierarchical regression analysis indicates that audit committee independence has a moderating effect on the extent of disclosure where it is found to reduce the negative effect between board ownership and the extent of disclosure, thus resulting in increased disclosure level and reduction in information asymmetry. Audit committee financial expertise is not found to be associated with the extent of disclosure. Among the control variables, the study finds that firm size and profitability are associated with the extent of disclosure.

Li et al. (2012) examine the impact of audit committee characteristics on the extent of intellectual capital disclosure based on a sample of 100 UK-listed firms. The result of their multiple regression analysis indicates that audit committee size has a significant positive association with the extent of disclosure. Additionally, the authors report that audit committee meeting frequency has a significant positive association with the extent of intellectual capital disclosure. On the other hand, unexpectedly, the results of the study indicate that audit committee financial expertise has a significant negative association with the extent of disclosure. The authors explain that the negative association may suggest that having members with financial expertise is more effective in influencing more financial disclosure than intellectual capital disclosure. The authors also find that audit committee directors' shareholding is negatively associated with the extent of disclosure.

Kusnadi et al. (2016) study the impact of audit committee characteristics on the quality of financial reporting for a sample of 423 Singaporean-listed firms.

The study considers audit committee independence, financial expertise, and cross-membership. The study controls for other audit committee characteristics (audit committee size, meeting frequency, etc.), board characteristics, and firm characteristics (size, performance, and operational efficiency variables). The result of their regression analysis shows that audit financial expertise has a significant positive association with the quality of financial reporting. Furthermore, the results document that audit committee independence and cross-membership are not associated with financial reporting quality. As for the control variables, the study finds that audit committee size and performance and operational efficiency characteristics are associated with the quality of financial reporting.

Appuhami and Tashakor (2017) conduct a study based on a sample of 300 Australian-listed firms to examine the impact of several audit committee characteristics on the extent of CSR disclosure. The audit characteristics considered include audit committee size, meeting frequency, independence, financial expertise, gender diversity, and independence of the audit committee chair. The study controls for firm size, profitability, leverage, industry type, and board independence. The study develops three indexes to measure the level of CSR disclosure by using content analysis of disclosure information obtained from the annual reports of the sample firms. The result of a multiple regression analysis documents that audit committee size, independence, meeting frequency, and gender diversity have a significant positive impact on the extent of disclosure. However, the study finds no impact for financial expertise or the independence of the audit committee chair. With regard to the control variables, the study documents that firm size and industry type have a significant positive association with the extent of disclosure. The remaining control variables are found to be insignificant. The overall findings of the study contribute to advancing the literature and provide evidence that a larger and more effective audit committee enhances the level of transparency and results in higher disclosure.

Habtoor et al. (2019) examine the impact of board committees, including the audit committee, on corporate risk disclosure based on a sample of 307 Saudi-listed firms for the period from 2008 to 2011. The audit committee characteristics investigated are audit committee size and meeting frequency as proxies for audit committee effectiveness. Using OLS regression and panel data analysis, the authors document that audit committee meeting frequency is significantly and positively associated with the extent of corporate risk disclosure. However, the authors do not find any relationship between audit committee size and the extent of corporate risk disclosure.

Buallay and Al-Ajmi (2020) examine the impact of audit committee characteristics on the extent of corporate sustainability disclosures based on a sample of 59 GCC banks for the period from 2013 to 2017. The authors consider audit committee size, independence, financial expertise, and meeting frequency. The study draws on select related theories, such as agency, legitimacy, and stakeholder theories, to develop the study hypotheses and examine the data. The result of their regression analysis indicates that audit committee independence and meeting frequency have a significant positive impact on the extent of sustainability disclosure. On the other hand, contrary to their hypothesis, the authors document a negative association between audit committee financial expertise and the extent of sustainability disclosures. Concerning the control variables, the authors report that size, age, and type of audit firm are all associated with the extent of sustainability disclosure.

In summary, prior studies examining the impact of audit committee characteristics on the extent of disclosure demonstrate that, overall, audit committee characteristics such as size, independence, meeting frequency, and financial expertise are associated with the information disclosure. However, the studies reviewed show mixed results. Moreover, it can be observed that most of these studies are focused mostly on European or other Asian regions. This book aims to fill this gap and examine the impact of audit committees on the extent of disclosure for Islamic and conventional banks in the GCC countries.

4.3.2. Internal Audit Function and Disclosure

The IAF is a critical component of the internal control environment and plays an important role in the overall governance structure of a firm (Jiang et al., 2018). The independence of the IAF and its direct reporting line to the board enable it to be an effective monitoring tool, which addresses gaps and weaknesses, including those related to the firm's disclosure practices (Al-Shetwi et al., 2011). Despite its importance, however, a review of the extant literature indicates that there is scarcity in research related to the role of the internal audit and that the effect of the IAF on disclosure is mostly unexplored, especially within the context of Islamic banks and developing countries (Sulub et al., 2020). The few relevant studies identified are discussed below.

Al-Shetwi et al. (2011) conduct a study of a sample of 44 Saudi-listed firms to examine the impact of the IAF on financial reporting quality. The study develops a composite comprising several IAF attributes, including independence and proficiency. The authors use several control variables, such as audit committee characteristics (size, independence, meeting frequency, financial expertise, etc.), the firm characteristics of size, leverage, and profitability, and audit firm type (small firm vs. Big 4). The result of their regression analysis indicates that there is no significant association between the IAF and financial reporting quality. Regarding the control variables, the study finds that audit committee financial expertise, leverage, and audit firm type are associated with the quality of financial reporting.

Lin et al. (2011) conduct a study based on a sample of 214 U.S. firms to examine the influence of the IAF on the disclosure of material weaknesses. The study considers several IAF attributes (e.g., competence, objectivity, independence, and investment) and IAF activities (audit fieldwork quality assurance, audit follow-up, and coordination with external auditors). The study controls for several related variables such as market value, firm age, sales growth, and institutional ownership. The result of a regression analysis indicates that IAF attributes have a marginal effect on material weakness disclosures. However, the study reports that IAF activity (audit fieldwork quality, audit follow-up, and coordination with external auditors) has a strong positive association with material weakness disclosures.

Razek (2014) studies the impact of corporate governance characteristics on the extent of CSR disclosure with a sample of Egyptian firms. The study examines several corporate governance characteristics, including internal audit quality and audit committee existence, size, and financial expertise. The study finds that internal audit quality has a significant impact on the extent of corporate social disclosure. Additionally, the study finds that audit committee characteristics (existence and skills and financial expertise) have a significant effect on the extent of disclosure. Overall, the study provides support for the effective role that internal audit plays as a corporate governance mechanism to enhance transparency and increase disclosure levels.

Ganesan et al. (2017) examine the impact of several corporate governance attributes on sustainability disclosure with a sample of 120 Malaysian-listed firms and use the IAF as moderating the relationship between the corporate governance attributes and the extent of sustainability disclosure. The corporate governance attributes considered for the study include board size, independence, and CEO role duality. The study controls for company size, profitability, and industry type. Using partial least squares structural equation modeling to test the hypotheses, the study finds that the IAF has a moderating effect on the relationship between corporate governance attributes and the extent of sustainability disclosure, thus suggesting that the internal audit contributes to greater disclosures. With regard to corporate governance attributes, the study finds that CEO role duality is negatively associated with disclosure. However, no significant impact is documented for board size or independence.

Sulub et al. (2020) examine a sample of 14 Sudanese Islamic banks to determine the effect of corporate governance and Shariah governance strength on the use of an IAF by Islamic banks. The authors also investigate if there is an association between the IAF and the extent of corporate governance disclosure. Utilizing agency and stakeholder theories, the authors analyze the annual reports of Islamic banks in the sample for a 5-year period. The corporate governance mechanisms considered include board and audit committee characteristics and ownership structure. Furthermore, the authors develop an index for measuring Shariah governance strength based on Shariah Supervisory Board (SSB) characteristics such as size, multiple membership, and educational qualifications. The study uses bank size as a control variable. The result of their regression analysis finds that Shariah governance strength is associated with the existence of an IAF, suggesting Islamic banks which have strong Shariah governance mechanisms in place tend to have an IAF. Moreover, the results of the study document a significant association between the IAF and the extent of corporate governance disclosure, thus providing support for the important role that the IAF plays in enhancing transparency and the level of disclosures.

Tumwebaze et al. (2022) study the impact of audit committees and IAFs on the quality of sustainability reporting based on a sample of 48 Ugandan financial firms. Drawing on agency and legitimacy theories, the study analyzes the sustainability disclosure practices of the Ugandan financial firms and performs empirical tests to establish the influence of audit committee effectiveness and IAF on sustainability disclosures. The authors develop an index for both audit committee effectiveness and quality of IAF in line with prior studies. Furthermore, the study controls for firm age, firm size, and auditor type, which are often considered in studies due to their association with the extent and quality of disclosures. The result of their hierarchical regression analysis shows that both audit committee effectiveness and the quality of the IAF have a significant positive impact on the sustainability disclosure practices of the financial firms examined.

In summary, the prior studies examined show that internal control elements such as audit committee characteristics and IAF are associated with the extent of disclosure. However, the result is mixed, with some studies finding a significant positive effect while others find a negative or no impact. Based on the overall results of the studies examined, this book aims to examine the impact of audit committee and IAF characteristics on the extent of disclosure by Islamic and conventional banks.

4.4. Shariah Governance and Disclosure

Effective Shariah governance is central to ensuring compliance with Shariah principles and rules, earning the trust of stakeholders, and achieving the higher objectives of the Shariah (Al Mannai & Ahmed, 2018; Obid & Naysary, 2016). Therefore, it can be argued that effective Shariah governance is essential to the survival of Islamic banks (AlQassasr & Ahmed, 2021; Grais & Pellegrini, 2006). The whole business model of the Islamic bank requires that the bank's transactions be conducted in accordance with the principles and rules of Shariah (AlQasasr & Ahmed, 2021; Grais & Pellegrini, 2006).

There is a growing call for Islamic banks to embrace comprehensive Shariah governance aimed at putting in place appropriate arrangements to ensure compliance with Shariah rules and contribute to the achievement of the higher objectives of the Shariah. In addition to industry stakeholders, regulators are also putting forth requirements which demand that Islamic banks establish proper Shariah governance. In this regard, some of the key regulators in the GCC have introduced a new Shariah governance model, requiring Islamic banks to take a more holistic approach to their Shariah governance. As part of these initiatives, the central banks demand that Islamic banks be more transparent and report their adherence to the new Shariah governance model. For instance, in 2017, the Central Bank of Bahrain published new Shariah governance Standards which introduced several new requirements for Islamic banks, including the requirement to be subjected to an independent external Shariah compliance audit on an annual basis. Other requirements included enhanced disclosures for the effectiveness and performance of the SSB.

4.4.1. Shariah Supervisory Board

One of the key governance mechanisms for ensuring strict adherence to Shariah law is the SSB (Abdel Karim, 1995; Alnasser & Muhammed, 2012). The SSB is an integral part of the Islamic bank's corporate governance structure and contributes to enhancing its overall performance (Mollah & Zaman, 2015). According to the AAOIFI standards,[4] the SSB is defined as an independent body of specialized jurists in fiqh al muamalat[5] (Islamic commercial jurisprudence).

The extant literature suggests that the SSB is an integral part of the Islamic bank's governance system (Hasan, 2011) and is entrusted with monitoring management and overseeing full compliance with Shariah principles and rules (Grais & Pellegrini, 2006). Karim (1995, p. 288) notes that the SSB is responsible for ensuring that all the bank's transactions, new products, and contracts are in conformity with Shariah rules and issuing fatwas on the permissibility of transactions. As stipulated by the AAOIFI governance standards, the fatwas and rulings of the SSB are binding on the Islamic bank. The SSB also works with external auditors and the bank's management in setting the bank's accounting policy on issues which are either not covered by the accounting principles enforced in the country or are in violation of the Shariah (Karim, 1995, p. 288).

Suleiman (2000) argues that the SSB's role is crucial as it provides assurance to the Islamic bank customers that the bank's transactions are conducted according to Shariah principles, and any transactions violating the Shariah rules are properly addressed and disclosed. Hence, an important aspect of the assurance provided by the SSB is to ascertain that the transactions identified as being in violation of Shariah rules are properly addressed and disclosed in a transparent manner. For instance, let us assume that the SSB, through its Shariah audits or review of transactions and contracts, finds that certain income generated by the bank is illegal according to Shariah rules. In this case, it becomes extremely important that the SSB ensure that the bank not only excludes this illegal income from its profits and disperses the income to charitable causes under the supervision of the SSB but also makes adequate disclosures about these transactions to customers and other stakeholders.

An examination of the literature on Islamic corporate governance reveals that transparency and disclosure are important principles of Islamic corporate governance (Baydoun & Willet, 1997; Grais & Pellegrini, 2006). Ariffin et al. (2007) argue that information disclosure in Islamic banks is crucial as it enables the bank's stakeholders to assess the bank's compliance with Shariah rules and principles. Moreover, one of the key responsibilities of the SSB is to advocate for transparency and disclosure not only about the Islamic bank's financial information but also about such nonfinancial information as CSR and Shariah compliance. It is also crucial that the Islamic bank discloses the SSB's duties, decision-making process, composition, and areas of expertise, hence enhancing the confidence of stakeholders and strengthening the credibility of the SSB (Grais & Pellegrini, 2006).

Numerous studies examine the role of Shariah governance characteristics (SSB, Shariah audit department, external Shariah audit, etc.) and its impact on different

---

[4] *Source*: AAOIFI Governance Standards, Section 2, p. 4.

[5] It is worth noting that, according to the AAOIFI governance standards, the SSB can have members other than those with a specialty in *fiqh al muamalat*. However, they have to be experts in the field of Islamic banks with knowledge about *fiqh al muamalat*.

aspects of the Islamic bank, including the extent of voluntary disclosure (Ahmed & Chapra, 2002; Archer et al., 1998; Elamer et al., 2019; Ghayad, 2008; Grais & Pellegrini, 2006; Hasan, 2011; Nathan & Ribière, 2007; Neifar et al., 2020; Suleiman, 2000). Selected prior studies examining the impact of Shariah governance elements on the extent of disclosure by Islamic banks are discussed next.

Farook et al. (2011) study a sample of 47 Islamic banks in 14 countries, including GCC countries, to examine the determinants of social responsibility disclosure by Islamic banks. The authors consider several corporate and Shariah governance mechanisms as the independent variables which are expected to have an impact on the extent of social responsibility disclosure. These include the type of political system (ratio of 1 for the country with the most freedom to 14 for the country with the most repression), the size of the Muslim population, SSB characteristics, and ownership structure. For SSB characteristics, the authors develop an index of Shariah governance strength, which is comprised of SSB characteristics used in prior studies, such as size of the SSB, educational qualifications, and cross-membership. The study uses bank size as a control variable in line with numerous prior studies which find size to influence the level of disclosure. For the dependent variable, the authors develop a disclosure index in line with prior studies; it is comprised of 32 items. Overall, the authors find that social responsibility disclosure in Islamic banks is very low (with a mean of 16.8%, approximately). Furthermore, the result of OLS regression analysis reveals that the proportion of the Muslim population has a significant impact on the extent of CSR disclosure by Islamic banks. Also, the authors find that the Shariah governance strength index is significantly and positively associated with the extent of CSR disclosure. A moderately significant positive association is also reported between the ownership structure (proportion of IAH funds) and the extent of CSR disclosure.

Wan Abdullah et al. (2013) conduct a study of a sample of 23 Islamic banks in Malaysia and Indonesia to investigate the impact of Shariah governance on the extent of Shariah-related disclosures. The authors consider SSB size, financial expertise, and cross-membership as explanatory variables. Regarding the dependent variable, the authors develop a disclosure index made up of 30 Shariah-related disclosure items. Overall, the result of the content analysis reveals that the level of Shariah disclosure in Islamic banks is below 50% except for four banks which disclose above 50% of the disclosure index. Further, the result of the regression analysis shows that some SSB characteristics have an impact on the extent of disclosure. The study finds that cross-membership and SSB financial expertise have a strong and positive association with Shariah-related disclosures. However, no association is found between SSB size and Shariah disclosures. The study concludes that a more effective SSB with members who are sitting on various Shariah boards and who have financial expertise are more likely to encourage greater Shariah disclosures.

El-Halaby and Hussainey (2015) conduct a study of 138 Islamic banks located in 25 countries, including the GCC, to examine the impact of the Shariah audit function along with several firm characteristics, including size, accounting standard, auditor type, profitability, leverage and age of the firm, on the extent of CSR disclosure. The authors control for some country-level variables, such as

GDP growth rate, culture, legal system, corruption index, and literacy rate. Using regression analysis, the empirical result shows that the existence of the Shariah audit function in the Islamic bank is positively associated with the extent of CSR disclosure. The authors also find a positive association between the accounting standard, bank size, and auditor type.

Grassa et al. (2018) study a sample of 78 Islamic banks from 11 countries, including GCC countries, for the period from 2004 to 2012 to examine the impact of corporate governance on the extent of product and services disclosures by Islamic banks. The corporate governance characteristics considered by the study are ownership structure (blockholder, institutional ownership, etc.), board characteristics (board size, independence, CEO role duality, etc.), and SSB size. Additionally, the study controls for profitability, leverage, size, Islamic finance share, listing status, business extent of disclosure index by the World Bank, and compliance with AAOIFI standards. The results of a regression analysis indicate that blockholder ownership, IAHs and CEO tenure and role duality are associated with the extent of the product and services disclosures by Islamic banks. On the other hand, institutional ownership has a negative association with the extent of product and services disclosure. The authors also document that both board size and SSB size have positive and significant effects on the extent of product and service disclosure by Islamic banks. Regarding the control variables, the study finds that bank profitability, age, leverage, listing, and compliance with AAOIFI standards have a positive impact on the extent of product and services disclosure.

In a longitudinal study, Elamer et al. (2019) investigate the effects of SSB characteristics and corporate governance mechanisms on the extent of operational risk disclosure for a sample of 63 banks in 10 countries, including the GCC. The authors use SSB characteristics related to SSB such as SSB existence, membership, and meeting frequency to construct their SSB quality index, which is used along with corporate governance characteristics (board size, proportion of independent board members, ownership structure, country-level governance quality index, etc.) as the explanatory variables for the study. The result of a panel data fixed effects regression analysis reveals that SSB characteristics (SSB existence, size, and meeting frequency) are significantly and positively associated with the extent of operational risk disclosure. The authors postulate that effective SSBs play an important governance role in Islamic banks and are likely to promote transparency and greater risk governance disclosure. The study also finds that block ownership, board independence, and the country-level governance quality index are all significantly and positively associated with the extent of disclosure.

In more recent work, Ridwan and Mayapada (2020) perform a study to examine the effect of corporate governance and SSB characteristics on the extent of CSR disclosure for a sample of Indonesian Islamic banks. The corporate governance characteristics considered include board size and meeting frequency as well as audit committee size and independence. The SSB characteristics used in the study are SSB size, educational background, and the reputation of the Shariah scholars in the SSB. The study controls for profitability and bank size. The results of their regression analysis show that board size has a significant negative impact on the extent of CSR disclosure. The study also finds that board meeting frequency has a significant positive association with the extent of CSR disclosure by Islamic banks. The study found no significant association between audit committee characteristics and the extent of CSR disclosure. Similarly, the authors report that SSB characteristics (SSB size, educational qualifications, and member reputations) have no impact on the extent of CSR disclosure by Islamic banks. Regarding the control variables, only bank size is found to be associated with the extent of CSR disclosure.

In summary, the extant literature provides support that Shariah governance, such as SSB size, meeting frequency and financial expertise and a Shariah audit unit, do have an effect on the Islamic bank's disclosure practices. However, most of these studies are focused on specific aspects of disclosure, such as Shariah or CSR disclosure. This book aims to fill this gap by considering various categories of disclosure, including Shariah, CSR, governance, risk, and financial information.

4.5. Firm- and Country-level Characteristics

Firm- and country-level characteristics provide important explanations and have been used in the literature as control variables. A review of the extant literature reveals that there are several firm- and country-level characteristics which have an effect on the extent of disclosure. These include size, profitability, leverage, cost-to-income (C2INC) ratio, and capital adequacy ratio (CAR). Besides the firm-level, country-level characteristics such as regulatory quality are also discussed in the literature and considered in prior studies, as these characteristics have an influence on the level of disclosure (Elamer et al., 2019; Ernstberger & Grüning, 2013). The regulatory environment of a country plays an important role and has a macro-level impact on the overall governance of firms. Legal and regulatory environments can provide an explanation for a firm's disclosure practices. Cheng and Courtenay (2006) assert that the legal and regulatory environment affects how the board monitors various aspects of the firm, including disclosure practices. They further postulate that in regulatory regimes where transparency is promoted, independent board members generally push for more disclosure by the firm. Beekes et al. (2016) argue that disclosure and transparency are likely to be higher in countries where there is a legal system that provides greater protection for investors and effective enforcement of rules. They further assert that firms are likely to provide timely and greater levels of disclosure to avoid potential penalties which may be imposed on them if they fail to disclose.

Numerous studies have examined firm characteristics such as size, performance, and leverage to determine their impact on the extent of corporate disclosure (Ahmed & Nicholls, 1994; Al-Hadi et al., 2019; Baldini et al., 2018; Barako et al., 2006; Belkaoui & Kahl, 1978; Buzby, 1975; Chow & Wong-Boren, 1987; Cooke, 1989; Hossain et al., 1995; Meek et al., 1995; Naser et al., 2002; Owusu-Ansah, 1998; Singhvi & Desai, 1971; Uyar et al., 2013; Wallace et al., 1994). A select number of these studies are discussed next.

Hossain et al. (1995) conduct a study of a sample of 55 New Zealand-listed firms to examine the impact of firm characteristics on the extent of disclosure.

The firm characteristics considered in the study are firm size, leverage, assets in place, auditor type (Big 6 or small firm), and foreign listing status. Drawing on prior studies and using content analysis, the study develops a disclosure index comprising 95 voluntary disclosure items. The disclosure index is employed as the dependent variable and used in investigating the relationship between the firm characteristics and the level of voluntary disclosure. The authors perform an OLS regression analysis to evaluate the impact of the firm characteristics on the extent of voluntary disclosure. The result of the regression analysis indicates that firm size and foreign listing have a significant positive impact on the extent of disclosure. Moreover, the authors find that leverage has a significant positive association with the extent of voluntary disclosure. The authors explain that as firms increase leverage, they are inclined to make more voluntary disclosures in order to reduce agency costs.

AlSaeed (2006) performs a study of a sample of 40 Saudi-listed firms to investigate the impact of firm characteristics on the extent of disclosure. The firm characteristics considered for the study are firm size, ownership dispersion, firm age, profitability, liquidity, leverage, industry type, and audit firm size. Using content analysis, the author develops a disclosure index consisting of 20 items and analyzes the extent of disclosure as reported in the annual reports of the sample firms. The analysis of the disclosure levels reveals that the level of disclosure is relatively low for the sample firms tested (the mean score is 33%). The author performs multiple regression analyses using OLS regression techniques to examine the impact of the firm characteristics on the extent of disclosure. The results of the regression analysis indicate that firm size has a significant positive association with the extent of disclosure. However, the study finds no significant association for the remaining variables. While the study sheds light on the low disclosure levels of firms in Saudi Arabia, the small sample size and the limited number of disclosure items considered (20 items) make it difficult for the results to be generalized.

Mohamed and Basuony (2015) conduct a study of a sample of 266 GCC firms to examine the impact of several firm characteristics on the extent of financial disclosure. These characteristics include firm size, profitability, leverage, industry type, and audit firm size. The study also analyzes the disclosure practices of the GCC countries in the sample to determine if there is any significant difference in the level of disclosure. The result of their regression analysis finds that firm size has a significant positive impact on the extent of disclosure. However, the remaining firm characteristics are found to have no significant impact on the extent of Internet financial disclosure. On the other hand, the study reports that there is a significant difference in disclosure practices among the GCC countries in the sample. In particular, the study finds that there is a significant difference in disclosure practices between Saudi and Omani firms.

Baldini et al. (2018) conduct a cross-country study to examine the impact of firm- and country-level characteristics on the extent of ESG disclosures for a sample of 14,174 observations for the period from 2005 to 2012 from firms of various industries, including financials, consumer goods, industrials, and basic materials. Drawing on institutional and legitimacy theories, the authors use select country- and firm-level characteristics as determinants of ESG disclosures.

The firm-level characteristics considered in the study are firm size, leverage, analyst coverage, and cross-listing. The country-level characteristics used in the study are political system (level of corruption, strength of legal framework), labor system (degree of labor protection, unemployment rate), and cultural system (social cohesion, equal opportunities). The result of multivariate regression analysis shows that all three country-level characteristics (i.e., political, labor, and cultural systems) have a significant impact on the extent of ESG disclosures. Moreover, the study finds that firm-level characteristics, namely, firm size, leverage, analyst coverage, and cross-listing, have a significant positive association with the extent of ESG disclosures.

In summary, the survey of the prior studies reveals that, overall, country- and firm-level characteristics (e.g., firm size, profitability, and leverage) and country-level characteristics (political system, regulatory quality, GDP growth rate, etc.) have an effect on firm disclosure and transparency. Furthermore, the extant literature provides support that these firm- and country-level characteristics have been used as control variables due to their association with disclosures.

4.6. Identifying the Literature Gap

This book aims to examine the impact of corporate governance on the extent of disclosure for Islamic and conventional banks in the GCC countries. While a significant number of studies have been done on the impact of corporate governance mechanisms on disclosure, which contribute greatly to advance research on the subject, a survey of the extant literature reveals notable gaps. First, it is observed that most studies, especially those related to GCC countries, are focused on examining specific types of disclosure, such as risk, corporate governance, intellectual property, or CSR-related information. This book fills this gap by examining six categories of disclosure, specifically strategy, governance, risk, CSR, Shariah, and financial information.

Second, prior studies have mostly used a limited number of corporate governance dimensions as explanatory variables and have not considered a comprehensive set of dimensions to fully determine their impact on disclosure. This book attempts to fill this gap by considering a comprehensive set of corporate governance dimensions as proxies, including board, internal control, and Shariah governance characteristics.

Third, most prior studies, especially those related to the GCC countries, examine corporate governance characteristics such as board size, independence, and meeting frequency as individual variables and do not consider their aggregate impact. Even the few studies which develop an index of corporate governance (e.g., Al-Hadi et al., 2019) tend to focus only on the impact of overall corporate governance quality. This book aims to extend the literature and address this gap in two ways. First, the study develops an index for three main thematic areas of corporate governance, which are board effectiveness, internal control strength, and Shariah governance strength (specific to Islamic banks). For each of the three thematic areas, an empirical analysis is performed at two levels, first at the composite level and then at the individual variable level. Moreover, this book considers various corporate governance characteristics, some of which are less explored in prior studies related to the GCC countries, such as the existence of an independent IAF.

4.7. Hypothesis Development

This book examines the impact of certain corporate governance characteristics on the extent of disclosure by Islamic and conventional banks in GCC countries. The main question that the study aims to answer is: How does corporate governance affect the extent of disclosure by Islamic and conventional banks in GCC countries? Based on a review of the extant literature, this book identifies certain corporate governance characteristics as independent variables that affect the extent of disclosure by Islamic and conventional banks. These are classified into three main categories, namely, board effectiveness, internal control strength, and Shariah governance strength. Board effectiveness characteristics include board size, independence, meeting frequency, diversity, and CEO role duality. The internal control strength characteristics include audit committee size, independence, meeting frequency, financial expertise, internal audit existence, and independence. Shariah governance characteristics comprise SSB size, meeting frequency, educational qualifications, financial expertise, and internal and external Shariah audits. To answer the research questions, this book develops three main hypotheses and sub-hypotheses, based on the independent (i.e., the corporate governance mechanisms described above) and dependent (i.e., the extent of disclosure) variables which are considered in this book, in line with prior studies.

4.7.1. Board Effectiveness and Extent of Disclosure

Following methods used by prior studies (e.g., Al-Hadi et al., 2019; Beekes & Brown, 2006; CIBAFI, 2107; Ishak & Al-Ebel, 2013; Sulub et al., 2020), this book develops an index to measure board effectiveness, comprising several board characteristics which are commonly associated with disclosure in the extant literature. These include board size, independence, meeting frequency, CEO duality, and board diversity. These board characteristics, which are discussed in further detail in the following subsections, have been identified in the literature as influencing the extent of disclosure. In line with prior studies and drawing from agency theory, which postulates that effective boards promote higher disclosure as a means of mitigating agency problems between management and stakeholders (Kent & Steward, 2008), this book expects that board effectiveness has a positive association with the extent of disclosure by Islamic and conventional banks. Accordingly, the following hypothesis is formulated:

H1. Board effectiveness is positively associated with the extent of disclosure.

4.7.1.1. Board Size

Board size is seen as an important determinant of effectiveness in monitoring, oversight, and decision-making (Allegrini & Greco, 2013; Allini et al., 2016; Anderson et al., 2004; Kilic et al., 2015; Yermack, 1996). However, as there is no globally agreed-upon specific board size, different views have been put forth in the extant literature about the ideal board size, with some researchers arguing for small board sizes, while others suggest larger board sizes (Hawkamah, 2017). For instance, some research studies (Cheng & Courtenay, 2006; John & Senbet, 1998; Yermack, 1996) contend that smaller boards (i.e., fewer than 10 members) are more effective. These studies argue that large boards lead to slower decision-making, poorer communication, and other inefficiencies. However, most studies (Abeysekera, 2010; Akhtaruddin et al., 2009; Allegrini & Greco, 2013; Al-Musalli & Ismail, 2012; Kilic et al., 2015; Larmou & Vafeas, 2010) strongly suggest that a larger board is likely to be more effective at discharging its responsibilities, in part because the workload can be distributed in a more manageable way. For instance, Allini et al. (2016) argue that a larger board enhances effectiveness and enables greater monitoring. They conclude that large boards are likely to advocate for greater disclosure. The argument is premised on the postulation that boards with a large number of members are likely to include experienced members who will monitor management more effectively and promote better governance, including disclosure and transparency. Furthermore, they contend that a larger board is in a better position to distribute roles more effectively and to allocate responsibilities among its members more equitability, thus enhancing board performance.

Hawkamah (2017) reports that the mean global board size is 10.4, suggesting that most companies do maintain a large board. This is especially true in companies with large and complex business operations such as the banking sector. Boone et al. (2007) find that firms tend to increase their board size over time due to growth in the business' scope and complexity or to changes in senior management structure. Large boards increase the capacity to monitor management, provide more effective distribution of the workload, and bring a greater pool of diverse skills and expertise (Al-Musalli & Ismail, 2012).

Prior studies have examined the effect of board size on different aspects of the firm, such as performance (Dalton et al., 1998; John & Senbet, 1998; Yermack, 1996), firm value (Mak & Kusnadi, 2005), executive compensation (Laksmana, 2008), CEO monitoring (Hermalin & Weisbach, 1998), and voluntary disclosure (Abeysekera, 2010; Akhtaruddin & Rouf, 2012; Akhtaruddin et al., 2009; Barros et al., 2013; Boone et al., 2007; Cheng & Courtenay, 2006; Cheung et al., 2007; Donnelly & Mulcahy, 2008; Eng & Mak, 2003; Gul & Leung, 2004; Jizi et al., 2014; Lim et al., 2007; Uyar et al., 2013). Overall, these studies, including those that examine a board's impact on the extent of disclosure, show mixed results, as discussed below.

Akhtaruddin et al. (2009) investigate the impact of board size on the extent of voluntary disclosure for a sample of 110 Malaysian-listed companies. The result of their study reveals a significant positive association between board size and the extent of voluntary disclosure. The authors suggest that a larger board size is more effective in influencing management to disclose more information. Abeysekera (2010) studies a sample of 26 Kenyan-listed firms, examining the impact of board size on the extent of intellectual capital disclosure. Using the annual reports of the sample firms for 2002 and 2003, the author finds that board size is positively and significantly associated with the extent of disclosure. Hidalgo et al. (2011) find that board size is significantly and positively associated with the extent of disclosure. The authors further postulate that the maximum board size should be 15 members, as recommended by corporate governance codes and best practices. Akhtaruddin and Rouf (2012) study the impact of board characteristics, including board size, on the extent of disclosure by a sample of 94 companies listed in the Bangladesh market. Their study finds that board size is positively associated with the extent of disclosure. Jizi et al. (2014) study the effect of board size on CSR disclosure in the U.S. banking sector and find a positive and significant relationship between board size and CSR disclosure, noting that firms with larger board sizes are more likely to make greater disclosures. Samaha et al. (2015) conduct a meta-analysis of studies examining the link between board and audit committee characteristics and voluntary disclosure. Their study concludes that board size has a significant positive association with the extent of disclosure. Grassa and Chakroun (2016) find that board size is associated with higher corporate governance disclosure. Ghabayen et al. (2016) find that board size is significantly and positively associated with the extent of disclosure for a sample of Jordanian banks.

Albassam and Ntim (2017) examine a sample of 75 Saudi-listed firms from 2004 to 2010 in order to study Islamic value and corporate governance characteristics. Using multivariate regression analysis, their study reveals that a larger board size is associated with a greater level of corporate governance disclosure. Grassa et al. (2018) examine a sample of 78 Islamic banks located in 11 countries to determine the impact of corporate governance mechanisms on product and service disclosures. Their study concludes that board size has a positive association with the extent of product and service disclosures by Islamic banks. In line with the above studies, this book postulates that board size contributes to an increased level of disclosure.

While a significant number of studies seem to suggest a positive association between board size and the extent of voluntary disclosure, several other studies report either an insignificant or a negative association. For example, Cheng and Courtenay (2006) study a sample of 114 firms listed on the Singapore Stock Exchange and find no association between board size and the extent of disclosure. Similarly, Arouri et al. (2011) find no significant relationship between board size and performance of banks in the GCC markets. Saha and Akter (2013) study a sample of financial and nonfinancial firms listed in the Dhaka Stock Exchange and also find no significant association between board size and the extent of voluntary disclosure. Shehata (2017) also examines a sample of GCC banks and finds that board size is not associated with the extent of corporate governance disclosure. Ridwan and Mayapada (2020) find that board size has a significant negative impact on the extent of CSR disclosure for a sample of Indonesian Islamic banks.

In summary, overall, the extant literature suggests that board size is an important variable which sheds light on the relationship between corporate governance and the extent of disclosure. While some studies have found a negative or insignificant relationship, most studies suggest that board size positively influences the extent of voluntary disclosure. Accordingly, the following hypothesis is postulated:

H2. There is a positive association between board size and the extent of disclosure.

4.7.1.2. Board Independence

Independence is the cornerstone to effective control and governance of firms (Hopt & Leyens, 2004), helping to address agency problems[6] that arise from the separation of ownership and management of a firm (Dalton et al., 1999). Fama (1980) defines independent directors as professional referees whose primary task is to monitor management and stimulate and oversee competition among the firm's top management. Cheng and Courtenay (2006) describe independent directors as board members who are not directly involved in the firm's operations.[7]

A substantial body of studies (Allini et al., 2016; Barros et al., 2013; Fama, 1980; Forker, 1992; Chen & Jaggi, 2000; Cheng & Courtenay, 2006; Haniffa & Cooke, 2005; Huafang & Jianguo, 2007; Kilic et al., 2015; Klein, 2002) suggests that independent board members play an instrumental role in monitoring management, contributing to the effectiveness of boards in discharging their responsibilities. Fama (1980, p. 293) posits that independent board members enhance the viability of the board of directors and provide a low-cost internal mechanism for monitoring management. Cheng and Courtenay (2006) argue that independent directors play a vital role in enhancing board effectiveness because they are seen as neutral and do not have a vested interest in the firm or its management. Haniffa and Cooke (2005) argue that independent board members provide important checks and balances for the company and are vital to ensuring the protection of the interests of all stakeholders.

While these studies strongly argue that independent directors are indispensable, not all researchers agree. Some studies hold the view that independent board members are not effective at monitoring management's behavior. For instance, Hart (1995) argues that independent board members may not be effective for several reasons, including lack of time, a financial interest in the firm, or loyalty to the management that appointed them. Larcker and Tayan (2011) give other reasons that may render independent directors ineffective, such as inadequate business acumen,

---

[6] See Chapter Three for extensive discussion on agency theory and agency problems and its impact on the firm's governance structure and disclosure policies.

[7] The literature distinguishes between independent directors who are affiliated with management through family or business relations and those who have no relationship with management. The former group are known as "grey directors" while the latter group are considered "independent directors" (Cheng & Courtenay, 2006).

irrelevant professional background, lack of ethical standards, an ongoing relationship with the CEO, or financial dependence on their directorship fees.

Critical responsibilities of independent board members include advocating for a better disclosure policy and monitoring the firm's financial reporting. Klein (2002) asserts that independent board members are more effective than their non-independent counterparts at scrutinizing the financial accounting and reporting processes of firms. Haniffa and Cooke (2002) suggest that, as part of their role, independent board members are expected to campaign for more disclosure and that the higher the number of independent board members (i.e., more than 50%), the greater the extent of voluntary disclosure made by the firm. Lim et al. (2007) postulate that independent board members argue for more voluntary disclosure to reduce information asymmetry between shareholders and managers and are likely to avoid risks of reputational damage and/or legal liabilities. Moreover, Allegrini and Greco (2013) suggest that independent board members are motivated to encourage greater disclosure so as to send a message to the market that they are not in collusion with any dominant personalities on the board and also to enhance their own professional reputation.

A review of the extant literature reveals several research studies that examine the association between board independence and disclosure (Chen & Jaggi, 2000; Cheng & Courtenay, 2006; Donnelly & Mulcahy, 2008; Eng & Mak, 2003; Garas and ElMassah, 2018; Grassa & Chakroun, 2016; Haniffa & Cooke, 2002; Ho & Shun Wong, 2001; Jizi et al., 2014; Kilic et al., 2015; Lim et al., 2007; Samaha et al., 2015; Wan-Hussin, 2009). While the majority of these studies report a positive association between board independence and voluntary disclosure, other studies report a negative or no association. Some of these studies are discussed next.

Cheng and Courtenay (2006) examine the association between board monitoring and the level of voluntary disclosure and find a significant positive association between board independence and level of disclosure. They assert that firms with boards with a majority of independent members have a higher level of voluntary disclosure than firms with a minority of independent board members. Similarly, Huafang and Jianguo (2007) investigate the effect of board composition on voluntary disclosure for a sample of 559 Chinese-listed firms for the year 2002. Their study finds that board independence is positively associated with the extent of voluntary disclosure. The results of the study suggest that a higher proportion of independent board members leads to a greater level of voluntary disclosure.

Donnelly and Mulcahy (2008) find a strong positive association between the number of independent board members and the extent of disclosure, noting that the extent of voluntary disclosure increases with the number of independent board members. Moreover, Donnelly and Mulcahy report that firms with independent chairpersons have higher voluntary disclosure than those without, which seems to further corroborate their findings that board independence significantly contributes to greater transparency. Akhtaruddin et al. (2009) examine the impact of corporate governance on the extent of voluntary disclosure for a sample of 110 companies listed in Bursa Malaysia at the end of 2002. The results of the analysis reveal a positive association between the proportion of independent board members and the extent of voluntary disclosure. Accordingly, the authors conclude that a higher percentage of independent board members results in enhanced transparency and a greater level of information disclosure. Jizi et al. (2014) find a positive and significant relationship between board independence and size and CSR disclosure. They also suggest that firms with independent board members are likely to focus on long-term sustainability and are, therefore, more engaged in CSR disclosure. Kilic et al. (2015) find a positive and significant relationship between board independence and the extent of CRS disclosure. Nerantzidis and Tsamis (2017) examine a sample of Greek-listed firms and find that board independence has a significant positive impact on the extent of corporate governance disclosure.

Despite the research findings listed here, the overall results are not conclusive. Some studies suggest a negative association, while others do not find any relationship. For example, Haniffa and Cooke (2002) use a sample of 167 Malaysian-listed firms to examine the impact of corporate governance and cultural factors on the extent of voluntary disclosure by Malaysian companies. The study finds a negative association between an independent chairperson and the extent of disclosure, which indicates that the presence of an independent chairperson results in lower levels of disclosure. Similarly, Eng and Mak (2003) report a negative association between independent board members and the extent of disclosure, in which an increased level of board independence results in reduced disclosure. In a similar vein, Barako et al. (2006) examine the annual reports of Kenyan-listed companies from 1992 to 2001 to determine the impact of independent board members on the extent of disclosure. Their study also finds a negative association between the number of independent board members and the extent of disclosure. Ghabayen et al. (2016) find that board independence is negatively associated with the extent of disclosure for a sample of Jordanian banks. Al-Hadi et al. (2019) examine a sample of GCC-listed financial firms to determine the impact of corporate governance on the extent of risk disclosure. Their study finds that board independence is negatively associated with the extent of disclosure.

While the above studies report a negative relationship, there are a number of other studies that find no significant relationship between independent board members and voluntary disclosure. For instance, Wan-Hussin (2009) investigates the effect of board composition on the extent of disclosure. The study, based on a sample of 32 Malaysian firms, finds no evidence to support the idea that independent board members promote greater disclosure or enhance corporate transparency. Similar results are also reported by Ho and Shun Wong (2001), who examine the effect of independent board members on the extent of voluntary disclosure by using a sample of 98 firms listed on the Hong Kong Stock Exchange. They develop a disclosure index that takes into account the user's perceptions about the value of the items included in their index. Their study finds no significant association between the number of independent board members and the extent of disclosure by the firm.

The negative association between board independence and disclosure may be attributed to undue influence of the management of the firm. Of particular concern is the role that the CEO plays in appointing board members. Research indicates that CEOs play a crucial role in the selection of board members. Hermalin and Weisbach (1998) cite several previous studies, such as Mace (1971) and Vancil (1987), which suggest that the CEO plays a significant role in choosing the board of directors. Farinha (2003) suggests that the inherent domination of boards by managers may limit the ability of independent board members to effectively discharge their monitoring role. These studies underscore the challenge posed by managers and the undue influence that they can exert, thus hindering an independent board member's ability to monitor management objectively and effectively and influence the firm's disclosure practices.

In summary, while the evidence is inconclusive, it appears that the majority of studies investigating the impact of board independence on disclosure support the view that independent board members enhance board effectiveness and contribute to a greater level of disclosure. Consistent with prior studies, this book anticipates the existence of a positive relationship between board independence and the extent of disclosure by Islamic and conventional banks. Accordingly, the following hypothesis is postulated:

> *H3*. The proportion of independent board members is positively associated with the extent of disclosure.

4.7.1.3. Board Meeting Frequency

The board of directors is ultimately responsible for monitoring the firm's management. Board meetings[8] provide a crucial venue for members to conduct business in a formal setting, review and approve key strategies and policies, and ratify decisions. Board meetings provide members the opportunity to have direct, face-to-face discussion and exchange of ideas on important strategies and policies, thus enhancing the board's effectiveness (Adawi & Rwegasira, 2011). Therefore, the frequency of board meeting is considered an indication of the board's commitment, diligence, and effectiveness in discharging its governance responsibilities (Abbott et al., 2004; Barros et al., 2013; Brick & Chidamabaran, 2010; Laksmana, 2008; Vafeas, 1999). Board members who meet more frequently are able to demonstrate greater commitment and diligence to the firm's business. Accordingly, a limited number of studies have used the frequency of board meetings in examining various aspects of the firm, including performance and the extent of voluntary disclosure. These studies are discussed below.

Vafeas (1999) studies a sample of 307 firms from 1990 to 1994 to examine the impact of the board's meeting frequency on the company's performance. The result of the multivariate study reveals that the number of board meetings during the year is negatively associated with the firm's value. The author suggests that more frequent board meetings are associated with poor performance in part

---

[8] Generally, boards of listed firms, including banks, are required to meet on a quarterly basis. Also, most corporate governance codes, including Sarbanes Oxley in the United States and the Cadbury Report in the United Kingdom, require that boards hold at least four (4) meetings annually. Nevertheless, the global practice of companies appears to be converging on having eight (8) meetings annually (Adawi & Rwegasira, 2011).

because the market perceives the frequency as a sign of an ineffective board, leading to higher operational costs. Kent and Stewart (2008) examine the impact of frequency of board meetings on the extent of disclosure for a sample of 965 Australian-listed companies. The result of their regression analysis indicates that the frequency of board meetings is positively associated with the extent of the disclosure of information. In a similar vein, Laksmana (2008) studies the impact of corporate governance characteristics such as frequency of board meetings on the extent of voluntary disclosure of executive compensation information for a sample of firms listed on the S&P 500. The author finds a positive association between the board's meeting frequency and the extent of voluntary disclosure of executive compensation information.

Barros et al. (2013) find a positive association between meeting frequency and the level of disclosure, thus suggesting that boards which meet often have a positive effect on the firm's disclosure practice and greater transparency. Nerantzidis and Tsamis (2017) examine a sample of Greek-listed firms and find that board meeting frequency has a significant positive impact on the extent of corporate governance disclosure. Alnabsha et al. (2018) examine the impact of several corporate governance characteristics, including frequency of board meetings, on the extent of disclosure for a sample of Libyan companies. Their study concludes that board meeting frequency has a significant impact on the extent of voluntary disclosure. Ridwan and Mayapada (2020) find that board meeting frequency has a significant positive impact on the extent of CSR disclosure for a sample of Indonesian Islamic banks.

On the other hand, Allini et al. (2016) examine the impact of board meeting frequency on the extent of risk disclosure for a sample of state-owned Italian firms and find no significant association between the board's meeting frequency and extent of risk disclosure by the firm. Based on the above studies, the current research takes the position that board meeting frequency is associated with the extent of voluntary disclosure and, therefore, proposes the following hypothesis:

> *H4*. There is a positive relationship between the number of board meetings and the extent of disclosure.

4.7.1.4. CEO Duality

CEO duality refers to the phenomenon in which the CEO assumes the role of the board chairman in addition to his or her role as CEO of the firm (Garas & ElMassah, 2018; Haniffa & Cooke, 2002). Numerous studies have taken the position that combining the roles of CEO and chairman is unhealthy because it allows the CEO to control the board's agenda and hinders the board's ability to monitor management's performance (Haniffa & Cooke, 2002; Wan Abdullah et al., 2015), resulting in poor disclosure, thus further exacerbating information asymmetry among management, the board, and stakeholders (Al-Shammari & Al-Sultan, 2010). On the other hand, agency theory suggests that when the CEO and board chairmanship are combined it creates an environment in which the CEO could potentially engage in opportunistic behavior, thereby advancing his or her interests at the expense of shareholders (Al-Shammari & Al-Sultan, 2010; Jizi et al., 2014). Therefore, it can be observed from the review of the literature that separating the roles of CEO and board chairmanship enhances the firm's corporate governance environment, particularly for the Islamic banking sector, which has additional agency relationships due to the nature of its business model (CIBAFI, 2017; Wan Abdullah et al., 2015).

On the other hand, some studies do suggest that combining the roles of CEO and board chairmanship leads to greater efficiency, streamlines the decision-making process, and creates a more unified and coherent board. These studies are premised on the view that management has stewardship responsibility and is genuinely pursuing the interest of the firm's shareholders. Therefore, the board and management function most effectively when they are combined, with oversight and decision-making processes under one leader (i.e., the CEO) in order to deliver on the firm's objectives (Gul & Leung, 2004; Haniffa & Cooke, 2002). In this regard, a few studies find that this role duality is positively related to the extent of disclosure. For instance, Jizi et al. (2014) examine the impact of corporate governance characteristics, including CEO role duality, on the extent of CSR disclosure in the U.S. commercial banking sector. Their study concludes that CEO role duality is positively and significantly associated with banks' CSR disclosure. The authors suggest that powerful CEOs do encourage greater transparency of a bank's CSR activities for their own benefit. In a similar vein, Grassa and Chackroun (2016) find that CEO duality is positively associated with the extent of corporate governance disclosure for a sample of 74 GCC banks.

However, overall, a significant body of literature suggests that CEO duality tends to have a negative, insignificant, or no association with the extent of disclosure. For instance, Gul and Leung (2004) find that CEO duality results in a lower level of disclosure. Other studies that find a negative and/or insignificant association between CEO duality and disclosure are Haniffa and Cooke (2002, Malaysia); Cheng and Courtenay (2006, Singapore); Huafang and Jianguo (2007, China); Donnelly and Mulcahy (2008, Ireland); Al-Shammari and Al-Sultan (2010, Kuwait); Allegrini and Greco (2013, Italy); Giannarakis (2014, USA); Shehata (2017, GCC); Neifar and Jarboui (2018, Middle East and Southeast Asia); and Tessema (2019, GCC). Accordingly, this book postulates the following hypothesis:

> *H5*. There is a negative relationship between CEO role duality and the extent of disclosure.

4.7.1.5. Board Diversity

Board diversity has gained significant attention in recent years. Research suggests that board diversity contributes to overall effectiveness of boards in discharging their oversight and monitoring responsibilities and contributing to the success of the organization. Gender diversity within the board, which refers to the number of women on the board, is an area that has received significant attention over the last two decades.

While more progress has been made in including female members on the board in Europe and North America, in the Middle East, female representation on company boards is lagging significantly. For instance, the percentage of female board members in the Fortune 500 increased from 15.7% from early 2010 to 22.5% in 2018 (Fucci & Cooper, 2019). On the other hand, the figures in the Middle East remain significantly lower compared to other parts of the world. In the United Arab Emirates, females represent only 1.9% of board members of all listed companies (Hawkamah, 2017).

Board diversity has been used in the literature as one of the explanatory variables for board effectiveness. However, the findings of these studies show mixed results. Kilic et al. (2015) find that board diversity is significantly and positively associated with the extent of disclosure for a sample of Turkish-listed firms. Allini et al. (2016) report that board diversity has a significant positive impact on the extent of risk disclosure for a sample of Italian-listed firms. Ghabayen et al. (2016) study the impact of board characteristics, including board diversity, on the extent of CSR disclosure for a sample of 16 Jordanian banks. Using content analysis, the authors develop a disclosure index which consists of 100 disclosure items. The result of their empirical analysis reveals that board diversity has a negative significant association with the extent of disclosure. On the other hand, Shehata (2017) examines the impact of board characteristics, including board diversity, on the extent of corporate governance disclosure for a sample of GCC banks. The result of the study indicates that board diversity is not associated with the extent of disclosure. However, Nerantzidis and Tsamis (2017) find that board diversity has a significant positive association with the extent of corporate governance disclosure for a sample of Greece firms. Hollindale et al. (2019) examine the association between board diversity and the extent of greenhouse gas emissions-related disclosure for a sample of Australian-listed firms. Their study finds that companies with a greater number of female board members tend to provide higher greenhouse gas emission disclosures. Based on the prior literature discussed above, this book expects that board diversity will have a positive impact on the extent of disclosure and that a higher number of women board members will result in greater disclosure. Accordingly, the following hypothesis is proposed:

> *H6*. There is a positive relationship between the proportion of women on the board and the extent of disclosure.

4.7.2. Internal Control Strength

4.7.2.1. Overall Internal Control Strength Score

This book develops an index of internal control strength to examine its impact on the extent of disclosure by Islamic and conventional banks in GCC countries. The index comprises internal control dimensions most commonly associated with disclosure, including audit committee size, independence, meeting frequency, financial expertise, and the existence of an independent IAF. Numerous prior studies suggest that audit committee and IAF characteristics are positively associated with the extent of disclosure. Accordingly, an aggregated score comprising these internal control dimensions is expected to have a positive association with the extent of disclosure. Accordingly, and in line with the findings of the study undertaken by CIBAFI (2017), this book postulates the following hypothesis:

> *H7*. Internal control strength has a positive association with the extent of disclosure.

4.7.2.2. Individual Dimensions of the Internal Control Environment

4.7.2.2.1. Audit Committee Size. The size of the audit committee, which comprises the total number of audit committee members, is an important element of corporate governance that influences the extent of disclosure by firms (DeZoort et al., 2002). The complexity of the monitoring duties and responsibilities assigned to the audit committee requires that an adequate number of directors be appointed to the committee. Several studies suggest that three members is the minimum size for an audit committee (Abbott et al., 2004).

A substantial body of literature examines the impact of the audit committee, including its size, on the extent of disclosure. Mangena and Pike (2005) find no significant relationship between committee size and the extent of disclosure for a sample of UK-listed firms. Hidalgo et al. (2011) conduct a study of Mexican-listed firms and find that more audit committee members result in greater disclosure of information. Akhtaruddin and Rouf (2012) investigate the impact of size on the extent of disclosure for a sample of Bangladeshi-listed firms. Their results reveal that committee size is positively associated with the extent of disclosure. Li et al. (2012) find that audit committee size is positively associated with the extent of intellectual property disclosure by UK firms. Madi et al. (2014) study the effect of audit committee size on the extent of voluntary disclosure for a sample of 146 Malaysian-listed firms for the year of 2009. Their study finds that audit committee size is positively associated with the extent of voluntary disclosure by firms. Appuhami and Tashakor (2017) conduct study of a sample of Australian-listed firms to examine the impact of several audit committee characteristics, including audit committee size, on the extent of CSR disclosure. Their study finds that the audit committee has a strong positive impact on the extent of voluntary CSR. Ridwan and Mayapada (2020) examine the impact of audit committee characteristics, including size, on the extent of CSR disclosure for a sample of Indonesian Islamic banks. Their study concludes that audit committee size has no significant impact on the extent of CRS disclosure.

Collectively, the results of the previous studies lend support to the premise that audit committee size strengthens the committee's effectiveness, enhances the firm's transparency, and contributes to greater levels of disclosure. Accordingly, the following hypothesis is proposed:

> *H8*. The size of the audit committee has a positive relationship with the extent of disclosure.

4.7.2.2.2. Audit Committee Independence. Independence is essential for the audit committee's oversight role and its ability to monitor effectively. Klein (2002) defines independent audit committee members as those members who have no relationship with the company that may impair their independence from management and the company. The proportion of independent audit committee members is used as a measure for the effectiveness of the committee (Abbott et al., 2004). Studies suggest that the proportion of independent board members is associated with the extent of disclosure (Li et al., 2012).

While most studies find a positive association between audit committee independence and disclosure, the result is not conclusive, as some studies report negative or insignificant relationships. For instance, Kent and Stewart (2008) examine a sample of Australian-listed firms to determine the impact of corporate governance quality on the extent of disclosure. Their study concludes that audit committee independence has no significant impact on the extent of disclosure. In a similar vein, Li et al. (2012) examine the impact of audit committee characteristics, including independence, on the extent of intellectual property disclosure for a sample of UK firms. Their study finds no significant association between audit committee independence and the extent of intellectual property disclosure. Ridwan and Mayapada (2020) also find no significant association between the independence of the audit committee and the extent of CRS disclosure for Indonesian Islamic banks.

As noted earlier, most studies seem to suggest a positive association between audit committee independence and disclosure. For instance, Madi et al. (2014) find that audit committee independence is positively associated with the extent of voluntary disclosure. Barros et al. (2013) investigate the impact of certain corporate governance characteristics, including audit committee independence, for listed firms in the French markets. They find that audit committee independence is positively associated with the extent of disclosure. Appuhami and Tashakor (2017) find a strong positive association between audit committee independence and the extent of voluntary CSR disclosure for a sample of listed Australian firms. Garas and ElMassah (2018) conduct a study of the impact of corporate governance characteristics including audit committee independence on the extent of CSR disclosure for a sample of 147 firms in the GCC countries. The study reports a positive association between audit committee independence and the extent of CSR disclosure, concluding that an independent audit committee contributes to greater transparency and information disclosure. Buallay and Al-Ajmi (2020) find that audit committee independence is positively associated with the extent of sustainability-related disclosures by a sample of GCC banks. Based on the above studies, and in line with the overall direction of the extant literature, this study postulates that an independent audit committee contributes to greater disclosure:

> *H9*. The proportion of independent members in the audit committee has a positive relationship with the extent of disclosure.

4.7.2.2.3. Audit Committee Meeting Frequency. The literature suggests that meeting frequency is one of the key measures for assessing the effectiveness of the audit committee (DeZoort et al., 2002). Meeting frequency refers to the number of meetings held during a given year. The literature suggests that frequent meetings are associated with greater diligence and monitoring (Abbott et al., 2004).

Barros et al. (2013) argue that more frequent meetings of audit committees and boards require management to prepare more information, contribute to enhancing the level of monitoring and oversight, and encourage management to be transparent.

A number of studies examine the effect of audit committee meetings on the extent of disclosure. For instance, Kent and Stewart (2008) report that audit committee meeting frequency has a significant influence over the extent of disclosure. Similarly, Li et al. (2012) find that meeting frequency is positively associated with the extent of intellectual property disclosure. Allegrini and Greco (2013) examine the impact of audit committee meeting frequency on the extent of voluntary disclosure for a sample of Italian-listed firms. Their study finds a positive association between the frequency of meetings and the extent of voluntary disclosure. On the other hand, Barros et al. (2013) find that the frequency of audit committee meetings is negatively associated with the extent of voluntary disclosure for French-listed firms. Similarly, Madi et al. (2014) examine a sample of Malaysian-listed firms to determine the impact of audit committee characteristics on the extent of disclosure. Their study finds no significant association between audit committee meeting frequency and the extent of disclosure. Appuhami and Tashakor (2017) report that audit committee meeting frequency has a significant positive association with the extent of voluntary CSR disclosure for a sample of listed Australian firms. In a similar vein, Buallay and Al-Ajmi (2020) report that audit committee meeting frequency is positively associated with the extent of sustainability disclosure by GCC banks. Considering the overall findings of the above studies, this book posits that more frequent audit committee meetings will lead to greater disclosure and transparency. Accordingly, the below hypothesis is postulated:

> *H10.* The number of audit committee meetings held during the year is positively associated with the extent of disclosure.

4.7.2.2.4. Audit Committee Financial Expertise, The audit committee plays crucial oversight and monitoring roles in management. The increasingly complex business operations and sophisticated financial and accounting issues that organizations face necessitate that audit committees include individuals with appropriate financial expertise and accounting knowledge (Abbott et al., 2004; Kusnadi et al., 2016). A review of the literature suggests that the financial expertise of audit committee members is one of the measures that determines the committee's effectiveness and its ability to duly discharge its oversight and monitoring responsibilities. Research suggests that the financial expertise of audit committee members influences the firm's transparency and disclosure level (Haniffa & Cooke, 2002). For instance, Mangena and Pike (2005) undertake an empirical study to examine the impact of audit committee characteristics, including size and financial expertise, on the extent of disclosure for a sample of 262 UK-listed firms. Their study concludes that an audit committee's financial expertise is positively associated with the extent of the firm's disclosure. In a similar vein, Li et al. (2012) examine the effect of the audit committee's financial expertise on the extent of intellectual property disclosure. Their study reveals that a greater level of financial expertise is associated with increased disclosure. Kusnadi et al. (2016) conduct a study of Singaporean-listed firms to examine the impact of audit committee characteristics on the quality of financial reporting. Their study finds that audit committee financial expertise has a significant positive association with the quality of financial reporting by Singaporean-listed firms.

While the majority of studies indicate a positive relationship between audit committee financial expertise and the extent of disclosure, some studies find an insignificant or a negative association. For example, Kent and Stewart (2008) find that audit committee expertise has a negative impact on the extent of disclosure. In a study of 124 Malaysian-listed companies, Akhtaruddin and Haron (2010) find no significant association between audit committee expertise and voluntary disclosure. In a similar vein, Madi et al. (2014) examine the impact of audit committee characteristics, including size, independence, and financial expertise, on the extent of voluntary disclosure for a sample of 146 Malaysian-listed firms. The study finds no significant relationship between financial expertise and the extent of disclosure. Buallay and Al-Aljmi (2020) find that audit committee financial expertise is negatively associated with the extent of sustainability disclosure. Considering the overall direction of prior studies, this book expects that audit committee financial expertise does enhance the audit committee's effectiveness and contributes to greater transparency:

> *H11*. The proportion of audit committee members with financial expertise has a positive relationship with the extent of disclosure.

4.7.2.2.5. Internal Audit Function Existence and Independence. The internal audit plays a pivotal role in the governance structure of firms and contributes to the establishment of an effective control environment (BCBS, 2015; Hermanson & Rittenburg, 2003; Sarens et al., 2012; Sulub et al., 2020). It operates as the eyes and the ears of the board, providing assurance to the board, the audit committee, and senior management on the effectiveness of the governance processes, risk management, and the internal control environment (BCBS, 2015; Hermanson & Rittenburg, 2003). In the past two decades and following high-profile accounting scandals such as Enron and WorldCom, the role of the IAF has taken more prominence, providing valuable advice to management on sound corporate governance practices (Sulub et al., 2020).

The existence of an independent IAF is a crucial part of the governance structure of organizations and enhances both the overall control environment and disclosure of information to stakeholders (Ganesan et al., 2017; Gramling et al., 2004; Karagiorgos et al., 2010; Lin et al., 2011; Zou, 2019). BCBS (2015) asserts in its corporate governance guidelines for the banking sector that banks should establish an independent IAF which reports directly to the board or the audit committee. A review of the extant literature reveals that the existence of an independent IAF has been used as a proxy for effective corporate governance (Sarens et al., 2012). For example, Holt (2012) finds that the disclosure credibility of firms is perceived by investors to be significantly higher when an independent internal audit exists, one which is reporting directly to the audit committee or the board. Ganesan et al. (2017) examine the impact of several corporate governance attributes on sustainability disclosure for a sample of Malaysian firms and use the IAF as moderating the relationship between corporate governance attributes and the extent of sustainability disclosure. Their study concludes that the IAF does have a moderating effect on the relationship between corporate governance attributes and the extent of sustainability disclosure. In line with the literature, this book uses IAF attributes, namely, the existence of an independent IAF, to examine the impact of such governance attributes on the extent of disclosure. Accordingly, the below hypotheses are postulated:

H12. The existence of an IAF has a positive association with the extent of disclosure.

H13. The independence of the IAF has a positive association with the extent of disclosure.

4.7.3. Shariah Governance Strength

The survey of the extant literature suggests that strong Shariah governance is of great importance to the overall success and long-term survival of Islamic banks. Furthermore, the literature suggests that Shariah governance is associated with the extent of disclosure. To examine the effect of the SSB on the extent of disclosure of Islamic banks, studies have used several explanatory variables, such as SSB size, meeting frequency, educational qualification, and the financial expertise of members (Abdallah et al., 2015; Abdul Raman & Bukair, 2013; Elamer et al., 2019; Farook et al., 2011; Nomran et al., 2018; Ridwan & Mayapada, 2020; Wan Abdullah et al., 2013). Most of these studies have developed a Shariah governance score which includes these variables and is designed to assess the overall impact of the SSB on the extent of disclosure (Farook et al., 2011). In line with prior studies, this study develops a Shariah governance strength index using the SSB and other Shariah governance-related characteristics which are discussed below. The Shariah governance index enables the researcher to assess the overall impact of Shariah governance on disclosure more effectively and to gain greater insight. Moreover, this approach has been used widely in the literature and is consistent with Farook et al. (2011), Abdul Raman and Bukair (2013), CIBAFI (2017), and Elamer et al. (2019). Accordingly, the following hypothesis is proposed:

H14. Shariah governance strength score has a positive relationship with the extent of disclosure.

4.7.3.1. SSB Size

In general, corporate literature has considered the size of boards as one of the variables which determine their effectiveness. Given the SSB's supervisory and oversight role, similar to the role of the board of directors (Farook et al., 2011), a number of studies have examined the SSB's size to shed light on its impact on the level of disclosure and transparency by Islamic banks (Abdul Raman & Bukair, 2013; Farook et al., 2011; Wan Abdullah et al., 2015). For the most part, these studies suggest that a large SSB results in more disclosure. For instance, Wan Abdullah et al. (2013) argue that larger SSBs are better positioned to enhance an Islamic bank's transparency and address the needs of various stakeholders. Moreover, they assert that a large SSB is more likely to contain diverse skills and education, including business and financial expertise, to engage in in-depth discussions and thorough analysis and reviews and to promote greater transparency and better disclosure practices.

The extant literature indicates that there is a relationship between SSB size and the level of voluntary disclosure. Farook et al. (2011) study the impact of the SSB and its characteristics such as size, cross-membership of the directors, their reputations, and educational qualifications on the extent of CSR disclosure, based on a sample of 47 banks from 14 countries. Referring to earlier studies (e.g., Gompers et al., 2003), the authors develop an Islamic governance score consisting of the SSB characteristics noted above. The study reveals that overall, the Islamic governance score is positively associated with the extent of CSR disclosure by Islamic banks. Abdul Raman and Bukair (2013) examine a sample of 58 Malaysian Islamic banks to determine the impact of SSB size on the extent of CSR disclosure by the bank. Their study shows a significant positive association between the size of the SSB and the extent of CRS disclosure by Islamic banks. Mallin et al. (2014) study a sample of 90 Islamic banks in 13 countries to analyze the CSR disclosure of Islamic banks and its determinants as well as its impact on the performance of Islamic banks. The study finds that CSR disclosure is positively associated with performance. Moreover, the study finds that SSB characteristics such as size have a significant positive impact on the extent of CSR disclosure. Elamer et al. (2019) investigate the impact of SSB and other corporate governance characteristics on the extent of operational risk disclosure by Islamic banks in the MENA region. The study finds a strong and positive association between SSB characteristics, including size, and the extent of operational risk disclosure by Islamic banks.

4.7.3.2. SSB Meeting Frequency

In general, the meeting frequency of governing bodies has been used widely in the literature as an explanatory for the effectiveness of a governing body in fulfilling its responsibilities (Abbott et al., 2004; Alnabsha et al., 2018; Brick & Chidamabaran, 2010; Laksmana, 2008; Vafeas, 1999). Being the main governing body responsible for ensuring Shariah compliance, SSBs hold regular meetings in which they review an Islamic bank's financial transactions to ensure compliance with Shariah rules. Several studies use the meeting frequency of SSBs as a proxy for the effectiveness of the SSBs in discharging their oversight responsibilities (Abdul Raman & Bukair, 2013; Kasim, 2012; Neifar et al., 2020; Nugraheni & Anuar, 2014; Othman et al., 2009; Ousama & Fatima, 2010; Rafay & Farid, 2018).

4.7.3.3. SSB Educational Qualifications

The educational qualifications of the SSB play an important role in ensuring that the SSB has the knowledge required to effectively discharge its duties and responsibilities. Accordingly, SSB members who possess a doctoral degree are more capable of performing their duties and discharging their Shariah oversight responsibilities, which often involve analyzing complex financial transactions and determining compliance with Shariah rules and requirements (Nomran et al., 2018). Based on this, several prior studies have used educational qualifications (i.e., SSB members having a PhD) as a proxy for measuring the effectiveness and/or strength of the SSB in discharging its duties (Abdul Raman & Bukair, 2013; Kasim, 2012; Neifar et al., 2020; Nugraheni & Anuar, 2014; Othman et al., 2009; Ousama & Fatima, 2010; Zirman et al., 2019). For instance, Nomran et al. (2018) find that the possession of a doctoral degree by SSB members is positively associated with the bank's performance. Accordingly, this book uses the educational qualifications of the SSB as one of the dimensions for examining the strength of the Shariah governance of Islamic banks and its impact on the extent of disclosure.

4.7.3.4. SSB Financial Expertise

An examination of the extant literature reveals that an SSB member's financial expertise (proxied by holding a business-related educational degree) influences an Islamic bank's level of voluntary disclosure. Farook et al. (2011) argue that SSB members who are equipped with a business-related doctoral degree are in a better position to influence an Islamic bank's disclosure policy than those without one. Wan Abdullah et al. (2013) find that SSB expertise has an influence over the extent of Shariah-related disclosures by Islamic banks.

CIBAFI (2017) highlight in their corporate governance study the lack of diverse expertise among the members of SSBs as one of the most significant challenges facing Islamic banks. In line with prior literature, this book uses the financial expertise of the SSB as one of the explanatory variables for the impact of the SSB on the extent of disclosure by Islamic banks.

4.7.3.5. SSB Duties and Responsibilities

The SSB plays a central role in ensuring an Islamic bank's compliance with Shariah rules. It is, therefore, essential that the terms, roles, and responsibilities of the SSB are well-defined and formally articulated in the Islamic bank's publications (Al Mannai & Ahmed, 2018). The literature identifies several key responsibilities of the SSB. These include the issuance of clear and detailed fatwas, reviews of the Islamic bank's transactions, as well as overseeing the internal Shariah review unit. AlQassar and Ahmed (2021) highlight the key roles and responsibilities of the SSB. They state that the SSB's role is to provide direction, conduct ongoing reviews, and closely supervise the activities of the Islamic bank to ensure proper compliance with Shariah rules and principles. Given the significant role that the SSB plays in the overall governance structure of Islamic banks, having well-defined duties and responsibilities for SSBs has been used in the literature as an important measure of SSB effectiveness. For instance, in their seminal Islamic corporate governance work, CIBAFI (2017) performed an analysis of whether

Islamic banks have well-defined duties and responsibilities for the SSB members. They report an overall rating score of 69 for Islamic banks having clearly defined roles and responsibilities, suggesting that Islamic banks still have some work to do to enhance the clarity of SSB roles and responsibilities. In line with prior studies, this book uses SSB duties and responsibilities as an explanatory variable for the strength of the overall Shariah governance of Islamic banks.

4.7.3.6. Internal Shariah Audit Unit

A key aspect of the Shariah governance structure of Islamic banks is having a robust internal Shariah audit unit which carries out audits designed to ascertain that the Islamic bank complies the Shariah rules in all its dealings and transactions (Al Mannai & Ahmed, 2018). The internal Shariah audit unit is also responsible for reviewing and assessing the operations and products of an Islamic bank to ensure that it is fully compliant with Shariah rules and principles (AlQassar & Ahmed, 2022). Moreover, the internal Shariah audit unit must have an adequate level of independence so that it can properly discharge its responsibilities for monitoring the Islamic bank's transactions and report any noncompliance with Shariah rules and principles (AlQassar & Ahmed, 2022). Despite its critical role, a survey of the extant literature suggests that not all Islamic banks maintain an internal Shariah audit unit. For instance, CIBAFI (2017) conduct an extensive review of governance of Islamic banks and find that only 65% of the Islamic banks examined have an internal Shariah audit unit.

Due to its key role, the Shariah audit unit has been used in the literature as one of the key characteristics for determining the effectiveness of the overall Shariah governance of the Islamic bank. Furthermore, the literature suggests that the existence of an internal Shariah audit unit has an impact on the extent of disclosure. For instance, Sencal and Asutay (2020) find the existence of an internal Shariah audit unit to be associated with the extent of ethical disclosure of annual Shariah reports issued by Islamic banks. In line with these studies, this book postulates that having an internal Shariah audit in Islamic banks contributes to greater levels of disclosure.

4.7.3.7. External Shariah Audit

In addition to the Shariah audits performed by the internal Shariah audit unit within the bank, there have been growing calls for an external Shariah audit performed by an independent external party with subject matter expertise. It is to be noted that external audit firms (such as the Big 4) are primarily focused on carrying out a financial statement audit and do not perform a separate Shariah audit. Instead, audit firms review the audit reports of the internal Shariah audit unit as part of the reviews they perform for the external financial statement audit (Al Mannai & Ahmed, 2018).

Having an external Shariah audit lends creditability to an Islamic bank's Shariah compliance efforts and provides further assurance to its stakeholders. While the external Shariah audit is not required by standard setters such as AAOIFI

(Al Mannai & Ahmed, 2018), there seems to be growing interest in having Islamic banks be subjected to an external audit to ascertain their level of compliance with Shariah rules. For instance, in 2018, the Central Bank of Bahrain published new Shariah governance standards which introduced a number of new requirements for Islamic banks, including the requirement to be subjected to an independent external Shariah compliance audit on an annual basis. In line with the literature, this book postulates that the performance of an external Shariah audit contributes to more effective Shariah governance and affects the extent of disclosure.

4.8. Control Variables

Firm- and country-level characteristics provide important explanations and have been used in the literature as control variables. These variables are used in this book as control variables to ensure that their effects are taken into account when examining the determinants of disclosure. The extant literature suggests that there are several firm- and country-level characteristics which have an effect on the extent of disclosure (Abdelsalam et al., 2008; Al-Hadi et al., 2019; Baldini et al., 2018; Barako et al., 2006; Uyar et al., 2013). This book considers several firm-level characteristics, such as size, profitability, leverage, efficiency ratio, and CAR. The C2INC ratio is used to assess the operational efficiency of the firm. The ratio is inversely related to operational efficiency, meaning the higher the ratio, the less efficient the firm is (Abselsalam et al., 2008). The CAR is a measure that is used in determining the capital that a bank is required to hold (Abdelsalam et al., 2008). The ratio, which comprises Tier 1 and Tier 2 capital divided by risk-weighted assets, is an important measure that is used by regulators to ensure that banks maintain adequate capital. The higher the CAR, the greater the level of capital maintained by the bank (Abdelsalam et al., 2008).

In addition to firm-level control variables, this book controls for some macro-level variables which have been associated with the extent of disclosure and used by some prior studies (Elamer et al., 2019; El-Halaby & Hussainey, 2015; Ernstberger & Grüning, 2013). These are the ease of doing business index, regulatory quality, political stability, and GDP growth rate. El-Halaby and Hussainey (2015) employ macro-level variables, including GDP growth rate, legal system, culture, and corruption index, to control for their effect on the extent of CSR disclosure by a sample of Islamic banks. Elamer et al. (2019) use some country-level data, mainly from the World Bank and including indicators for political stability, regulatory quality, and GDP growth rate, to examine their impact on the extent of operational risk disclosures for a sample of MENA Islamic banks. Consistent with prior studies, this book controls for the firm- and country-level characteristics summarized in Table 5.3.

4.9. Summary and Conclusion

In summary, this chapter provides an overview of the existing literature on corporate governance and voluntary disclosure. Additionally, the chapter has examined earlier studies on the effect of corporate governance mechanisms such as board characteristics (board independence, size, frequency of meetings), internal controls characteristics (audit committee size and independence, existence of internal audit and its independence, type of external audit firm, etc.), and SSB characteristics on the extent of voluntary disclosure by Islamic and conventional banks.

The overall findings of these research studies lend support to the claim that stronger corporate governance leads to a higher level of voluntary disclosure. Similarly, researchers have found a relationship between poor corporate governance and information asymmetry. For example, Ahmed and Chapra (2002) observe that in environments where corporate governance is weak, disclosure quality tends to be poor and lacking. Bonazzi and Islam (2007) also suggest that poor corporate governance leads to market failures, non-existence of markets, moral hazards, asymmetric information, incomplete contracts, and adverse selection, among other problems.

Chapter Five

Analysis of Disclosure Practices in GCC Banks

Abstract

The previous chapter outlined the research methodology used for this book to address the research questions. It reviewed the research philosophies and approaches and explained the sampling technique. Additionally, the chapter provided a detailed discussion of the data collection methods and the data analysis tools used to analyze the data and present the results.

This chapter presents the descriptive statistics of the variables included in the empirical part of the research. The chapter begins with an introduction that provides an overview of the banks in the sample examined. The second section analyzes the disclosure index adopted for the study. While the third section provides detailed descriptive statistics for the study variables for both Islamic and conventional banks, the fourth section presents a correlation analysis to examine intercorrelations among the variables. The chapter also discusses the findings, focusing on differences between Islamic and conventional banks.

Keywords: Corporate governance; Shariah governance; disclosure index; Islamic banks; conventional banks; descriptive statistics

5.1. Introduction

This book examines a sample of 52 GCC Islamic and conventional banks over 5 years (2015–2019), yielding a total of 260 observations. Table 5.1 provides descriptive statistics for banks by type (Islamic vs. conventional) and by country. A total of 25 Islamic banks are included in this book, representing 48% of the total sample, while the remaining 27 banks in the sample are comprised of conventional banks, which represent 52% of the total banks in the sample. Table 5.2 provides

Corporate Governance and Disclosure in GCC Banks:
Islamic Perspectives, Empirical Insights and Policy Implications, 101–125

doi:10.1108/978-1-80686-279-520261005

Table 5.1. Descriptive Statistics of the Banks by Type.

Bank Type	Frequency	Percent	Cumulative Percent
Islamic	25	48.1	48.1
Conventional	27	51.9	100
Total	52	100	

Table 5.2. Descriptive Statistics of the Banks by Country.

Country	Frequency	Percent	Cumulative Percent
Bahrain	13	25.0	25.0
Kuwait	10	19.2	44.2
Oman	6	11.5	55.8
Qatar	8	15.4	71.2
Saudi Arabia	8	15.4	86.5
The United Arab Emirates	7	13.5	100.0
Total	52	100.0	

a breakdown of banks by country. The largest number of banks in the sample is based in Bahrain (25% of the banks in the sample), while Kuwait has the second largest (19%), with Oman having the smallest (11%). The remaining GCC countries each have approximately 15%. It is worth noting that the sample is based on Islamic and conventional banks whose annual reports are published and available.

5.2. Overall Disclosure Index Analysis

This book develops a disclosure index which is comprised of six categories, namely, bank profile and strategic information (BPSI), corporate governance, risk governance, Shariah governance, social responsibility, sustainability and value creation, and financial information, which together make up 70 items. Table 5.3 provides a summary of the categories and the number of disclosure items in each. Moreover, the following subsections provide an analysis of the disclosure scores by country, bank type, and year.

The extent of disclosure by country measures the average total disclosure score across all 5 years (2015–2019) for each GCC country. Table 5.4 provides a summary of the aggregate level of disclosure by country.

Table 5.4 shows that Oman has the highest score (76.79%), followed by Bahrain (73.38%), both of which exceed the average score across the countries in the sample (70.74%). Qatar also has an average disclosure score of 71.97%, slightly above the average score for all countries. On the other hand, Kuwait has

Table 5.3. Summary of Disclosure Items by Category.

No.	Category Description	Number of Items
1	Bank profile and strategic information	8
2	Corporate governance	11
3	Risk governance	6
4	Shariah governance	15
5	Social responsibility, sustainability, and value creation	19
6	Financial information	11
	Total	70

Table 5.4. Aggregate Disclosure Score by Country.

Oman	Bahrain	Qatar	Kuwait	The United Arab Emirates	Saudi Arabia	Overall Average for All Countries
76.79%	73.38%	71.97%	69.35%	66.30%	66.29%	70.74%

an average disclosure score of 69.35%, which is marginally lower than the mean score for all countries. However, the United Arab Emirates and Saudi Arabia have the lowest average disclosure scores when compared to the remaining countries (66.30% and 66.29%, respectively).

Table 5.5 illustrates that the aggregate disclosure level for all banks remains steady year over year, with most years having a slight increase, ranging from 69% in 2015 to 72% in 2019. The lowest disclosure is 69.09% in 2016, and the highest is 72.31% in 2019.

Overall, Table 5.5 shows a trend toward increased transparency and higher disclosure, in line with growing demand from bank stakeholders for more disclosure. Table 5.6 offers a detailed breakdown of disclosures by country and year. The table indicates that, for most countries, the disclosure score remains relatively steady over the years, with slight increases or decreases. However, the disclosure scores for Bahrain, Qatar, and Kuwait show a consistent rise from 2017 to 2019, signaling an improvement in transparency for these countries.

Table 5.5. The Extent of Total Disclosure Year over Year.

2015	2016	2017	2018	2019
69.20%	69.09%	71.58%	71.52%	72.31%

Table 5.6. Summary of Aggregate Disclosure Scores by Country and by Year.

Country	2015	2016	2017	2018	2019	Total
Oman	76.52%	76.82%	77.90%	76.62%	76.08%	76.79%
Bahrain	72.67%	72.37%	73.09%	74.01%	74.78%	73.38%
Qatar	71.40%	71.62%	70.91%	72.13%	73.78%	71.97%
Kuwait	66.78%	68.75%	69.22%	70.84%	71.17%	69.35%
The United Arab Emirates	65.75%	62.84%	69.17%	69.05%	64.69%	66.30%
Saudi Arabia	61.93%	61.33%	70.10%	66.04%	72.06%	66.29%
Total	69.20%	69.09%	71.58%	71.52%	72.31%	70.74%

5.2.1. Aggregate Disclosure Scores by Bank Type

The extent of disclosure can also be analyzed by bank type, namely, whether the bank is conventional or Islamic. Table 5.7 summarizes the extent of disclosure by bank type.

Overall, Table 5.7 shows that conventional banks are more transparent and provide greater disclosure in their annual reports. The overall average for conventional banks over the five years is 73.25%, whereas for Islamic banks, it is 68.02%, indicating that Islamic banks have lower disclosure levels than their conventional counterparts. This trend appears consistent throughout the 2015–2019 period covered in this book. In 2015, Islamic banks had a disclosure level of 65.83%, while their conventional counterparts were at 72.32%. Although the disclosure levels for both Islamic and conventional banks remained relatively stable in 2016, in 2017, disclosures increased to 74.4% for conventional banks and 68.51% for Islamic banks. In 2018, the overall disclosure score for conventional banks decreased slightly to 73.80%, while Islamic banks' score increased to 69.49%. In 2019, the disclosure level for conventional banks stayed roughly the same, whereas Islamic banks' score rose to 70.69%. Conversely, Table 5.8 presents the disclosure scores by bank type and country. Overall, the data indicate that, except for Bahrain and Kuwait, conventional banks tend to provide higher levels of disclosure than Islamic banks. In Bahrain and Kuwait, Islamic banks offer slightly higher disclosure levels compared to their conventional counterparts.

Table 5.7. Aggregate Disclosure by Year and by Bank Type.

Bank Type	2015	2016	2017	2018	2019	Overall Average
Islamic	65.83%	65.60%	68.51%	69.49%	70.69%	68.02%
Conventional	72.32%	72.32%	74.41%	73.40%	73.80%	73.25%

Table 5.8. Aggregate Disclosure by Country and by Bank Type.

Bank Type	Bahrain	Kuwait	Oman	Qatar	Saudi Arabia	The United Arab Emirates
Islamic	73.87%	69.54%	76%	62.10%	59.86%	55.14%
Conventional	72.27%	69.16%	77.18%	77.89%	72.73%	70.76%

However, as noted earlier, the overall results show that conventional banks provide greater disclosure than Islamic banks. The result is consistent with those of Wan Abdullah et al. (2013) and El-Halaby and Hussainey (2015), who report low disclosure levels for Islamic banks. However, the result contrasts with that of Grassa and Chakroun (2016), who find that Islamic banks provide better corporate governance disclosure than their conventional counterparts.

While Islamic banks lag in the extent of disclosure compared to their conventional counterparts, it is important to note that Islamic banks show a trend of improved disclosure levels over the study period (i.e., an increase from 65.83% in 2015 to 70.69% in 2019). This trend is consistent with that observed by Grassa and Chakroun (2016), who observe a gradual improvement in corporate governance disclosure by Islamic banks in the GCC countries.

It is worth noting that the difference in the extent of disclosure between Islamic and conventional banks is significant. The result of an independent samples *t*-test, as shown in Table 5.9, indicates that the disclosure difference between Islamic and conventional banks is significant ($t = -2.867$, df = 237, and $p = 0.002$). The findings are consistent with those of Aribi and Gao (2010), who report significant differences in the disclosure of CSR information between Islamic and conventional banks for a sample of GCC banks.

Given the recent establishment of Islamic banks in Oman, further analysis is conducted to determine whether differences in disclosure among banks in GCC countries are due to bank age. The banks are grouped into two categories: recent banks, which have been in existence for less than 25 years, and older banks, which have been in existence for more than 25 years. The results in Table 5.10 show that there is no significant difference in disclosure practices between recent and older banks, indicating that bank age does not have a significant impact on disclosure practices.

Table 5.9. Independent Sample *t*-test for the Disclosure Difference Between Islamic and Conventional Banks.

Dependent Variable	Bank Type	*N*	*M*	SD	*t*	df	*p*
Disclosure score	Islamic	125	0.68	0.121	−2.867	237	0.002
	Conventional	135	0.72	0.096			

Table 5.10. Independent Sample *t*-test for the Disclosure Difference Due to Bank Age.

Dependent Variable	Bank Age	*N*	*M*	SD	*t*	df	*p*
Disclosure score	Recent (<25 years)	65	0.69	0.077	1.288	85	0.201
	Older (>25 years)	60	0.67	0.154			

5.3. Category-level Disclosure Index Analysis

The disclosure index developed for this book consists of six main categories, as illustrated in Table 6.3. This section presents the disclosure index analysis for each of the six categories with a focus on comparing Islamic and conventional banks by country and year.

5.3.1. Category Level Disclosure Analysis by Year for All Banks

This section presents the evolution of the category-level disclosures over the years for all banks combined. As shown in Table 5.11, the corporate governance and risk governance categories have the highest disclosure scores (mostly 90% or above). The corporate governance disclosure score evolved from 90% in 2015 to approximately 92% in 2019, while the risk governance disclosure score increased from 92% in 2015 to 94% in 2019. On the other hand, the disclosure score for the social responsibility, sustainability, and value creation (SRSVC) category has the smallest disclosure score (approximately 50%), followed by the disclosure score for the BPSI category, which ranged from 55% in 2015 to 59% in 2019. This suggests that banks in GCC countries are lagging in their disclosure practices regarding SRSVC and BPSI information. The financial information category scored approximately 79%. Overall, the result shows a small but steady increase

Table 5.11. Category Level Disclosure Analysis by Year for all Banks.

Category	2015	2016	2017	2018	2019
Bank profile and strategic information	54.84%	55.63%	59.13%	58.38%	59.27%
Corporate governance	89.69%	89.16%	93.18%	91.61%	92.83%
Risk governance	92.31%	93.27%	93.91%	94.55%	94.23%
Shariah governance	64%	64.80%	67.20%	69.87%	70.93%
Social responsibility, sustainability, and value creation	49.60%	49.19%	52.02%	52.13%	53.44%
Financial information	79.37%	78.32%	79.37%	79.55%	79.72%

in disclosure scores for all the categories over the years, thus suggesting that there is a trend of incremental improvement in disclosure and transparency.

5.3.2. Category Level Disclosure Analysis by Country for All Banks

This section presents the category-level disclosures by country for all banks combined. As shown in Table 5.12, Bahrain scores highest in the BPSI category (94%), while Oman scores lowest (40%). For the corporate governance category, Oman and Bahrain have the highest scores (100% and 99%, respectively), and the UAE has the lowest score (75%). With regards to risk governance disclosure, Qatar scores the highest (98%), followed by Oman (96%) and the UAE (95%), and Bahrain had the lowest score (89%).

On the other hand, Oman has the highest score (87%) for the financial information disclosure category, followed by Qatar (82%) and the UAE (80%). Also, for disclosures related to SRSVC information, Oman scores highest (61%). Qatar and Kuwait come after Oman, scoring 54% and 52%, respectively. Overall, the results show that corporate and risk governance information is disclosed more than information in other categories, especially in the BPSI and SRSVC categories, which appear to be disclosed least.

5.3.3. Disclosure Analysis for the Shariah Governance Category: Specific to Islamic Banks

Table 5.13 provides an overview of Shariah governance-related disclosure by country. The table shows that Oman has the highest Shariah governance disclosure score (91%), followed by Bahrain (85%) and Kuwait (70%). On the other hand, Saudi Arabia has the lowest score (34%), followed by the UAE (45%).

Table 5.12. Category-level Disclosure Analysis by Country for All Banks.

Category	Bahrain	Kuwait	Oman	Qatar	Saudi Arabia	The United Arab Emirates
Bank profile and strategic information	63.96%	55.82%	39.88%	58.933%	59.51%	58.72%
Corporate governance	99.16%	89.27%	100%	91.59%	88.86%	74.55%
Risk governance	88.97%	94.67%	95.56%	98.33%	92.92%	94.76%
Shariah governance	85.04%	70.40%	91.33%	52%	34.33%	45.33%
Social responsibility, sustainability, and value creation	47.37%	52.32%	60.70%	53.82%	49.21%	48.42%
Financial information	79.16%	72.18%	87.27%	81.59%	79.32%	79.72%

Table 5.13. Shariah Governance Category Disclosure Analysis by Country.

Bahrain	Kuwait	Oman	Qatar	Saudi Arabia	The United Arab Emirates
85.04%	70.40%	91.33%	52.00%	34.33%	45.33%

Table 5.14. Shariah Governance Category Disclosure Analysis by Year.

2015	2016	2017	2018	2019
64.00%	64.80%	67.20%	69.87%	70.93%

Table 5.14 presents an overview of Shariah governance disclosures by year. The results show that the level of Shariah governance disclosure has gradually increased from 64% in 2015 to 71% in 2019. Although the improvement in Shariah governance disclosure is significant, it is also clear that Shariah governance disclosure still lags behind the disclosure of other information by Islamic banks, such as corporate and risk governance disclosures.

5.4. Descriptive Statistics for the Study Variables

The variables considered in this book are broadly categorized into two main categories: explanatory and control. The explanatory variables are those attributable to corporate governance mechanisms and are used to measure their impact on disclosure. These variables are further categorized into three main themes: board characteristics, internal control characteristics, and Shariah governance characteristics. The descriptive statistics for each thematic area are discussed below. The control variables considered for this book, which include bank size, profitability, leverage, efficiency, and regulatory compliance, are also discussed in this section.

5.4.1. Board Characteristics

Table 5.15 reports descriptive statistics for the board of directors, including board size, independence, meeting frequency, diversity, and CEO role duality. The table shows that the largest board size is 15, while the smallest is 4, and the mean board size is 9.36. The mean board size is consistent with other studies, which report an average board size of 9 for GCC-listed companies (Elamer et al., 2019; Grassa & Matoussi, 2014; Hawkamah, 2019). However, the average board size in the GCC is slightly smaller than the global average, which is 10 (Hawkamah, 2019).

On the other hand, the mean percentage of independent board members is 38%, while the highest percentage of independent board members is approximately 91% and the smallest is 0%. This is lower than the recommended minimum percentage of 50% for independent members (Hawkamah, 2019). Moreover, it lags significantly behind the percentage of independent members in other parts

Table 5.15. Descriptive Statistics for the Study Variables.

Variables	*N*	**Min**	**Max**	**Mean**	**Median**	**SD**
Board size	260	4	15	9.36	9	1.562
Board independence	260	0.00	0.91	0.379	0.40	0.260
Board meeting frequency	260	2	23	7.61	7	3.20
CEO role duality	259	0	1	0.04	0.00	0.193
Board diversity	260	0.000	0.273	0.023	0.00	0.054
Audit committee size	260	2	6	3.49	3	0.717
Audit committee independence	260	0.00	1.00	0.563	0.667	0.340
Audit committee meeting frequency	260	2	28	5.92	6	2.313
Audit committee financial expertise	260	0	1.00	0.421	0.333	0.269
Internal audit existence	260	0	1	0.96	1	0.202
Internal audit independence	260	0	1	0.77	1	0.420
Bank size	260	46.24	821,968.02	42,959.60	17,475.62	92,903.92
Return on average assets	260	−32.00	2.87	0.698	1.35	3.62
Return on average equity	260	−36.81	25.49	8.57	10.18	9.73
Earnings quality	234	1.0	94.0	50.67	52.00	25.07
Cost to income	260	12.15	791.20	53.55	39.08	66.45
Leverage	260	1.04	11.98	7.25	7.39	2.04
Capital adequacy ratio	257	−6.10	65.07	18.72	17.67	6.54
Ease of doing business	260	59.60	81.30	67.08	66.8100	5.24
Regulatory quality	260	48.56	82.69	65.96	67.7900	10.00
GDP growth rate	260	−4.71	5.11	1.81	1.78	2.14

of the world, including Europe (62%) and the United States (85%).[1] On average, boards held 8 meetings per year, while the highest number of annual meetings held is 23, and the lowest is 2. The mean CEO role duality is 4%, suggesting that the majority of banks in the GCC comply with corporate governance standards and best practices that require the separation of the CEO and chairman of the board roles. The mean percentage of board diversity is 2.3%, indicating that very few boards have female board members, highlighting that GCC banks are lagging the global trend toward greater board gender diversity. This result is consistent with Hawkamah's (2019) findings, which report that the average percentage of female board members in the MENA region is 3.8%.

5.4.2. Internal Control Strength

Table 5.15 presents descriptive statistics for internal control strength, highlighting audit committee characteristics and the internal and external audit elements considered in the study. The table shows that the mean audit committee size is 3.5, with the highest number of audit committee members being 6 and the smallest being 2. The mean percentage of audit committee independence is 56.3%, with the range being between a maximum of 100% and a minimum of 0%. This seems to suggest that most banks in GCC do maintain some independent members within their audit committees. On the other hand, the highest number of audit committee meetings held during the year is 28, while the lowest is 2.

The mean number of audit committee meetings is approximately 6 per year. The standard division for audit committee meeting frequency is 2.313. The mean financial expertise for the audit committee is 42%, with a minimum of 0% and a maximum of 100%. The audit committee's financial expertise has a standard deviation of 0.269. The mean internal audit existence is 96%, which suggests that almost all banks in the GCC do have an IAF. The standard deviation for internal audit existence is 0.202. On the other hand, the mean internal audit independence is 77%, suggesting that even though most banks have an IAF, not all are set up as an independent function. The standard division for internal audit independence is 0.420. The mean external audit type is 100%, suggesting that all the banks in the GCC do retain a Big 4 audit firm. The standard deviation for the external audit type is 0.062.

5.4.3. Control Variables

This book considers several bank- and country-level control variables, as summarized in Table 5.15. The mean bank size is 42,960 (in millions USD), while the minimum is 46.24, and the maximum bank size is 821,968. This suggests that there is considerable disparity in bank sizes, as some of the banks have very large asset sizes, while others have small asset sizes. In terms of profitability, the mean

---

[1]For further details, refer to Hawkamah's (2019) report on Board Best Practices in the Middle East.

ROAA is 0.70, while the mean ROAE is 8.57. Another measure of profitability that has recently gained more importance is earnings quality.[2] As the above table shows, the mean percentile of earnings quality is 50.67, suggesting that a considerable number of banks have current earnings that may not be indicative of future earnings. The mean cost-to-income ratio is 53.55, and the mean leverage ratio is 7.25, while the minimum is 1.04 and the maximum is 11.98. The mean CAR is 18.72, which is above the required minimum adequacy ratio, thus suggesting a high degree of compliance with regulatory requirements. The mean regulatory quality ranking is 67.08, while the mean GDP growth rate is 1.81, both indicating that at the country level, overall regulatory quality and economic growth are rather slow and lagging.

5.4.4. Sharia Governance Strength (Specific to Islamic Banks)

Table 5.16 presents the descriptive statistics for the Shariah governance variables examined in this book. The mean SSB size is 3.91, and the size ranges from a minimum of three members to a maximum of six members. The SSB meeting frequency has a mean score of 7.14, and the number of meetings ranges from 0 to 49. The mean SSB duties defined is 96%, indicating that the majority of Islamic banks define the duties and responsibilities of their Shariah boards. The mean financial expertise among the SSBs is 23.2%, and the standard deviation is 0.246. The mean SSB educational qualification is 79.3%, indicating that a significant

Table 5.16. Descriptive Statistics of Shariah Governance Strength.

Variables	***N***	**Min**	**Max**	**Mean**	**Median**	**SD**
SSB size	125	3	6	3.91	4	0.984
SSB meeting frequency	86	0	49	10.29	5	12.45
SSB duties defined	125	0	1.00	0.96	1	0.197
SSB financial expertise	125	0.00	0.67	0.232	0.20	0.246
SSB educational qualification	125	0.20	1.00	0.793	1	0.222
Internal Shariah audit unit exist	125	0	1	0.94	1	0.246
External Shariah audit performed	125	0	1	0.13	0.00	0.335

[2]A proprietary profitability model developed by Refinitiv, which measures the quality and reliability of earnings and their likely sustainability in the future. The model ranks companies as a percentage based on the quality of earnings, with the highest rank being 100 (source: Refinitiv.com).

number of SSB members hold doctorate-level qualifications. The mean for internal Shariah audit unit existence is 0.94, while the mean external Shariah audit existence is 0.13, which reveals that while most Islamic banks maintain an internal Shariah audit unit, only a few have an external Shariah audit as part of their Shariah governance.

5.5. Correlation Testing

This section presents the results of the correlation testing performed for this book to determine the nature and direction of the association between the study variables. A bivariate correlation analysis is performed using Pearson's and Spearman's correlation tests to examine the relationship between corporate governance characteristics (independent variables) and the extent of disclosure (dependent variable). Correlational testing is used to establish the validity of the model's constructs and confirm its appropriateness. Correlation testing is also used to detect multicollinearity issues (Saunders et al., 2012; Wheeler & Tiefelsdorf, 2005). Furthermore, the correlation analysis helps the research test the association among variables and supports the inferential analysis to test the hypotheses and address the research questions.

5.5.1. Association of Corporate Governance Dimensions and Disclosure

This book considers several corporate governance characteristics which relate to board of directors, internal control strength, and Shariah governance. The board dimensions include board size, independence, board meeting frequency, board diversity, and CEO role duality. For internal control strength, audit committee-related characteristics, and internal audit quality, dimensions are considered. The Shariah governance dimensions include SSB size, educational qualifications, financial expertise, etc. Fig. 5.1 summarizes the three corporate governance thematic areas and their respective individual dimensions.

Table 5.17 provides the Pearson correlation test results for the association between disclosure and corporate governance dimensions, along with the control variables considered for this book. As shown in the table, the Pearson correlation test indicates that board size and independence are positively and significantly correlated with the extent of disclosure. Audit committee size, independence, and financial expertise are also found to be significantly and positively associated with disclosure. Aside from the audit committee-related characteristics, the independence of the IAF is significantly and positively associated with the extent of disclosure. The result of the Pearson correlation analysis for the corporate governance variables is generally consistent with the hypotheses and research questions developed for this book both in terms of the significance and direction of the correlation. The remaining corporate governance dimensions do not show any significant association with disclosure.

With regard to the control variables, the Pearson correlation analysis shows that bank size is significantly and positively associated with disclosure. Additionally,

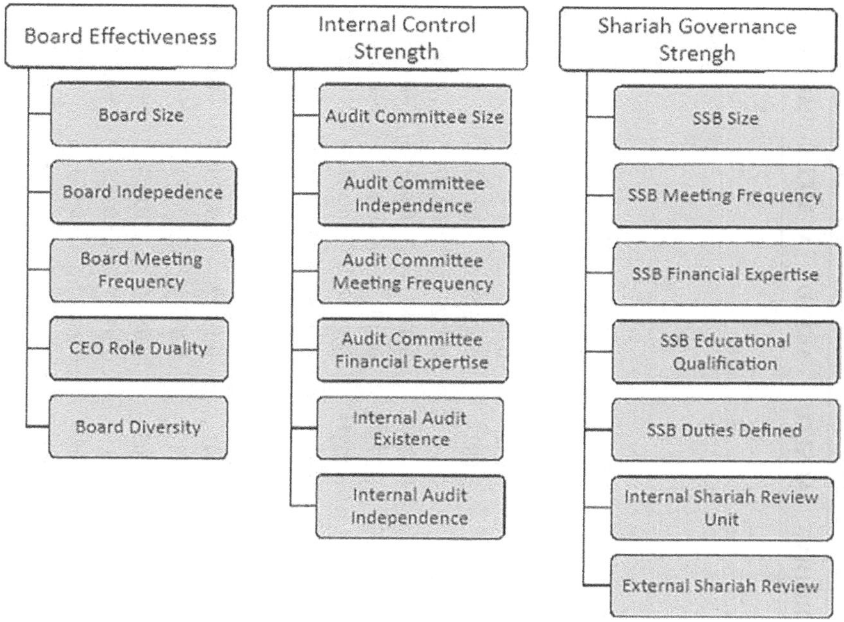

Fig. 5.1. Corporate Governance Thematic Areas and Their Individual Dimensions.

leverage is found to be significantly and positively associated with the extent of disclosure. The other control variables do not have any significant relationship with the extent of disclosure.

Table 5.18 illustrates the results for the Spearman's correlation test to determine the association between the corporate governance dimensions and disclosure for both conventional and Islamic banks included in the study. As shown in the table, the correlation test indicates that board size and independence have a significant and positive correlation with the extent of disclosure. Audit committee size, independence, and financial expertise are all found to be significantly and positively associated with disclosure. Aside from the audit committee-related characteristics, the existence of an internal audit has a positive association with the extent of disclosure, while the independence of the internal audit function is significantly and positively associated with the extent of disclosure. The result of the Spearman's correlation analysis for the corporate governance variables is generally consistent with the hypotheses and research questions developed for this book both in terms of the significance and direction of the correlation. The remaining corporate governance dimensions do not show any significant association with disclosure.

With regard to the control variables, the Spearman correlation analysis shows that leverage is significantly and positively associated with disclosure. Additionally, the CAR is found to be negatively associated with the extent of disclosure. The other control variables do not have any significant relationship with the extent of disclosure.

Table 5.17. Pearson Correlation of Corporate Governance Characteristics and Disclosure for Islamic and Conventional Banks.

	DISCORE	BDSIZE	BDIND	BDMEET	CDUO	BDDIV	ACSIZE	ACIND	ACMEET	ACEXP
DISCORE	1									
BDSIZE	0.201**	1								
BDIND	0.201**	0.205**	1							
BDMEET	0.09	−0.016	−0.184**	1						
CDUO	0.032	−0.161**	−0.056	−0.159*	1					
BDDIV	0.087	0.257**	0.017	0.082	−0.035	1				
ACSIZE	0.251**	0.408**	0.122*	0.054	−0.157*	0.141*	1			
ACIND	0.131*	0.168**	0.347**	−0.264**	0.027	−0.049	0.019	1		
ACMEET	0.041	0.055	0.039	0.219**	0.028	−0.013	0.052	−0.048	1	
ACEXP	0.156*	−0.002	0.212**	−0.054	0.112	−0.052	0.082	0.301**	−0.019	1
IAEXST	0.087	−0.11	0.066	−0.019	0.033	0.074	−0.065	0.022	0.150*	0.068
IAIND	0.329**	0.095	−0.069	0.011	0.105	0.057	−0.013	−0.028	0.063	−0.025
SIZE	0.161**	0.146*	−0.117	0.145*	−0.07	−0.08	0.272**	−0.101	0.028	−0.059
ROAA	0.033	0.141*	−0.116	0.249**	0.01	0.062	0.173**	−0.02	0.495**	0.061
ROAE	−0.066	0.152*	−0.211**	0.274**	−0.049	−0.004	0.214**	−0.06	0.334**	0.01
ERQ	−0.002	0.164**	−0.083	−0.03	−0.034	0.015	0.267**	0.013	−0.044	0.023
C2INC	−0.004	−0.054	0.252**	−0.242**	−0.009	−0.079	−0.150*	0.152*	−0.146*	−0.032
LEV	0.124*	0.114	−0.193**	0.359**	−0.148*	−0.046	0.041	−0.197**	0.329**	−0.007
CAR	−0.054	0.138*	0.027	−0.158*	0.12	0.124*	−0.12	0.092	−0.332**	−0.074
DBNDX	−0.062	0.063	0.065	−0.166**	−0.048	0.12	0.065	0.089	−0.004	−0.008
REGQ	0.077	−0.026	0.031	−0.11	−0.051	0.082	−0.09	0.109	−0.003	−0.07
PS	−0.019	−0.033	−0.027	0.056	0.027	−0.005	−0.006	−0.042	−0.033	0.091
GDP	0.004	0.095	0.11	−0.179**	0.031	0.002	0.052	0.197**	−0.049	0.058

	IAEXIST	IAIND	SIZE	ROAA	ROAE	EARQ	C2INC	LEV	CAR	BNDX	REGQ	PS	GDP
DISCORE													
BDSIZE													
BDIND													
BDMEET													
CDUO													
BDDIV													
ACSIZE													
ACIND													
ACMEET													
ACEXP													
IAEXST	1												
IAIND	0.317**	1											
SIZE	−0.162**	−0.047	1										
ROAA	0.169**	−0.023	0.126*	1									
ROAE	0.054	−0.052	0.216**	0.758**	1								
ERQ	0.002	0.014	0.190**	0.07	0.194**	1							
C2INC	0.016	0.062	−0.136*	−0.746**	−0.617**	−0.078	1						
LEV	0.107	0.158*	0.064	0.455**	0.484**	0.031	−0.405**	1					
CAR	−0.06	−0.049	−0.067	−0.089	0.023	0.01	0.023	−0.347**	1				
DBNDX	0.018	0.123*	0.211**	−0.019	0.056	0.106	0.036	−0.078	−0.088	1			

(*Continued*)

Table 5.17. (Continued)

	IAEXIST	IAIND	SIZE	ROAA	ROAE	EARQ	C2INC	LEV	CAR	BNDX	REGQ	PS	GDP
REGQ	0.053	0.241**	0.076	−0.076	0.014	−0.068	0.072	−0.06	−0.065	0.766**	1		
PS	0.058	0.039	0.074	0.051	0.014	0.068	−0.09	0.025	0.022	−0.049	−0.094	1	
GDP	−0.076	0.01	−0.018	−0.065	−0.042	0.018	0.07	−0.127*	0.032	0.414**	0.416**	0.051	1

**Correlation is significant at the 0.01 level (2-tailed). *Correlation is significant at the 0.05 level (2-tailed).

DISCORE, disclosure score; BDSIZE, board size; BDIND, board independence; BDMEET, board meeting frequency; CDUAL, CEO role duality; BDDIV, board diversity; ACSIZE, audit committee size; ACIND, audit committee independence; ACMEET, audit committee meeting frequency; ACEXP, audit committee financial expertise; IAEXST, internal audit existence; IAIND, internal audit independence; SIZE, natural logarithm of bank assets; ROAA, return on average assets; ROAE, return on average equity; EARQ, earnings quality; C2INC, cost to income ratio; LEV, leverage; CAR, capital adequacy ratio; DBNDX, ease of doing business index; REGQ, regulatory quality; PS, political stability; GDPG, GDP growth rate.

Table 5.18. Spearman's Correlation of Corporate Governance Characteristics and Disclosure for Conventional and Islamic Banks.

	DISCORE	BDSIZE	BDIND	BDMEET	CDUO	BDDIV	ACSIZE	ACIND	ACMEET	ACEXP
DISCORE	1									
BDSIZE	0.201**	1								
BDIND	0.237**	0.205**	1							
BDMEET	0.095	−0.016	−0.184**	1						
CDUO	−0.01	−0.161**	−0.056	−0.159*	1					
BDDIV	0.114	0.257**	0.017	0.082	−0.035	1				
ACSIZE	0.233**	0.408**	0.122*	0.054	−0.157*	0.141*	1			
ACIND	0.209**	0.168**	0.347**	−0.264**	0.027	−0.05	0.019	1		
ACMEET	0.096	0.055	0.039	0.219**	0.028	−0.01	0.052	−0.048	1	
ACEXP	0.160**	−0.002	0.212**	−0.054	0.112	−0.05	0.082	0.301**	−0.019	1
IAEXIST	0.146*	−0.11	0.066	−0.019	0.033	0.074	−0.065	0.022	0.150*	0.068
IAIND	0.337**	0.095	−0.069	0.011	0.105	0.057	−0.013	−0.028	0.063	−0.025
SIZE	0.079	0.140*	−0.179**	0.267**	−0.204**	−0.127*	0.363**	−0.096	0.140*	−0.027
ROA	−0.114	0.234**	−0.153*	0.003	−0.03	−0.01	0.256**	0.097	0.083	0.038
ROE	−0.056	0.165**	−0.210**	0.188**	−0.12	−0.04	0.217**	−0.01	0.144*	0.001
EARQ	0.028	0.148*	−0.072	−0.012	−0.045	0.013	0.253**	0.01	−0.038	0.012
C2INC	−0.017	−0.160**	0.336**	−0.139*	−0.074	−0.04	−0.192**	0.198**	−0.158*	0.076
LEV	0.150*	0.053	−0.174**	0.336**	−0.149*	−0.06	−0.066	−0.232**	0.201**	−0.037
CAR	−0.133*	0.07	0.057	−0.170**	0.149*	0.014	−0.042	0.102	−0.201**	0.11
DBINDX	0.082	0.096	0.102	−0.251**	−0.031	0.086	0.045	0.220**	−0.035	0.013
REGQ	0.12	−0.043	−0.009	−0.068	−0.059	0.084	−0.09	0.04	0.026	−0.108
PS	0.021	−0.029	−0.012	0.071	0.021	0.009	0.01	0.007	−0.023	0.145*
GDP	0.013	0.105	0.104	−0.200**	0.018	0.004	0.039	0.169**	−0.058	0.037

(*Continued*)

Table 5.18. (Continued)

	IAEXIST	IAIND	SIZE	ROAA	ROAE	EARQ	C2INC	LEV	CAR	BINDX	REGQ	PS	GDP
DISCORE													
BDSIZE													
BDIND													
BDMEET													
CDUO													
BDDIV													
ACSIZE													
ACIND													
ACMEET													
ACEXP													
IAEXIST	1												
IAIND	0.317**	1											
SIZE	−0.124*	−0.1	1										
ROA	−0.061	−0.133*	0.564**	1									
ROE	−0.013	−0.04	0.615**	0.880**	1								
EARQ	0.006	−0.01	0.349**	0.305**	0.293**	1							
C2INC	0.032	−0.03	−0.537**	−0.627**	−0.598**	−0.253**	1						
LEV	0.112	0.256**	0.133*	−0.093	0.227**	0.009	−0.029	1					

CAR	−0.034	−0.12	−0.074	0.126*	−0.053	0.057	−0.059	−0.378**	1				
DBINDX	−0.023	0.111	−0.078	0.182**	0.132*	0.065	0	−0.124*	−0.294**	1			
REGQ	0.039	0.233**	−0.05	0.124*	0.198**	−0.051	−0.1	0.025	−0.290**	0.708**	1		
PS	0.055	−0.01	0.113	0.025	0.038	0.114	−0.064	0	0.052	−0.095	−0.04	1	
GDP	−0.078	0.053	−0.178**	0.038	0.02	−0.069	0.097	−0.084	−0.092	0.480**	0.395**	0	1

**Correlation is significant at the 0.01 level (2-tailed). *Correlation is significant at the 0.05 level (2-tailed).

DISCORE, disclosure score; BDSIZE, board size; BDIND, board independence; BDMEET, board meeting frequency; CDUAL, CEO role duality; BDDIV, board diversity; ACSIZE, audit committee size; ACIND, audit committee independence; ACMEET, audit committee meeting frequency; ACEXP, audit committee financial expertise; IAEXST, internal audit existence; IAIND, internal audit independence; SIZE, natural logarithm of bank assets; ROAA, return on average assets; ROAE, return on average equity; EARQ, earnings quality; C2INC, cost to income ratio; LEV, leverage; CAR, capital adequacy ratio; DBNDX, ease of doing business index; REGQ, regulatory quality; PS, political stability; GDPG, GDP growth rate.

5.5.2. Association of Shariah Governance Dimensions and Disclosure (Specific to Islamic Banks)

This research considers several Shariah governance dimensions in line with prior studies, including SSB size, educational qualifications, financial expertise, and the existence of internal and external Shariah audits. Pearson and Spearman's correlation tests are used to analyze the association between the variables considered in this book. The results of the correlation testing are summarized in Tables 5.19 and 5.20.

Table 5.19 presents the Pearson correlation test results for the association between disclosure and Shariah governance dimensions, along with the control variables considered in this book. Overall, the result shows that the Shariah governance strength score is significantly and positively associated with the extent of disclosure. For the individual Shariah governance dimensions, the Pearson correlation test indicates a significant, positive relationship between the "SSB duties defined" dimension and the extent of disclosure. External Shariah audit existence is also significantly and positively associated with the extent of disclosure. There are no significant associations between the extent of disclosure and SSB size, financial expertise, educational qualifications, or the existence of an internal Shariah audit function. The results of the Pearson correlation analysis for the Shariah governance variables are generally consistent with the hypotheses and research questions developed for this book, both in terms of significance and direction.

Regarding the control variables, the Pearson correlation analysis shows that bank size has a significant and negative association with disclosure. Additionally, return on average equity is found to be significantly and negatively associated with the extent of disclosure. The other control variables do not have any significant relationship with the extent of disclosure.

Table 5.20 provides the Spearman correlation test results for the association of disclosure and Shariah governance dimensions, along with the control variables considered for this book. Overall, the result shows that the Shariah governance strength score is significantly and positively associated with the extent of disclosure. For the individual Shariah governance dimensions, the results show a significant, positive relationship between SSB financial expertise and the extent of disclosure by Islamic banks.

Moreover, the table shows a significant, positive relationship between "SSB duties defined" and the extent of disclosure. External Shariah audit existence is also significantly and positively associated with the extent of disclosure. There are no significant associations between the extent of disclosure and SSB size, SSB duties, educational qualifications, or the existence of an internal Shariah audit function. The results of Spearman's correlation analysis for the Shariah governance variables are generally consistent with the hypotheses and research questions developed for this book, both in terms of significance and direction.

Regarding the control variables, the Spearman's correlation analysis shows that bank size has a significant negative association with disclosure. Additionally, both return on average equity and return on average assets are found to be significantly and negatively associated with the extent of disclosure. The cost-to-income

Table 5.19. Pearson Correlation of Shariah Governance Dimensions and the Extent of Disclosure for Islamic Banks.

	DISCORE	SSBGOV	SSBSIZE	SSBEXP	SSBEDU	SSBDD	SSBMEET	ISAUD	ESAUD	SIZE
DISCORE	1									
SSBGOV	0.328**	1								
SSBSIZE	0.122	0.768**	1							
SSBEXP	0.214**	0.609**	0.318**	1						
SSBEDU	0.046	0.256**	0.11	0.209**	1					
SSBDD	0.286**	0.355**	0.153*	0.234**	−0.05	1				
SSBMEET	0.131	0.295**	0.314**	−0.309**	−0.218**	0.105	1			
ISAUD	0.14	0.401**	0.196*	0.102	−0.064	0.781**	0.134	1		
ESAUD	0.292**	0.185*	−0.287**	0.092	−0.011	0.078	−0.196*	0.1	1	
SIZE	−0.197*	0.074	0.499**	−0.404**	0.018	−0.021	0.253**	0.061	−0.382**	1
ROAA	−0.405**	−0.04	0.267**	−0.237**	0.095	−0.203*	−0.002	−0.057	−0.308**	0.682**
ROAE	−0.341**	0.028	0.397**	−0.264**	0.079	−0.199*	0.073	−0.056	−0.348**	0.819**
EARQ	−0.123	0.172*	0.319**	0.094	0.181*	0.094	0.106	0.058	−0.378**	0.316**
C2INC	0.224**	0.136	−0.182*	0.378**	0.012	0.160*	−0.107	0.014	0.344**	−0.657**
LEV	0.173*	0.032	0.211**	−0.192*	0.047	−0.026	0.285**	−0.177*	−0.192*	0.402**
CAR	−0.201*	−0.101	−0.150*	−0.123	0.006	0.077	0.101	0.169*	−0.097	−0.127
DBNDX	0.09	0.290**	0.158*	0.600**	0.249**	0.012	−0.400**	−0.039	0.098	−0.178*
REGQ	0.062	0.068	0.005	0.374**	0.229**	−0.187*	−0.400**	−0.220**	0.1	−0.127
PS	−0.016	0.08	0.131	0.036	0.031	0.039	0.032	0.009	−0.066	0.129
GDP	0.049	0.143	0.029	0.367**	0.204*	0.027	−0.242**	−0.071	0.068	−0.287**

(*Continued*)

Table 5.19. (Continued)

	ROAA	ROAE	EARQ	C2INC	LEV	CAR	DBNDX	REGQ	PS	GDP
DISCORE										
SSBGOV										
SSBSIZE										
SSBEXP										
SSBEDU										
SSBDD										
SSBMEET										
ISAUD										
ESAUD										
SIZE										
ROAA	1									
ROAE	0.887**	1								
EARQ	0.254**	0.255**	1							
C2INC	−0.750**	−0.712**	−0.145	1						
LEV	0.049	0.306**	0.054	−0.107	1					
CAR	0.05	−0.135	0.037	−0.072	−0.412**	1				
DBNDX	0.087	0.04	0.109	0.108	−0.234**	−0.279**	1			
REGQ	0.096	0.146	−0.095	0.005	−0.203*	−0.178*	0.659**	1		
PS	0.007	0.05	−0.014	−0.064	0.005	0.093	−0.206*	−0.099	1	
GDP	−0.128	−0.142	−0.01	0.196*	−0.224**	0.006	0.511**	0.416**	0.009	1

**Correlation is significant at the 0.01 level. *Correlation is significant at the 0.05 level.

DISCORE, disclosure score; SSBGOV, Shariah governance strength score; SSBSIZE, the total number of Shariah; SSBEXP, the number of Shariah board members with financial expertise; SSBEDU, the number of Shariah board members with a PhD; SSBDD, dummy variable for having defined duties for the Shariah board; SSBMEET, the total number of Shariah board meetings during the year; ISAUD, dummy for the existence of internal Shariah audit unit; ESAUD, dummy for the performance of external Shariah audit; SIZE, natural logarithm of bank assets; ROAA, return on average assets; ROAE, return on average equity; EARQ, earnings quality ratio; C2INC, cost to income ratio; LEV, leverage; CAR, capital adequacy ratio; DBNDX, a World Bank index measuring the ease of doing business index; REGQ, an indicator of regulatory quality; PS, political stability indicator; GDPG, GDP growth rate.

Table 5.20. Spearman's Correlation of Shariah Governance Dimensions and the Extent of Disclosure for Islamic Banks.

	DISCORE	SSBGOV	SSBSIZE	SSBEXP	SSBEDU	SSBDD	SSBMEET	ISAUD	ESAUD	SIZE
DISCORE	1									
SSBGOV	0.219*	1								
SSBSIZE	−0.067	0.692**	1							
SSBEXP	0.091	0.602**	0.318**	1						
SSBEDU	0.013	0.241**	0.11	0.209*	1					
SSBDD	0.253**	0.568**	0.153	0.234**	−0.05	1				
SSBMEET	0.156	0.306**	0.314**	−0.309**	−0.218*	0.105	1			
ISAUD	0.128	0.552**	0.196*	0.102	−0.064	0.781**	0.134	1		
ESAUD	0.255**	0.179*	−0.287**	0.092	−0.011	0.078	−0.196*	0.1	1	
SIZE	−0.229*	0.145	0.500**	−0.354**	0.063	0.052	0.347**	0.114	−0.289**	1
ROAA	−0.029	0.003	0.225*	−0.226*	−0.047	−0.078	0.128	−0.065	−0.007	0.292**
ROAE	−0.271**	−0.028	0.369**	−0.288**	−0.006	−0.159	0.134	−0.085	−0.199*	0.531**
EQQ	−0.129	0.167	0.330**	0.092	0.184*	0.089	0.11	0.052	−0.405**	0.360**
C2INC	0.071	0.037	−0.186*	0.226*	0.056	0.076	−0.124	0.041	0.092	−0.287**
LEV	0.087	0.015	0.262**	−0.204*	−0.015	−0.052	0.270**	−0.205*	−0.158	0.218*
CAR	−0.071	−0.016	−0.128	0.021	0.027	0.045	−0.011	0.076	0.011	−0.084
DBNDX	−0.126	0.287**	0.240**	0.574**	0.222*	0.025	−0.386**	−0.011	0.072	0.014
REGQ	0.019	0.067	−0.007	0.458**	0.256**	−0.158	−0.432**	−0.198*	0.138	−0.161
PS	−0.023	0.04	0.079	−0.005	−0.006	0.045	0.07	0.019	−0.094	0.094
GDP	−0.014	0.14	0.069	0.366**	0.193*	0.018	−0.287**	−0.061	0.075	−0.143

(Continued)

Table 5.20. (Continued)

	ROAA	ROAE	EQQ	C2INC	LEV	CAR	DBNDX	REGQ	PS	GDP
DISCORE										
SSBGOV										
SSBSIZE										
SSBEXP										
SSBEDU										
SSBDD										
SSBMEET										
ISAUD										
ESAUD										
SIZE										
ROAA	1									
ROAE	0.767**	1								
EQQ	0.006	0.118	1							
C2INC	−0.736**	−0.623**	−0.02	1						
LEV	0.498**	0.527**	0.05	−0.426**	1					
CAR	−0.087	0.032	0.002	−0.005	−0.347**	1				
DBNDX	−0.075	0.039	0.139	0.097	−0.185*	−0.067	1			
REGQ	−0.142	−0.032	−0.081	0.144	−0.232**	−0.031	0.753**	1		
PS	0.079	0.046	−0.013	−0.128	0.038	0.037	−0.127	−0.141	1	
GDP	−0.111	−0.115	0.051	0.106	−0.231**	0.06	0.454**	0.426**	0.057	1

**Correlation is significant at the 0.01 level. *Correlation is significant at the 0.05 level.

DISCORE, disclosure score; SSBGOV, Shariah governance strength score; SSBSIZE, the total number of Shariah; SSBEXP, the number of Shariah board members with financial expertise; SSBEDU, the number of Shariah board members with a PhD; SSBDD, dummy variable for having defined duties for the Shariah board; SSBMEET, the total number of Shariah board meetings during the year; ISAUD, dummy for the existence of internal Shariah audit unit; ESAUD, dummy for the performance of external Shariah audit; SIZE, natural logarithm of bank assets; ROAA, return on average assets; ROAE, return on average equity; EARQ, earnings quality ratio; C2INC, cost to income ratio; LEV, leverage; CAR, capital adequacy ratio; DBNDX, a World Bank index measuring the ease of doing business index; REGQ, an indicator of regulatory quality; PS, political stability indicator; GDPG, GDP growth rate.

ratio and leverage are positively associated with the extent of disclosure, whereas the CAR is negatively associated with it. The other control variables do not have any significant relationship with the extent of disclosure.

5.6. Conclusion

This chapter thoroughly discusses the descriptive and correlation statistics used in the tests and analyses conducted to examine the relationship and effects of corporate governance mechanisms on disclosure. It offers a detailed analysis of the disclosure index by country, year, and bank type. The chapter also explores the descriptive statistics related to Islamic and conventional banks in the sample, showing that, overall, the former tend to have lower average disclosure scores than the latter. Finally, it provides a detailed analysis of the Pearson and Spearman correlation tests performed and presents the results.

Chapter Six

Corporate Governance and Disclosure Practices in GCC Banks

Abstract

The previous chapter presented the descriptive statistics for the variables of interest for this book. The chapter provided an overview of the sample bank profiles and analyzed the disclosure index. Moreover, the previous chapter discussed in detail the descriptive statistics for the study variables and presented the results of the correlation analysis, shedding light on the intercorrelations found among the study variables. This chapter tests the hypotheses and presents the results and findings. The chapter begins with an overview of the inferential analyses. It then presents the OLS regression results and provides a detailed account. The chapter also discusses the results of the OLS regression analysis, with robust standard errors testing performed. The chapter then presents the results of PLS-SEM analysis. The chapter concludes with a summary of the main points discussed.

Keywords: Islamic banks; corporate governance; Shariah governance; hypothesis testing; regression analysis

6.1. Introduction

A hierarchical multiple regression analysis was conducted to test the hypotheses developed for this book. The study examines three main hypotheses under three thematic areas related to board effectiveness (BDEFFCT), internal control strength (ICSTRENGTH), and Shariah governance strength. Additional sub-hypotheses are developed to test the individual dimensions within each of the three thematic governance areas to examine their impact on the disclosure index of conventional and Islamic banks while taking the control variables' effects into consideration. These individual governance thematic area and its individual dimensions are listed

Corporate Governance and Disclosure in GCC Banks:
Islamic Perspectives, Empirical Insights and Policy Implications, 127–154

Published under exclusive licence by Emerald Publishing Limited
doi:10.1108/978-1-80686-279-520261006

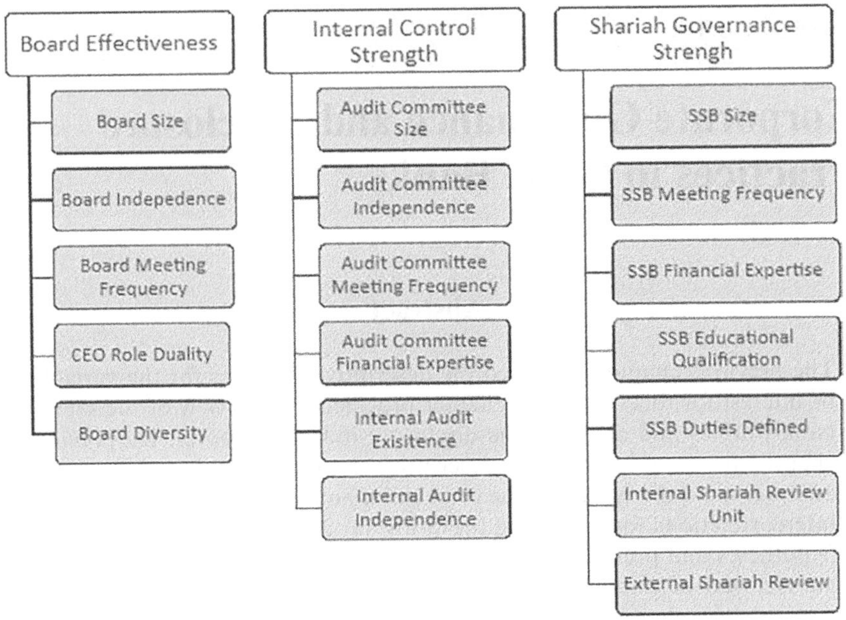

Fig. 6.1. Corporate Governance Thematic Areas and Their Individual Dimensions.

in Fig. 6.1. Several control variables at the bank and country levels, which prior studies have consistently associated with disclosure, are considered along with the corporate governance dimensions of interest. These control variables include size, profitability (ROAA, ROAE), leverage, efficiency (C2INC), regulatory quality (REGQ), political stability score, and GDP growth rate. Multiple regression models were run to examine the hypotheses and address the research questions.

6.2. Hypothesis Testing

This book first conducts an OLS regression analysis to test the main hypotheses and the sub-hypotheses. The use of OLS regression analysis as the main regression model is deemed appropriate for the study given the religious, political, and cultural homogeneity and geographic proximity of the GCC countries. Furthermore, the economies, capital markets, and regulatory environments of the GCC countries have many similarities (Shehata, 2017; Tessema, 2019). To validate the robustness and fit of the regression model, additional inferential analyses are performed. OLS regression analysis with robust standard errors is undertaken to confirm the consistency of the main OLS regression results. Additionally, PLS-SEM analysis is employed using SmartPLS software to attest the robustness of the regression results and ascertain the consistency of the findings (Hair et al., 2017; Sarstedt et al., 2021). The results of the OLS regression analysis with robust standard errors and the PLS-SEM analyses are discussed in Sections 7.4 and 7.5, respectively.

6.3. OLS Regression Analysis

This book proposes three main hypotheses and several sub-hypotheses as discussed in Chapter Five. OLS regression analysis is employed to test the main and sub-hypotheses and determine the impact of (1) BDEFFCT, (2) ICSTRENGTH, and (3) Shariah Governance[1] on the extent of disclosure for Islamic and conventional banks. Individual dimensions within each of the three thematic areas are further analyzed and tested to determine their impact on disclosure levels. Multiple regression models are run to examine the hypotheses and address the research questions. The results of the regression test are exhibited in Table 6.2.

6.3.1. Multicollinearity Test

Multicollinearity refers to the presence of high correlations among independent variables, which is considered to make the model less reliable in predicting the effects of the individual variables (Chatterjee & Yilmaz, 1992). A variance inflation factor (VIF) and tolerance level are calculated using SPSS to test the multicollinearity and ensure that the VIF is within the tolerance levels suggested by prior studies (Chatterjee & Yilmaz, 1992; Field, 2009). To be acceptable, the VIF should be less than 5. Table 6.1 summarizes the multicollinearity tests conducted for the linear regression model.

Table 6.1 shows that the highest VIF is 3.099, while the lowest is 1.072, and the mean is 1.642. On the other hand, Table 7.1 indicates that the lowest tolerance is 0.3230. Therefore, the result confirms that the variables do not have a multicollinearity problem.

6.3.2. OLS Regression Analysis for the Impact of Corporate Governance Dimensions on Disclosure for Conventional and Islamic Banks

OLS regression analysis is conducted to examine the impact of corporate governance dimensions on the extent of disclosure. Six models are developed and tested, with the first three models focusing on the three main corporate governance dimensions and the remaining three covering the individual variables related to the main corporate governance dimensions. Model (1) tests the impact of the BDEFFCT dimension, along with the control variables, on the extent of disclosure. Model (2) tests the impact of the ICSTRENGTH dimension on the extent of disclosure. Model (3) tests the effect of BDEFFCT and internal control dimensions on the extent of disclosure. Model (4) tests the effect of the individual variables related to the BDEFFCT dimension on the extent of disclosure. Model (5) tests the individual variables pertaining to the ICSTRENGTH dimension on the extent of disclosure. Finally, Model (6) tests all individual corporate governance variables considered for this book. Table 7.2 summarizes the results of the OLS regression analysis performed for the study.

Model (1) tests the impact of the board's effectiveness on the extent of disclosure. BDEFFCT is an index comprised of several board-related dimensions, such

[1]The results of the Shariah governance inferential analysis are discussed in Chapter Eight.

Table 6.1. VIF for Corporate Governance Variables.

Independent Variable	Tolerance	VIF	Control Variable	Tolerance	VIF
BDSIZE	0.6110	1.636	SIZE	0.7430	1.345
BDIND	0.6690	1.496	ROAE	0.3980	2.511
BDMEET	0.7080	1.412	EARQ	0.8200	1.219
CDUAL	0.8380	1.193	C2INC	0.5420	1.846
BDDIV	0.7920	1.263	LEV	0.4970	2.014
ACSIZE	0.6000	1.666	CAR	0.6190	1.616
ACIND	0.7150	1.399	DBNDX	0.3360	2.98
ACMEET	0.6910	1.447	REGQ	0.3230	3.099
ACEXP	0.8100	1.234	PS	0.9330	1.072
IAEXST	0.7910	1.264	GDP	0.7260	1.377
IAIND	0.7200	1.388			

Mean VIF 1.642.

BDSIZE, board size; BDIND, board independence; BDMEET, board meeting frequency; CDUAL, CEO role duality; BDDIV, board diversity; ACSIZE, audit committee size; ACIND, audit committee independence; ACMEET, audit committee meeting frequency; ACEXP, audit committee financial expertise; IAEXST, internal audit existence; IAIND, internal audit independence; SIZE, natural logarithm of bank assets; ROAA, return on average assets; ROAE, return on average equity; EARQ, earnings quality; C2INC, cost to income ratio; LEV, leverage; CAR, capital adequacy ratio; DBNDX, ease of doing business index; REGQ, regulatory quality; PS, political stability; GDPG, GDP growth rate.

as board size (BDSIZE), independence, meeting frequency, CEO duality, and board diversity (BDDIV). As shown in Table 6.2, the adjusted R^2 for the model is 0.207, suggesting that BDEFFCT, along with the control variables, explains 20.7% of the variance in disclosure. The model for these dimensions was significant ($F = 6.199$, $p < 0.01$). The results also indicated that BDEFFCT had a significant positive impact ($\beta = 0.279$, $t = 4.856$, $p < 0.01$) on the dependent variable (disclosure score). The significant impact of BDEFFCT indicates that boards with higher effectiveness (i.e., more independent board members, more frequent meetings, and greater diversity) contribute to greater transparency and disclosure in banks. The findings provide evidence supporting the hypothesis regarding BDEFFCT. Several control variables show a significant impact on the extent of disclosure.

With regards to the firm-level control variables, the result shows that bank size (SIZE) has a significant positive impact ($\beta = 0.215$, $t = 3.552$, $p < 0.01$) on the extent of disclosure. ROAA also has a marginally significant positive impact ($\beta = 0.184$, $t = 1.729$, $p < 0.10$), while ROAE has a significant negative impact ($\beta = -0.362$, $t = -3.770$, $p < 0.01$) on the extent of disclosure. It is also noted that leverage (LEV) has a statistically significant positive association ($\beta = 0.191$, $t = 2.660$, $p < 0.01$) with the extent of disclosure. For the macro-level control

Table 6.2. OLS Regression Analysis for Impact of Corporate Governance Dimensions on Disclosure for Conventional and Islamic Banks.

Predictive Variables	**Model (1) Beta (*t*)**	**Model (2) Beta (*t*)**	**Model (3) Beta (*t*)**	**Model (4) Beta (*t*)**	**Model (5) Beta (*t*)**	**Model (6) Beta (*t*)**
BDEFFCT	0.279*** (4.856)		0.156*** (2.863)			
ICSTRENGTH		0.464*** (8.619)	0.416*** (7.471)			
BDSIZE				0.133** (2.092)		0.020 (0.315)
BDIND				0.278*** (4.467)		0.230*** (3.732)
BDMEET				0.029 (0.450)		0.045 (0.757)
CDUAL				0.144** (2.487)		0.093* (1.696)
BDDIV				0.042 (0.689)		0.040 (0.708)
ACSIZE					0.252*** (4.206)	0.191*** (2.939)
ACIND					0.124** (2.124)	0.079 (1.318)
ACMEET					0.011 (0.151)	−0.032 (−0.462)

(Continued)

Table 6.2. (Continued)

Predictive Variables	**Model (1) Beta (*t*)**	**Model (2) Beta (*t*)**	**Model (3) Beta (*t*)**	**Model (4) Beta (*t*)**	**Model (5) Beta (*t*)**	**Model (6) Beta (*t*)**
ACEXP					0.166*** (2.935)	0.135** (2.420)
IAEXST					0.005 (0.088)	−0.007 (−0.115)
IAIND					0.277*** (4.712)	0.285*** (4.810)
SIZE	0.215*** (3.552)	0.245*** (4.404)	0.239*** (4.365)	0.221*** (3.584)	0.213*** (3.648)	0.224*** (3.841)
ROAE	−0.362*** (−3.770)	−0.362*** (−4.113)	−0.341*** (−3.920)	−0.339*** (−3.526)	−0.378*** (−4.151)	−0.321*** (−3.528)
ROAA	0.184* (1.729)	0.076 (0.772)	0.042 (0.426)	0.143 (1.356)	0.174 (1.475)	0.137 (1.178)
EARQ	0.046 (0.764)	−0.008 (−0.140)	−0.004 (−0.069)	0.042 (0.704)	−0.024 (−0.418)	−0.008 (−0.142)
C2INC	0.049 (0.572)	−0.026 (−0.324)	−0.043 (−0.543)	0.015 (0.173)	0.033 (0.367)	0.009 (0.096)
LEV	0.191*** (2.660)	0.260*** (3.958)	0.238*** (3.642)	0.243*** (3.281)	0.208*** (2.975)	0.216*** (3.015)
CAR	0.033 (0.520)	0.109* (1.885)	0.078 (1.349)	0.041 (0.641)	0.113* (1.799)	0.080 (1.244)

DBNDX	−0.395***	−0.372***	−0.389***	−0.408***	−0.376***	−0.393***
	(−4.242)	(−4.371)	(−4.626)	(−4.358)	(−4.300)	(−4.520)
REGQ	0.378***	0.338***	0.355***	0.390***	0.321***	0.322***
	(4.119)	(4.027)	(4.282)	(4.295)	(3.520)	(3.602)
PS	−0.029	−0.041	−0.037	−0.026	−0.051	−0.053
	(−0.517)	(−0.783)	(−0.723)	(−0.464)	(−0.951)	(−1.016)
GDP	0.024	−0.024	−0.025	0.001	0.003	0.003
	(0.379)	(−0.414)	(−0.438)	(0.008)	(0.050)	(0.047)
IBDUMMY	−0.149**	−0.183***	−0.171***	−0.225***	−0.147**	−0.197***
	(−2.470)	(−3.303)	(−3.115)	(−3.523)	(−2.487)	(−3.197)
Constant	0.866***	0.722***	0.736***	0.827***	0.811***	0.860***
	(8.178)	(7.320)	(7.562)	(7.528)	(6.758)	(7.066)
Adjusted R^2	0.207	0.333	0.351	0.229	0.309	0.343
F Statistics	6.199	10.924	3.396	5.523	7.422	6.886
Number of observations	260	260	260	260	260	260

$^{***}p < 0.01$, $^{**}p < 0.05$, $^{*}p < 0.1$.

BDEFFCT, board effectiveness index; ICSTRENGTH, internal control strength index; BDSIZE, board size; BDIND, board independence; BDMEET, board meeting frequency; CDUAL, CEO role duality; BDDIV, board diversity; ACSIZE, audit committee size; ACIND, audit committee independence; ACMEET, audit committee meeting frequency; ACEXP, audit committee financial expertise; IAEXST, internal audit existence; IAIND, internal audit independence; SIZE, natural logarithm of bank assets; ROAA, return on average assets; ROAE, return on average equity; EARQ, earnings quality; C2INC, cost to income ratio; LEV, leverage; CAR, capital adequacy ratio; DBNDX, ease of doing business index; REGQ, regulatory quality; PS, political stability; GDP, GDP growth rate; IBDUMMY, Islamic banks dummy number.

variables, the result indicates that the ease of doing business index (DBNDX) has a significant negative impact ($\beta = -0.395$, $t = -4.242$, $p < 0.01$) on the extent of disclosure, while REGQ has a significant positive impact ($\beta = 0.378$, $t = 4.119$, $p < 0.01$) on the extent of disclosure. The result also shows that the Islamic bank dummy (IBDUMMY) variable has a significant negative impact ($\beta = -0.149$, $t = -2.470$, $p < 0.05$) on the extent of disclosure. This suggests that conventional banks have significantly higher disclosures when compared to their Islamic bank counterparts. No significant impact is detected for the remaining control variables.

Model (2) presents the results of the regression analysis for the ICSTRENGTH dimension along with the control variables. The ICSTRENGTH dimension is a self-developed index that comprises audit committee characteristics (size, independence, financial expertise, etc.) and the existence and independence of the internal audit function (IAF). As demonstrated in Table 6.2, the adjusted R^2 for the model is 0.333, suggesting that the ICSTRENGTH dimension, along with the control variables in the model, explains about 33.3% of the variance in disclosure. The model for the internal control dimension is significant ($F = 10.924$, $p < 0.01$). The result indicates that the ICSTRENGTH dimension has a significant, positive impact ($\beta = 0.464$, $t = 8.619$, $p < 0.01$) on the extent of disclosure. Accordingly, the ICSTRENGTH hypothesis is supported.

For the firm-level control variables, the results show that bank size has a significant positive impact ($\beta = 0.245$, $t = 4.404$, $p < 0.01$) on the extent of disclosure. On the other hand, return on average equity has a significant negative impact ($\beta = -0.362$, $t = -4.9113$, $p < 0.01$) on the extent of disclosure, while no significant association is found between return on average assets (ROAA) and the extent of disclosure. Leverage also has a statistically significant positive association ($\beta = 0.260$, $t = 3.958$, $p < 0.01$) with the extent of disclosure.

For the macro-level control variables, the result indicates that the World Bank index for ease of doing business has a significant negative impact ($\beta = -0.372$, $t = -4.371$, $p < 0.01$) on the extent of disclosure, while REGQ has a significant positive impact ($\beta = 0.338$, $t = 4.027$, $p < 0.01$) on the extent of disclosure. This suggests that countries with simpler, more efficient business requirements tend to have less disclosure. However, the result indicates that a stronger regulatory environment with robust, effective policies contributes to greater transparency and higher disclosure. The result also shows that the Islamic bank dummy variable has a significant negative impact ($\beta = -0.183$, $t = -3.303$, $p < 0.01$) on the extent of disclosure. This suggests that conventional banks have significantly higher disclosures than their Islamic bank counterparts. No significant impact on disclosure is detected for the remaining control variables.

Model (3) presents the results of the regression analysis for BDEFFCT and ICSTRENGTH along with the control variables. As shown in Table 6.2, the adjusted R^2 for the model is 0.351, indicating that the BDEFFCT and internal control dimensions, along with the control variables, explain 35.1% of the variance in disclosure. The model for these two dimensions is significant ($F = 3.396$, $p < 0.01$). The result indicates that both dimensions (BDEFFCT and ICSTRENGTH) have a significant and positive impact ($\beta = 0.378$, $t = 4.119$, $p < 0.01$ and $\beta = 0.378$, $t = 4.119$, $p < 0.01$, respectively) on the extent of disclosure.

For the firm-level control variables, the results show that bank size has a significant positive impact ($\beta = 0.239$, $t = 4.365$, $p < 0.01$) on the extent of disclosure. On the other hand, return on average equity has a significant negative impact ($\beta = -0.341$, $t = -3.920$, $p < 0.01$) on the extent of disclosure, while no significant association is found between ROAA and the extent of disclosure. Leverage also has a statistically significant positive association ($\beta = 0.238$, $t = 3.642$, $p < 0.01$) with the extent of disclosure.

For the macro-level control variables, the result indicates that the World Bank index for ease of doing business has a significant negative impact ($\beta = -0.389$, $t = -4.626$, $p < 0.01$) on the extent of disclosure, while REGQ has a significant positive impact ($\beta = 0.355$, $t = 4.282$, $p < 0.01$) on the extent of disclosure. This suggests that countries with simpler, more efficient business requirements tend to have less disclosure. However, the result indicates that a stronger regulatory environment with robust and effective policies contributes to more transparency and higher disclosure. The result also shows that the Islamic bank dummy variable has a significant negative impact ($\beta = -0.171$, $t = -3.115$, $p < 0.01$) on the extent of disclosure. This suggests that conventional banks have significantly higher disclosures when compared to their Islamic bank counterparts. No significant impact on disclosure is detected for the remaining control variables.

Model (4) presents the results of the regression analysis for the individual variables within the BDEFFCT dimension, along with the control variables. As shown in Table 6.2, the adjusted R^2 for the model is 0.229, indicating that the BDEFFCT subdimensions, along with the control variables, explain 22.9% of the variance in disclosure. The model for the BDEFFCT subdimensions is significant ($F = 5.523$, $p < 0.01$). The result indicates that BDSIZE has a positive and significant impact ($\beta = 0.133$, $t = 2.092$, $p < 0.05$) on the extent of disclosure. Board independence (BDIND) also has a significant positive impact ($\beta = 0.278$, $t = 4.467$, $p < 0.01$) on the extent of disclosure. CEO role duality (CDUAL) is found to be significantly and positively associated with the extent of disclosure ($\beta = 0.144$, $t = 2.487$, $p < 0.01$). On the other hand, board meeting frequency (BDMEET) and BDDIV were found to have no impact on the extent of disclosure. This suggests that more board meetings and board member diversity do not affect the level of disclosure by the bank.

For the firm-level control variables, the results show that bank size has a significant positive impact ($\beta = 0.221$, $t = 3.584$, $p < 0.01$) on the extent of disclosure. On the other hand, return on average equity has a significant negative impact ($\beta = -0.339$, $t = -3.526$, $p < 0.01$) on the extent of disclosure, while no significant association is found between ROAA and the extent of disclosure. Leverage also has a statistically significant positive association ($\beta = 0.243$, $t = 3.281$, $p < 0.01$) with the extent of disclosure.

For the macro-level control variables, the result indicates that the World Bank index for ease of doing business has a significant negative impact ($\beta = -0.408$, $t = -4.358$, $p < 0.01$) on the extent of disclosure, while REGQ has a significant positive impact ($\beta = 0.390$, $t = 4.295$, $p < 0.01$) on the extent of disclosure. This seems to suggest that countries with easier and more efficient business requirements tend to have less disclosure. However, the result indicates that a stronger regulatory environment with robust and effective policies contributes to more transparency and higher disclosure. The result also shows that the Islamic bank dummy variable has a significant negative impact ($\beta = -0.225$, $t = -3.523$, $p < 0.01$) on the extent of disclosure. This suggests that conventional banks have significantly higher disclosures when compared to their Islamic bank counterparts. No significant impact on disclosure is detected for the remaining control variables.

Model (5) presents the results of the regression analysis for the individual variables within the ICSTRENGTH dimension, along with the control variables. As shown in Table 6.2, the adjusted R^2 for the model is 0.309, indicating that the BDEFFCT subdimensions, along with the control variables, explain 30.9% of the variance in disclosure. The model for the ICSTRENGTH subdimensions is significant ($F = 7.422$, $p < 0.01$). The result indicates that audit committee size (ACSIZE) has a positive and significant impact ($\beta = 0.252$, $t = 4.206$, $p < 0.01$) on the extent of disclosure. Audit committee independence (ACIND) also has a significant positive impact ($\beta = 0.124$, $t = 2.124$, $p < 0.05$) on the extent of disclosure. Audit committee financial expertise (ACEXP) is also found to be significantly and positively associated ($\beta = 0.166$, $t = 2.935$, $p < 0.01$) with the extent of disclosure. Moreover, the result indicates that internal audit independence (IAIND) has a positive significant impact ($\beta = 0.277$, $t = 4.712$, $p < 0.01$) on the extent of disclosure. Unexpectedly, audit committee meeting frequency (ACMEET) and internal audit existence (IAEXIST) were found to have no impact on the extent of disclosure. This suggests that more audit committee meetings and the existence of IAFs do not affect the level of disclosure by the bank.

For the firm-level control variables, the result shows that bank size has a significant positive impact ($\beta = 0.213$, $t = 3.648$, $p < 0.01$) on the extent of disclosure. On the other hand, return on average equity has a significant negative impact ($\beta = -0.378$, $t = -4.151$, $p < 0.01$) on the extent of disclosure, while no significant association is found between ROAA and the extent of disclosure. Leverage also has a statistically significant positive association ($\beta = 0.208$, $t = 2.975$, $p < 0.01$) with the extent of disclosure.

For the macro-level control variables, the result indicates that both the World Bank index for ease of doing business and REGQ have a significant negative impact ($\beta = -0.051$, $t = -0.951$, $p < 0.01$; $\beta = -0.376$, $t = -4.300$, $p < 0.01$, respectively) on the extent of disclosure. The result also shows that the Islamic bank dummy variable has a significant negative impact ($\beta = -0.225$, $t = -3.523$, $p < 0.01$) on the extent of disclosure. Consistent with prior studies, this suggests that Islamic banks lag in their disclosure practices and that conventional banks disclose significantly more than their Islamic bank counterparts. No significant impact on disclosure is detected for the remaining control variables.

Model (6) presents the results of the regression analysis for all the individual corporate governance variables within the model, along with the control variables. The results in Table 6.2 show that the adjusted R^2 for the model is 0.343, which suggests that the corporate governance-related variables, along with the control variables in the model, explain 34.3% of the variance in disclosure. The model for the individual corporate governance variables is significant ($F = 6.886$, $p < 0.01$). The result indicates that BDIND also has a positive significant impact ($\beta = 0.230$, $t = 3.732$, $p < 0.01$) on the extent of disclosure. CDUAL has a marginally positive association ($\beta = 0.093$, $t = 1.696$, $p < 0.10$) with the extent of disclosure. The result also indicates that ACSIZE has a positive and significant impact ($\beta = 0.191$, $t = 2.939$, $p < 0.01$) on the extent of disclosure. ACEXP also has a significant and positive impact ($\beta = 0.135$, $t = 2.420$, $p < 0.01$) on the extent of disclosure. Moreover, the result indicates that IAIND has a positive significant impact ($\beta = 0.285$, $t = 4.810$, $p < 0.01$) on the extent of disclosure.

For the firm-level control variables, the results show that bank size has a significant positive impact ($\beta = 0.224$, $t = 3.841$, $p < 0.01$) on the extent of disclosure. On the other hand, return on average equity has a significant negative impact ($\beta = -0.321$, $t = -3.528$, $p < 0.01$) on the extent of disclosure, while no significant association is found between ROAA and the extent of disclosure. Leverage also has a statistically significant positive association ($\beta = 0.216$, $t = 3.015$, $p < 0.01$) with the extent of disclosure.

For the macro-level control variables, the result indicates that both the World Bank index for ease of doing business and REGQ have a significant negative impact ($\beta = -0.053$, $t = -1.016$, $p < 0.01$ and $\beta = -0.393$, $t = -4.520$, $p < 0.01$) on the extent of disclosure. The result also shows that the Islamic bank dummy variable has a significant negative impact ($\beta = -0.197$, $t = -3.3197$, $p < 0.01$) on the extent of disclosure. This suggests that conventional banks have significantly higher disclosures when compared to their Islamic bank counterparts. No significant impact on disclosure is detected for the remaining control variables.

6.3.3. OLS Regression Analysis with Robust Standard Error

To further confirm the results of the main OLS regression analysis, this book undertakes an OLS regression analysis with robust standard errors. The results of the OLS analysis with robust standard errors are presented in Table 6.3.

Table 6.3 presents the results of the OLS regression analysis with robust standard errors for the impact of corporate governance on the extent of disclosure. As shown in Table 6.3, the result of the OLS regression analysis with robust standard errors is generally consistent with the main OLS regression analysis, thus confirming and further attesting to the robustness of the findings. There are a few insignificant differences noted between the two models, as discussed below.

For Model (1), the result is consistent with the main OLS regression analysis for all variables both in terms of the significance of the findings and its direction, except for the ROAA where the level of significance has changed from 10% to 5%. Model (2) results between the main OLS regression analysis and the OLS regression analysis with the robust errors show one difference in the level of significance for the control variables, where the level of significance for the impact of the CAR has increased from 10% to 1% after applying the robust standard error analysis. No other differences are noted, as the remaining variables are consistent with the main OLS regression analysis findings. Model (3) shows that the result of the OLS regression analysis with robust standard errors is consistent for all the variables, except for the CAR, where the model indicates that it has a marginally significant impact on the extent of disclosure. The remaining variables are the same and consistent with the main OLS regression analysis.

Table 6.3. OLS Regression Analysis with Robust Standard Error for the Impact of Corporate Governance Dimensions on Disclosure for Conventional and Islamic Banks.

Predictive Variables	**Model (1) Beta (*t*)**	**Model (2) Beta (*t*)**	**Model (3) Beta (*t*)**	**Model (5) Beta (*t*)**	**Model (6) Beta (*t*)**	**Model (7) Beta (*t*)**
BDEFFCT	0.279*** (4.468)		0.156*** (2.950)			
ICSTRENGTH		0.464*** (7.674)	0.416*** (7.192)			
BDSIZE				0.133** (2.032)		0.020 (0.297)
BDIND				0.278*** (3.874)		0.230*** (3.501)
BDMEET				0.029 (0.360)		0.045 (0.661)
CDUAL				0.144*** (3.203)		0.093** (2.126)
BDDIV				0.042 (0.716)		0.040 (0.758)
ACSIZE					0.252*** (4.564)	0.191*** (3.444)
ACIND					0.124** (2.009)	0.079 (1.229)
ACMEET					0.011 (0.136)	−0.032 (−0.439)

ACEXP					0.166***	0.135**
					(2.721)	(2.340)
IAEXST					0.005	−0.007
					(0.121)	(−0.136)
IAIND					0.277***	0.285***
					(3.984)	(4.038)
SIZE	0.215***	0.245***	0.239***	0.221***	0.213***	0.224***
	(4.052)	(4.601)	(4.448)	(4.048)	(3.997)	(4.102)
ROAE	−0.362***	−0.362***	−0.341***	−0.339***	−0.378***	−0.321***
	(−2.765)	(−3.359)	(−3.105)	(−2.809)	(−3.063)	(−2.698)
ROAA	0.184**	0.076	0.042	0.143**	0.174	0.137
	(2.345)	(0.799)	(0.477)	(2.205)	(1.295)	(1.093)
EARQ	0.046	−0.008	−0.004	0.042	−0.024	−0.008
	(0.725)	(−0.135)	(−0.066)	(0.677)	(−0.392)	(−0.134)
C2INC	0.049	−0.026	−0.043	0.015	0.033	0.009
	(0.477)	(−0.367)	(−0.635)	(0.156)	(0.303)	(0.084)
LEV	0.191***	0.260***	0.238***	0.243***	0.208***	0.216***
	(2.821)	(4.668)	(3.642)	(3.217)	(3.417)	(2.880)
CAR	0.033	0.109***	0.078*	0.041	0.113*	0.080
	(0.741)	(2.783)	(1.936)	(0.920)	(1.932)	(1.353)
DBNDX	−0.395***	−0.372***	−0.389***	−0.408***	−0.376***	−0.393***
	(−4.452)	(−3.577)	(−3.869)	(−3.723)	(−3.418)	(−3.641)

(*Continued*)

Table 6.3. (Continued)

Predictive Variables	**Model (1) Beta (*t*)**	**Model (2) Beta (*t*)**	**Model (3) Beta (*t*)**	**Model (5) Beta (*t*)**	**Model (6) Beta (*t*)**	**Model (7) Beta (*t*)**
REGQ	0.378***	0.338***	0.355***	0.390***	0.321***	0.322***
	(4.090)	(3.875)	(4.281)	(4.131)	(3.544)	(3.725)
PS	−0.029	−0.041	−0.037	−0.026	−0.051	−0.053
	(−0.495)	(−0.748)	(−0.701)	(−0.441)	(−0.891)	(−0.972)
GDP	0.024	−0.024	−0.025	0.001	0.003	0.003
	(0.394)	(−0.432)	(−0.458)	(0.008)	(0.051)	(0.049)
IBDUMMY	−0.149**	−0.183***	−0.171***	−0.225***	−0.147**	−0.197***
	(−2.146)	(−2.880)	(−2.787)	(−3.126)	(−2.158)	(−2.740)
Constant	0.866***	0.722***	0.736***	0.827***	0.811***	0.860***
	(6.902)	(6.664)	(6.928)	(6.891)	(6.358)	(6.544)
Adjusted R^2	0.207	0.333	0.351	0.229	0.309	0.343
F Statistics	6.199	10.924	11.026	5.523	7.422	6.886
Number of observations	260	260	260	260	260	260

$^{***}p < 0.01$, $^{**}p < 0.05$, $^{*}p < 0.1$.

BDEFFCT, board effectiveness index; ICSTRENGTH, internal control strength index; BDSIZE, board size; BDIND, board independence; BDMEET, board meeting frequency; CDUAL, CEO role duality; BDDIV, board diversity; ACSIZE, audit committee size; ACIND, audit committee independence; ACMEET, audit committee meeting frequency; ACEXP, audit committee financial expertise; IAEXST, internal audit existence; IAIND, internal audit independence; SIZE, natural logarithm of bank assets; ROAA, return on average assets; ROAE, return on average equity; EARQ, earnings quality; C2INC, cost to income ratio; LEV, leverage; CAR, capital adequacy ratio; DBNDX, ease of doing business index; REGQ, regulatory quality; PS, political stability; GDP, GDP growth rate; IBDUMMY, Islamic banks dummy number.

Model (4) shows that there is a change in the level of significance for CDUAL ($p < 0.05$ under the main OLS regression analysis, whereas $p < 0.01$ under the OLS regression analysis with robust standard errors). Moreover, ROAA has a moderately significant impact on the extent of disclosure after applying the robust standard error analysis. Model (5) shows that there are no differences between the two analyses, and the result for all the variables is consistent with the main OLS regression analysis in terms of the level of significance of the impact and its direction. Model (6), which has all the individual variables in the study, shows few differences from the main OLS regression analysis. CDUAL has changed from being a marginally significant positive impact ($p < 0.10$) to a moderately significant positive impact ($p < 0.05$) after applying robust standard errors. ACIND has changed from having a moderately significant positive impact ($p < 0.05$) to no impact after applying the robust standard errors. The remaining individual variables are all consistent with the main OLS regression analysis.

Based on the results of the OLS regression analysis with robust standard errors, it can be concluded that, other than the few insignificant differences discussed above, the result is consistent with the main OLS regression analysis. This confirms the robustness of the main regression analysis and validates the result of the analysis.

6.4. Partial Least Squares Structural Equation Modeling Analysis

PLS-SEM analysis was performed to further validate and confirm the results of the main regression analysis and validate the hypotheses. As the purpose of PLS-SEM analysis is to support and validate the main OLS regression analysis, the focus of the analysis is to test the structural model by using bootstrapping techniques to determine the relationship and its significance among the variables of interest (Chin, 1998; Hair et al., 2017; Sarstedt et al., 2021; Xu & Akther, 2019). Six models are constructed and analyzed to test the main hypotheses and sub-hypotheses. These models are run using SmartPLS software version # 3. Models (1) through (3) are concerned with testing the main hypotheses of this book, while Models (4) through (6) are testing the sub-hypotheses. The results of the PLS-SEM analysis are summarized in Table 6.4. Moreover, Figs. 6.1–6.13 provide results of the PLS-SEM analysis in the form of graphical images. The results of each of the models are discussed next.

Model (1) tests the impact of BDEFFCT on the extent of disclosure, while controlling for the control variables used in this study. BDEFFCT is a self-developed index, which is comprised of several board-related dimensions such as BDSIZE, independence, meeting frequency, CDUAL, and BDDIV. As demonstrated in Table 6.4, the BDEFFCT dimension, along with the control variables, explains 20.7% of the variance (Adj. $R^2 = 0.207$). The result indicates that BDEFFCT has a significant positive impact ($\beta = 0.279$, $t = 4.658$, $p < 0.01$) on the dependent variable (disclosure score). The significant impact of BDEFFCT indicates that boards with higher effectiveness (i.e., more independent board members, more frequent meetings, and greater diversity) contribute to greater transparency and

Table 6.4. **PLS-SEM Analysis for Impact of Corporate Governance Dimensions on Disclosure for Conventional and Islamic Banks.**

Predictive Variables	**Model (1) Beta (*t*)**	**Model (2) Beta (*t*)**	**Model (3) Beta (*t*)**	**Model (4) Beta (*t*)**	**Model (5) Beta (*t*)**	**Model (6) Beta (*t*)**
BDEFFCT	0.279*** (4.658)		0.156*** (2.935)			
ICSTRENGTH		0.464*** (8.482)	0.416*** (8.395)			
BDSIZE				0.133** (2.238)		0.019 (0.303)
BDIND				0.278*** (4.049)		0.227*** (3.542)
BDMEET				0.029 (0.391)		0.043 (0.644)
CDUAL				0.144*** (3.113)		0.090** (2.172)
BDDIV				0.042 (0.744)		0.040 (0.809)
ACSIZE					0.252*** (5.207)	0.193*** (3.906)
ACIND					0.123* (1.833)	0.082 (1.182)
ACMEET					n/a n/a	n/a n/a

ACEXP					0.165***	0.137**
					(2.963)	(2.485)
IAEXST					0.005	−0.006
					(0.111)	(−0.116)
IAIND					0.277***	0.285***
					(4.487)	(4.296)
SIZE	0.215***	0.245***	0.239***	0.221***	0.213***	0.225***
	(2.929)	(2.325)	(3.051)	(2.915)	(2.955)	(3.092)
ROAE	−0.362***	−0.362***	−0.341***	−0.339***	−0.378***	−0.322***
	(−2.874)	(−3.649)	(−3.338)	(−2.832)	(−3.313)	(−2.769)
ROAA	0.184**	0.076	0.042	0.143	0.183*	0.111
	(2.026)	(0.863)	(0.516)	(1.571)	(1.806)	(1.030)
EARQ	0.046	−0.008	−0.004	0.042	−0.024	−0.007
	(0.748)	(−0.143)	(−0.068)	(0.747)	(−0.415)	(−0.130)
C2INC	0.049	−0.026	−0.043	0.015	0.039	0.007
	(0.509)	(−0.326)	(−0.569)	(0.148)	(0.416)	(0.065)
LEV	0.191***	0.260***	0.238***	0.243***	0.208***	0.214***
	(3.020)	(4.803)	(4.255)	(3.292)	(3.414)	(3.075)
CAR	0.033	0.109***	0.078**	0.041	0.110**	0.088
	(0.783)	(3.095)	(1.975)	(0.924)	(2.226)	(1.751)
DBNDX	−0.395***	−0.372***	−0.389***	−0.408***	−0.377***	−0.392***
	(−3.896)	(−3.755)	(−4.231)	(−4.252)	(−3.639)	(−4.028)

(Continued)

Table 6.4. (Continued)

Predictive Variables	Model (1) Beta (t)	Model (2) Beta (t)	Model (3) Beta (t)	Model (4) Beta (t)	Model (5) Beta (t)	Model (6) Beta (t)
REGQ	0.378***	0.338***	0.355***	0.390***	0.321***	0.321***
	(4.396)	(4.048)	(4.807)	(4.678)	(3.923)	(4.002)
PS	−0.029	−0.041	−0.037	−0.026	−0.051	0.052
	(−0.489)	(−0.777)	(−0.711)	(−0.469)	(−0.916)	(1.018)
GDP	0.024	−0.024	−0.025	0.001	0.003	0.003
	(0.382)	(−0.435)	(−0.453)	(0.009)	(0.053)	(0.050)
IBDUMMY	−0.149**	−0.183***	−0.171***	−0.225***	−0.147**	−0.196***
	(−2.380)	(−3.228)	(−3.071)	(−3.461)	(−2.308)	(−2.855)
Adjusted R^2	0.207	0.333	0.351	0.229	0.311	0.345
Number of observations	260	260	260	260	260	260

***$p < 0.01$, **$p < 0.05$, *$p < 0.1$.

BDEFFCT, board effectiveness index; ICSTRENGTH, internal control strength index; BDSIZE, board size; BDIND, board independence; BDMEET, board meeting frequency; CDUAL, CEO role duality; BDDIV, board diversity; ACSIZE, audit committee size; ACIND, audit committee independence; ACMEET, audit committee meeting frequency; ACEXP, audit committee financial expertise; IAEXST, internal audit existence; IAIND, internal audit independence; SIZE, natural logarithm of bank assets; ROAA, return on average assets; ROAE, return on average equity; EARQ, earnings quality; C2INC, cost to income ratio; LEV, leverage; CAR, capital adequacy ratio; DBNDX, ease of doing business index; REGQ, regulatory quality; PS, political stability; GDP, GDP growth rate; IBDUMMY, Islamic banks dummy number.

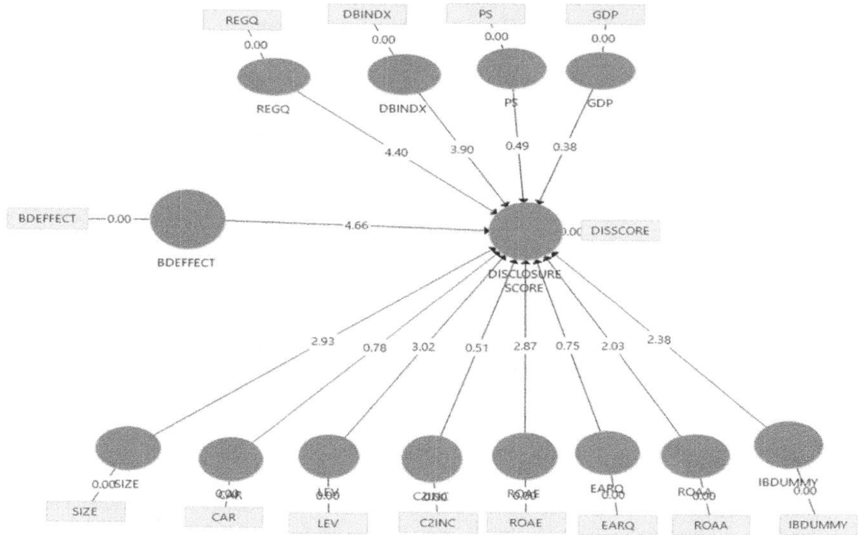

Fig. 6.2. Model 1 – Bootstrapping for the Impact of BDEFFCT on the Extent of Disclosure.

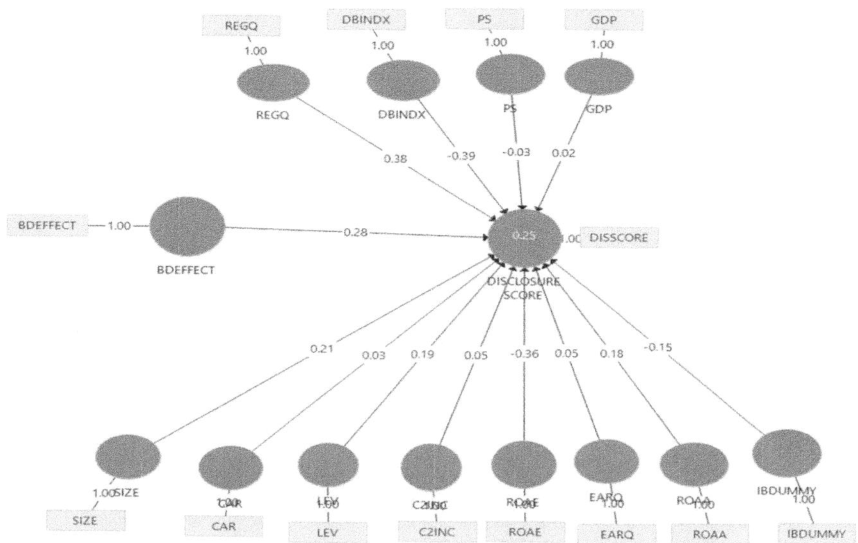

Fig. 6.3. Model 1 – Path for the Impact of BDEFFCT on the Extent of Disclosure.

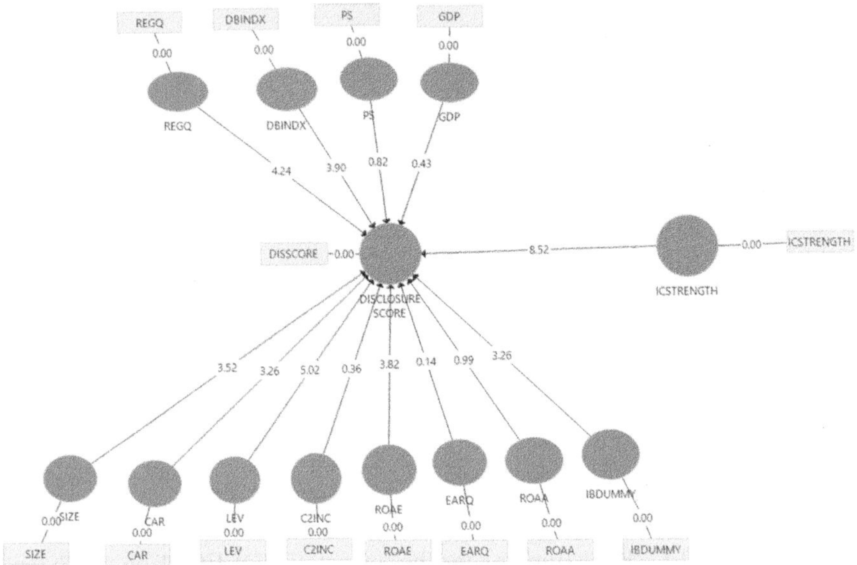

Fig. 6.4. Model 2 – Bootstrapping for the Impact of ICSTRENGTH on the Extent of Disclosure.

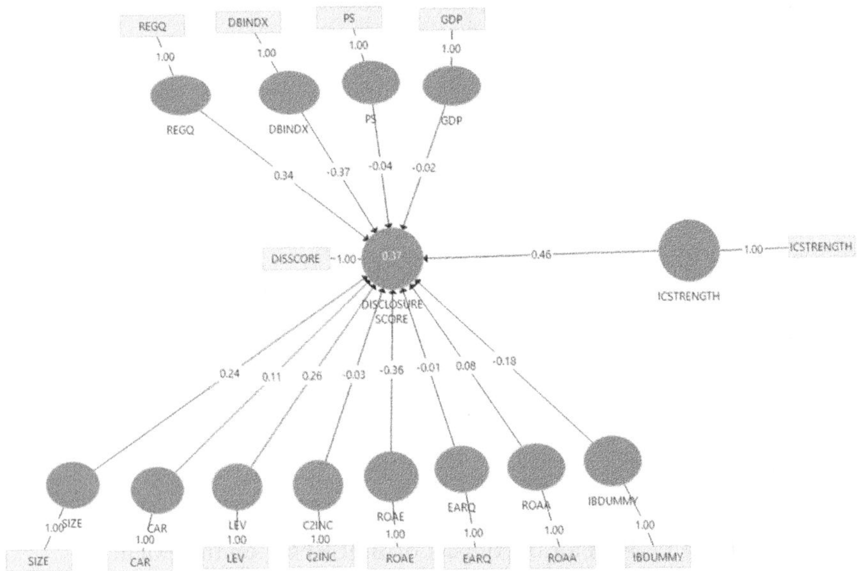

Fig. 6.5. Model 2 – Path for the Impact of ICSTRENGTH on the Extent of Disclosure.

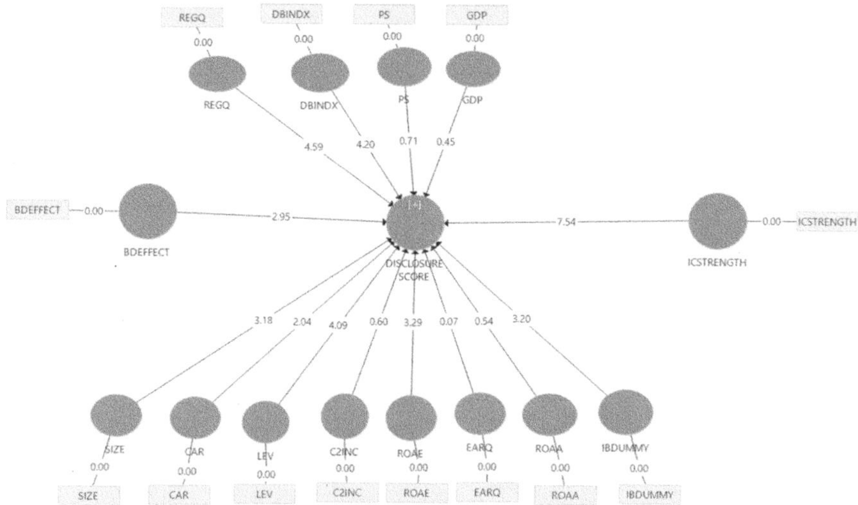

Fig. 6.6. Model 3 – Bootstrapping for Impact of BDEFFCT and ICSTRENGTH on the Extent of Disclosure.

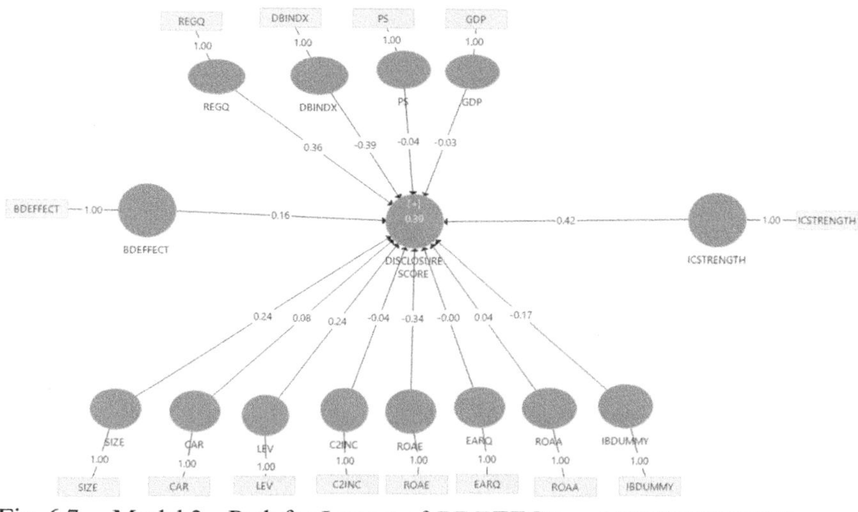

Fig. 6.7. Model 3 – Path for Impact of BDEFFCT and ICSTRENGTH on the Extent of Disclosure.

disclosure by banks. The PLS-SEM findings confirm and are consistent with the results of the main regression analysis performed in this book.

Several control variables show a significant impact on the extent of disclosure. Regarding the firm-level control variables, the results show that bank size has a significant positive impact ($\beta = 0.215$, $t = 2.929$, $p < 0.01$) on the extent of disclosure. ROAA has a moderately significant positive impact ($\beta = 0.184$,

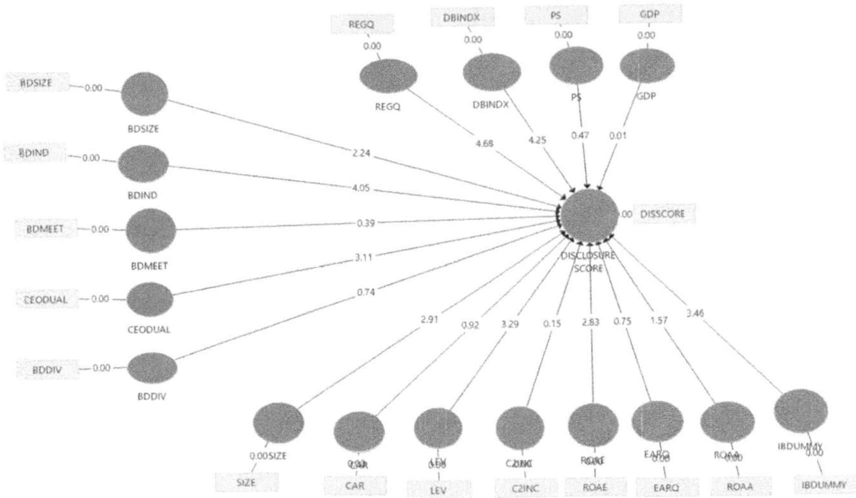

Fig. 6.8. Model 4 – Bootstrapping for Impact of Board Characteristics on the Extent of Disclosure.

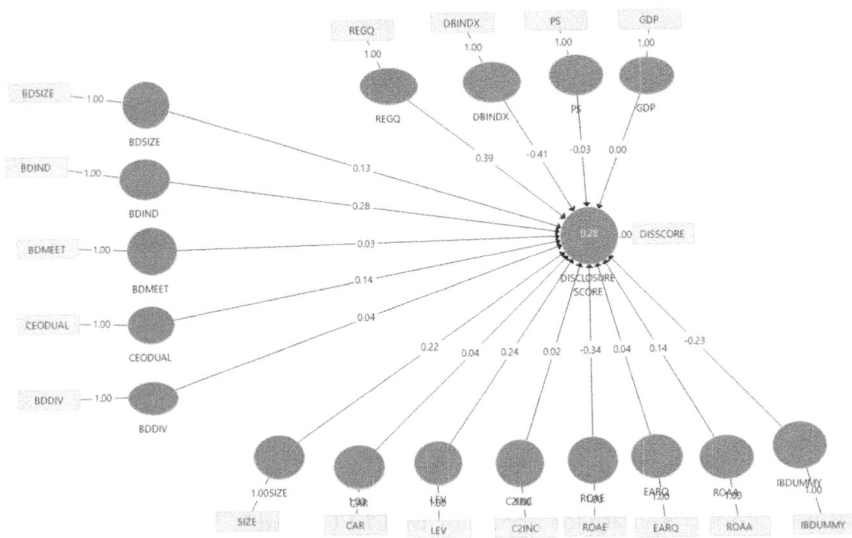

Fig. 6.9. Model 4 – Path for Impact of Board Characteristics on the Extent of Disclosure.

$t = 2.026, p < 0.05$), while return on average equity has a significant negative impact ($\beta = -0.362$, $t = -2.874$, $p < 0.01$) on the extent of disclosure. It is also noted that leverage has a statistically significant positive association ($\beta = 0.191$, $t = 3.020$, $p < 0.01$) with the extent of disclosure.

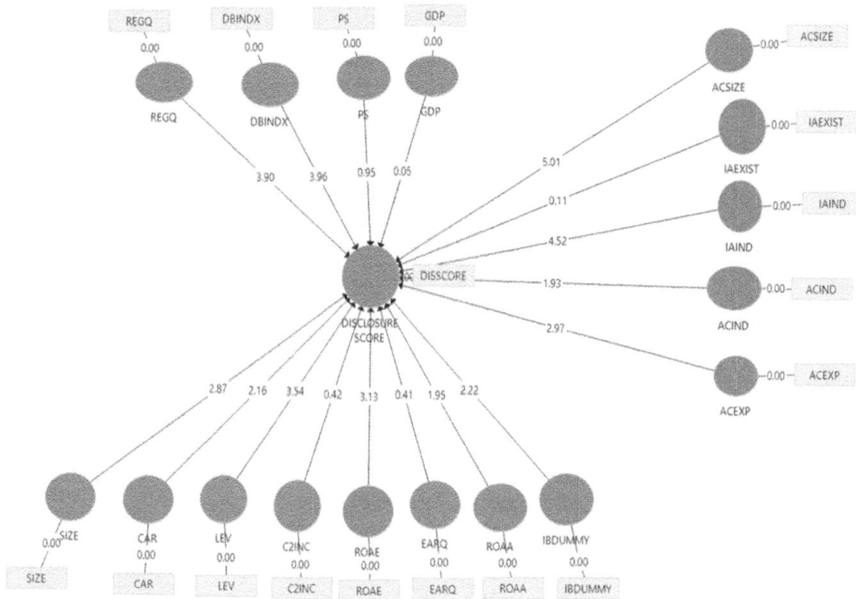

Fig. 6.10. Model 5 – Bootstrapping for Impact of ICSTRENGTH Characteristics on the Extent of Disclosure.

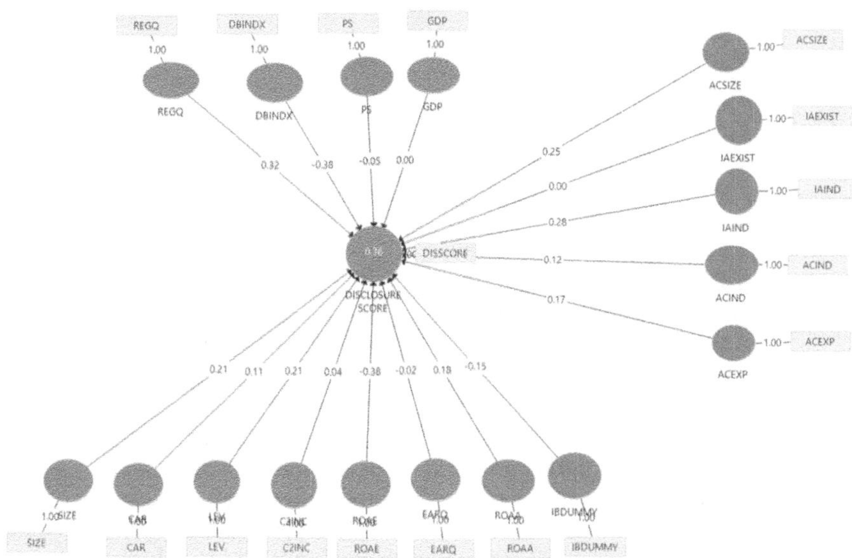

Fig. 6.11. Model 5 – Path for Impact of ICSTRENGTH Characteristics on the Extent of Disclosure.

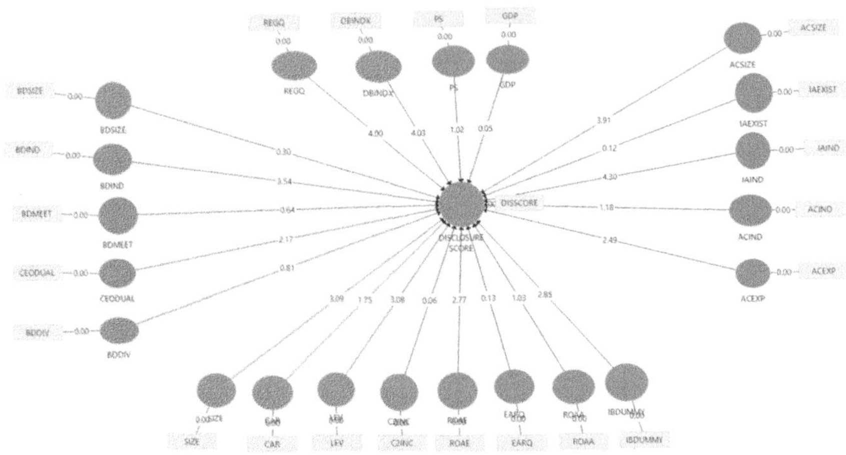

Fig. 6.12. Model 6 – Bootstrapping for the Impact of Board and Internal Control Characteristics on the Extent of Disclosure.

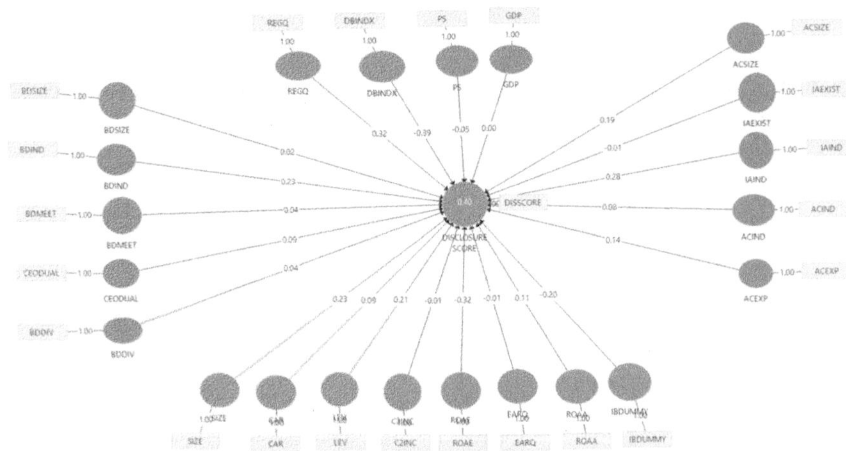

Fig. 6.13. Model 6 – Path for the Impact of Board and Internal Control Characteristics on the Extent of Disclosure.

For the macro-level control variables, the result indicates that the ease of DBNDX has a significant negative impact ($\beta = -0.395$, $t = -3.896$, $p < 0.01$) on the extent of disclosure while REGQ has a significant positive impact ($\beta = 0.378$, $t = 4.396$, $p < 0.01$) on the extent of disclosure. The result also shows that the Islamic bank dummy variable has a significant negative impact ($\beta = -0.149$, $t = -2.380$, $p < 0.05$) on the extent of disclosure. This suggests that conventional banks disclose significantly more than their Islamic bank counterparts. No significant impact is detected for the remaining control variables. Overall, the Model (1) results of the PLS-SEM analysis for both the explanatory and control variables are consistent with the OLS regression and validate the robustness of the main regression analysis.

Model (2) presents the result of the PLS-SEM analysis for the ICSTRENGTH dimension, along with the control variables considered for this book. ICSTRENGTH is a self-developed index comprising several related individual items, such as ACSIZE, independence, meeting frequency, and financial expertise, as well as the existence and independence of the IAF. As demonstrated in Table 6.4, the ICSTRENGTH dimension, along with the control variables, explains 33.3% of the variance (Adj. $R^2 = 0.333$). Furthermore, the result indicates that ICSTRENGTH has a significant positive impact ($\beta = 0.464$, $t = 8.482$, $p < 0.01$) on the dependent variable (disclosure score). The findings are consistent with the OLS regression analysis for the ICSTRENGTH dimension. The significant impact of the ICSTRENGTH dimension indicates that banks with strong audit committees and independent IAFs are more transparent and provide greater disclosure. Several control variables show a significant impact on the extent of disclosure.

With regards to the firm-level control variables, the result shows that bank size has a significant positive impact ($\beta = 0.245$, $t = 2.325$, $p < 0.01$) on the extent of disclosure. Furthermore, return on average equity has a significant negative impact ($\beta = -0.362$, $t = -3.649$, $p < 0.01$) on the extent of disclosure. It is also noted that leverage has a statistically significant positive association ($\beta = 0.260$, $t = 4.803$, $p < 0.01$) with the extent of disclosure.

For the macro-level control variables, the result indicates that the CAR has a significant positive impact ($\beta = 0.109$, $t = 3.095$, $p < 0.01$) on the extent of disclosure. On the other hand, the ease of DBINDX has a significant negative impact ($\beta = -0.372$, $t = -3.755$, $p < 0.01$) on the extent of disclosure, while REGQ has a significant positive impact ($\beta = 0.338$, $t = 4.048$, $p < 0.01$) on the extent of disclosure. The result also shows that the Islamic bank dummy variable has a significant negative impact ($\beta = -0.183$, $t = -3.228$, $p < 0.01$) on the extent of disclosure. This suggests that conventional banks have significantly higher disclosure when compared to their Islamic bank counterparts. No significant impact is detected for the remaining control variables. Overall, it can be observed that, except for the findings for one control variable (i.e., CAR), the Model (2) result of the PLS-SEM analysis is consistent with the OLS regression, thus validating the robustness of the findings of the main regression analysis.

Model (3) tests the BDEFFCT and ICSTRENGTH dimensions along with the control variables for this book. As demonstrated in Table 6.4, the BDEFFCT and ICSTRENGTH dimensions, along with the control variables, explain 35.1% of the variance (Adj. $R^2 = 0.351$). The result indicates that BDEFFCT has a significant positive impact ($\beta = 0.156$, $t = 2.935$, $p < 0.01$) on the dependent variable (disclosure score). On the other hand, ICSTRENGTH has a significant positive impact ($\beta = 0.416$, $t = 8.395$, $p < 0.01$) on the extent of disclosure. Several control variables show a significant impact on the extent of disclosure. The PLS-SEM findings for the BDEFFCT and ICSTRENGTH dimensions are consistent with the main regression analysis results in this book and confirm their validity.

Regarding the firm-level control variables, the results show that bank size has a significant positive impact ($\beta = 0.239$, $t = 3.051$, $p < 0.01$) on the extent of disclosure. Furthermore, return on average equity has a significant negative impact ($\beta = -0.341$, $t = -3.338$, $p < 0.01$) on the extent of disclosure. It is also noted that leverage has a statistically significant positive association ($\beta = 0.238$, $t = 4.255$, $p < 0.01$) with the extent of disclosure.

For the macro-level control variables, the result indicates that the CAR has a moderately significant positive impact ($\beta = 0.078$, $t = 1.975$, $p < 0.05$) on the extent of disclosure. On the other hand, the ease of DBINDX has a significant negative impact ($\beta = -0.389$, $t = -4.231$, $p < 0.01$) on the extent of disclosure, while REGQ has a significant positive impact ($\beta = 0.355$, $t = 4.807$, $p < 0.01$) on the extent of disclosure. The result also shows that the Islamic bank dummy variable has a significant negative impact ($\beta = -0.171$, $t = -3.071$, $p < 0.01$) on the extent of disclosure. This suggests that conventional banks have significantly higher disclosure when compared to their Islamic bank counterparts. No significant impact is detected for the remaining control variables. Overall, it can be observed that, except for one control variable (i.e., CAR), the Model (3) results of the PLS-SEM analysis are consistent with the OLS regression, thus validating the robustness of the main regression analysis.

Model (4) tests the impact of the individual board dimensions along with the control variables on the extent of disclosure. These include BDSIZE, independence and meeting frequency, CDUAL, and BDDIV. As demonstrated in Table 7.4, the individual BDEFFCT dimensions, along with the control variables, explain 22.9% of the variance (Adj. $R^2 = 0.229$). The result indicates that BDSIZE has a moderately positive and significant impact ($\beta = 0.133$, $t = 2.238$, $p < 0.05$) on the extent of disclosure. BDIND has a significant positive impact ($\beta = 0.278$, $t = 4.049$, $p < 0.01$) on the extent of disclosure. CDUAL is found to have a significant positive association ($\beta = 0.144$, $t = 3.133$, $p < 0.01$) with the extent of disclosure. On the other hand, BDMEET and BDDIV were found to have no impact on the extent of disclosure. The PLS-SEM findings for the individual board dimensions confirm and are consistent with the results of the main regression analysis performed in this book.

As for the firm-level control variables, the results show that bank size has a significant positive impact ($\beta = 0.221$, $t = 2.915$, $p < 0.01$) on the extent of disclosure. Return on average equity has a significant negative impact ($\beta = -0.339$, $t = -2.832$, $p < 0.01$) on the extent of disclosure. It is also noted that leverage has a statistically significant positive association ($\beta = 0.243$, $t = 3.292$, $p < 0.01$) with the extent of disclosure.

For the macro-level control variables, the result indicates that the ease of DBNDX has a significant negative impact ($\beta = -0.408$, $\tau = -4.252$, $p < 0.01$) on the extent of disclosure, while REGQ has a significant positive impact ($\beta = 0.390$, $t = 4.678$, $p < 0.01$) on the extent of disclosure. The result also shows that the Islamic bank dummy variable has a significant negative impact ($\beta = -0.225$, $t = -3.361$, $p < 0.01$) on the extent of disclosure. No significant impact is detected for the remaining control variables. Overall, it can be observed that the Model (4) result of the PLS-SEM analysis for both the individual board dimensions and control variables is consistent with the OLS regression and validates the robustness of the findings of the main regression analysis.

Model (5) presents the PLS-SEM analysis results for the individual variables of the ICSTRENGTH dimension along with the control variables. These individual dimensions include ACSIZE, ACIND, ACMEET, ACEXP, IAEXIST, and IAIND. As demonstrated in Table 7.4, the individual ICSTRENGTH dimensions along with the control variables explain 31.1% of the variance (Adj. $R^2 = 0.311$). The result indicates that ACSIZE has a positive and significant impact ($\beta = 0.252$, $t = 5.207$, $p < 0.01$) on the extent of disclosure. ACIND also has a marginally significant positive impact ($\beta = 0.123$, $t = 1.833$, $p < 0.10$) on the extent of disclosure. ACEXP is also found to be significantly and positively associated ($\beta = 0.165$, $t = 2.963$, $p < 0.01$) with the extent of disclosure. Moreover, the result indicates that IAIND has a positive significant impact ($\beta = 0.277$, $t = 4.487$, $p < 0.01$) on the extent of disclosure.

As for the firm-level control variables, the results show that bank size has a significant positive impact ($\beta = 0.213$, $t = 2.955$, $p < 0.01$) on the extent of disclosure. ROAA also has a marginally significant positive impact ($\beta = 0.183$, $t = 1.806$, $p < 0.10$), while return on average equity has a significant negative impact ($\beta = -0.378$, $t = -3.313$, $p < 0.01$) on the extent of disclosure. It is also noted that leverage has a statistically significant positive association ($\beta = 0.208$, $t = 3.414$, $p < 0.01$) with the extent of disclosure.

At the macro level, the result indicates that the CAR has a moderately significant positive impact ($\beta = 0.110$, $t = 2.226$, $p < 0.05$) on the extent of disclosure. On the other hand, the ease of DBINDX has a significant negative impact ($\beta = -0.377$, $t = -3.639$, $p < 0.01$) on the extent of disclosure, while REGQ has a significant positive impact ($\beta = 0.321$, $t = 3.923$, $p < 0.01$) on the extent of disclosure. The result also shows that the Islamic bank dummy variable has a moderately significant negative impact ($\beta = -0.147$, $t = -2.308$, $p < 0.05$) on the extent of disclosure. This suggests that conventional banks have significantly higher disclosure when compared to their Islamic bank counterparts. No significant impact is detected for the remaining control variables. Overall, it can be observed that, except for the findings for one control variable (i.e., CAR), the Model 6 result of the PLS-SEM analysis is consistent with the OLS regression, thus validating the robustness of the findings of the main regression analysis.

Model (6) presents the result of the PLS-SEM analysis for the individual corporate governance variables within the model along with the control variables. As demonstrated in Table 7.4, the individual corporate governance dimensions along with the control variables explain 34.5% of the variance (Adj. $R^2 = 0.345$). The result indicates that BDIND also has a positive significant impact ($\beta = 0.227$, $t = 3.542$, $p < 0.01$) on the extent of disclosure. CDUAL has a moderately positive association ($\beta = 0.090$, $t = 2.172$, $p < 0.05$) with the extent of disclosure. The result also indicates that ACSIZE has a positive and significant impact ($\beta = 0.193$, $t = 3.906$, $p < 0.01$) on the extent of disclosure. ACEXP has a moderately significant and positive impact ($\beta = 0.137$, $t = 2.485$, $p < 0.05$) on the extent of disclosure. Moreover, the result indicates that IAIND has a positive significant impact ($\beta = 0.285$, $t = 4.296$, $p < 0.01$) on the extent of disclosure.

Concerning the firm-level control variables, the results show that bank size has a significant positive impact ($\beta = 0.225$, $t = 3.092$, $p < 0.01$) on the extent of disclosure. Return on average equity has a significant negative impact ($\beta = -0.322$, $t = -2.769$, $p < 0.01$) on the extent of disclosure. It is also noted that leverage has a statistically significant positive association ($\beta = 0.214$, $t = 3.075$, $p < 0.01$) with the extent of disclosure.

For the macro-level control variables, the result indicates that the ease of DBNDX has a significant negative impact ($\beta = -0.392$, $t = -4.028$, $p < 0.01$) on the extent of disclosure, while REGQ has a significant positive impact ($\beta = 0.321$, $t = 4.002$, $p < 0.01$) on the extent of disclosure. The result also shows that the Islamic bank dummy variable has a significant negative impact ($\beta = -0.196$, $t = -2.855$, $p < 0.05$) on the extent of disclosure. This suggests that conventional banks have significantly higher disclosure when compared to their Islamic bank counterparts. No significant impact is detected for the remaining control variables.

Overall, the PLS-SEM results for both the explanatory and control variables are consistent with the OLS regression and validate the robustness of the main regression analysis. Figs. 6.2–6.13 provide the results of the PLS-SEM analysis in the form of graphical images.

6.5. Conclusion

This chapter discusses in detail the inferential statistics pertaining to the tests and analysis performed to establish the relationship and impact of corporate governance mechanisms on the extent of disclosure. Overall, the result of the regression analysis shows that both BDEFFCT and ICSTRENGTH dimensions have significant positive effect on the extent of disclosure. This suggests that strong corporate governance mechanisms contribute to greater disclosure and result in higher disclosure. Moreover, the study finds significant positive association between some of the individual corporate governance variables and extent of disclosure, including BDIND, CDUAL, ACSIZE, ACEXP, and IAIND.

In summary, the chapter starts with an introduction and then presents the hypotheses, which are tested in line with the research questions. The main OLS regression analysis used for this book is presented, and the findings are thoroughly discussed. Further analysis performed to support the main regression by using PLS-SEM techniques is then presented, along with the results. Finally, the chapter provides summaries of the data analysis performed and the findings which have been identified.

Chapter Seven

Shariah Governance and Disclosure in Islamic Banks

Abstract

The previous chapter discussed the first part of the empirical analysis examining the impact of corporate governance on the extent of disclosure by Islamic and conventional banks in GCC countries. Building on the chapter, this chapter provides a detailed account of the empirical results of the work performed on the Shariah governance of Islamic banks. The chapter starts by presenting the results of the regression analyses conducted for this book. The main regression analysis performed for this book is OLS regression. The chapter then presents the results of OLS regression analysis with robust standard errors. The chapter then discusses the results of an additional inferential analysis using PLS-SEM techniques to support and confirm the robustness of the main OLS regression results. The chapter concludes with a summary of the main topics and findings.

Keywords: Islamic banks; Shariah governance; Shariah Supervisory Board; hypothesis testing; regression analysis

7.1. Introduction

A hierarchical multiple regression analysis is conducted to test the hypotheses developed for this book. The study examines three main hypotheses across three thematic areas: board effectiveness, internal control strength, and Shariah governance strength. Additional sub-hypotheses are developed to test individual dimensions within the thematic governance areas, examining their impact on the disclosure index of conventional and Islamic banks while considering the effects of control variables.

Corporate Governance and Disclosure in GCC Banks:
Islamic Perspectives, Empirical Insights and Policy Implications, 155–169

Published under exclusive licence by Emerald Publishing Limited
doi:10.1108/978-1-80686-279-520261007

The main hypotheses related to board effectiveness, internal control strength, and overall corporate governance quality are analyzed and discussed in the chapter. The current chapter focuses on presenting and discussing the results of the inferential analysis for the Shariah governance dimension, which is specific to Islamic banks only.

The individual dimensions within the Shariah governance dimension are further analyzed and tested to determine their impact on the extent of disclosure. These individual dimensions within the Shariah governance thematic area are listed in Fig. 7.1.

Several control variables at the bank and country levels, which prior studies have consistently associated with disclosure, are considered along with the corporate governance dimensions of interest. These control variables include size, profitability (ROAA, ROAE), leverage, efficiency (C2INC), regulatory quality (REGQ), political stability score, and GDP growth rate. Multiple regression models are run to examine the hypotheses and address the research questions.

7.2. Hypothesis Testing

The current research first conducts an OLS regression analysis to test the main Shariah governance hypothesis. The use of OLS regression analysis as the main regression model is deemed appropriate for this study given the cultural

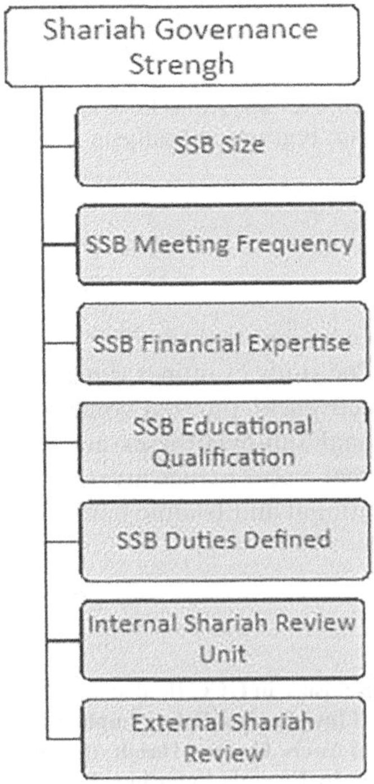

Fig. 7.1. Shariah Governance Thematic Area and Its Individual Dimensions.

homogeneity and geographic proximity of the GCC banks. To validate the robustness and fit of the regression model, additional inferential analyses are performed. OLS regression analysis with robust standard errors is undertaken to validate the consistency of the main OLS findings. The results of the main OLS regression and the OLS regression with robust standard errors are discussed in Section 7.3. PLS-SEM analysis is also employed using SmartPLS software to attest the robustness of the regression results and ascertain the consistency of the findings. The results of the PLS-SEM analysis are discussed in Section 7.4.

7.3. OLS Regression Analysis

This book proposes the main hypothesis for the Shariah governance dimension as discussed in Chapter Five. OLS regression analysis is employed to test the main hypothesis and determine the impact of Shariah governance on the extent of disclosure for Islamic banks. The individual dimensions within the Shariah governance dimension are further analyzed and tested to determine their impact on the extent of disclosure. Multiple regression models are run to examine the hypotheses and address the research questions. The results of the regression test are exhibited in Table 7.2.

7.3.1. Multicollinearity Test

Multicollinearity refers to the presence of high correlations among independent variables, which is considered to cause issues in the regression model (Chatterjee & Yilmaz, 1992). VIF and tolerance levels are calculated in SPSS to test for multicollinearity and ensure that the VIFs are within the tolerance levels suggested by prior studies (Chatterjee & Yilmaz, 1992). To be acceptable, the VIF should be less than 5. Table 7.1 summarizes the multicollinearity tests conducted for the linear regression model.

Table 7.1 shows that the highest VIF is 4.031, while the lowest is 1.102, and the mean is 2.481. On the other hand, Table 7.1 indicates that the lowest tolerance is 0.272. Therefore, the results confirm that the variables do not have multicollinearity problems.

7.3.2. OLS Regression Analysis for the Impact of Shariah Governance Dimensions on Disclosure for Islamic Banks

OLS regression analysis is conducted to examine the impact of Shariah governance dimensions on the extent of disclosure by Islamic banks. Two models are developed and tested to examine their impact on the extent of disclosure. Model (1) tests the impact of the overall Shariah governance strength dimension, along with the control variables, on the extent of disclosure. Model (2) tests the individual variables pertaining to the Shariah governance strength dimension on the extent of disclosure, along with the control variables considered for this book. Table 7.2 summarizes the results of the OLS regression analysis performed for this book.

Table 7.1. Variance Inflation Factor (VIF) for Shariah Governance Variables.

Variable	Tolerance	VIF
SSBSIZE	0.293	3.412
SSBEXP	0.248	4.031
SSBEDU	0.814	1.229
SSBDD	0.29	3.452
SSBMEET	0.556	1.798
ISAUD	0.284	3.525
ESAUD	0.734	1.363
SIZE	0.316	3.16
ROAE	0.291	3.442
EARQ	0.654	1.529
C2INC	0.571	1.75
LEV	0.375	2.664
CAR	0.696	1.437
DBNDX	0.272	3.683
REGQ	0.317	3.158
PS	0.907	1.102
GDP	0.696	1.436
Mean VIP		2.481

SSBSIZE, the total number of Shariah; SSBEXP, the number of Shariah board members with financial expertise; SSBEDU, the number of Shariah board members with a PhD; SSBDD, dummy variable for having defined duties for the Shariah board; SSBMEET, the total number of Shariah board meetings during the year; ISAUD, dummy for the existence of internal Shariah audit unit; ESAUD, dummy for the performance of external Shariah audit; SIZE, natural logarithm of bank assets; ROAA, return on average assets; ROAE, return on average equity; EARQ, earnings quality; C2INC, cost to income ratio; LEV, leverage; CAR, capital adequacy ratio; DBNDX, ease of doing business index; REGQ, regulatory quality; PS, political stability; GDPG, GDP growth rate.

Model (1) presents the results of the regression analysis for the overall Shariah governance strength dimension along with the control variables. Shariah governance strength is an index comprising SSB-related dimensions such as SSB size, meeting frequency, and financial expertise. As demonstrated in Table 7.2, the adjusted R^2 for the model is 0.246, suggesting that the overall Shariah governance strength dimension, along with the control variables, explains about 24.6% of the variance in disclosure. The model for the overall Shariah governance strength dimension is significant ($F = 4.380$, $p < 0.01$). The result indicates that the overall Shariah governance strength (SSBGOV) dimension has a significant and positive impact ($\beta = 0.283$, $t = 3.264$, $p < 0.01$) on the extent of disclosure.

Table 7.2. OLS Regression Analysis for the Impact of Shariah Governance Dimensions on Disclosure for Islamic Banks.

Predictive Variables	**Model (1) Beta (*t*)**	**Model (2) Beta (*t*)**
SSBGOV	0.283*** (3.264)	
SSBSIZE		0.126 (0.881)
SSBEXP		−0.107 (−0.690)
SSBEDU		0.040 (0.467)
SSBDD		0.245* (1.691)
SSBMEET		0.184* (1.768)
ISAUD		0.001 (0.009)
ESAUD		0.177* (1.907)
SIZE	0.012 (0.109)	−0.115 (−0.819)
ROAA	0.416*** (2.711)	0.361** (2.282)
ROAE	−0.695*** (−4.138)	−0.628*** (−3.424)
EARQ	−0.031 (−0.353)	0.038 (0.393)
C2INC	0.046 (0.388)	0.031 (0.261)
LEV	0.310*** (2.777)	0.287** (2.253)
CAR	0.090 (0.963)	0.072 (0.750)
DBNDX	−0.378*** (−2.757)	−0.284* (−1.910)
REGQ	0.391*** (2.972)	0.450*** (3.233)
PS	−0.038 (−0.468)	−0.010 (−0.126)

(*Continued*)

Table 7.2. (Continued)

Predictive Variables	**Model (1) Beta (*t*)**	**Model (2) Beta (*t*)**
GDP	−0.016 (−0.178)	−0.011 (−0.118)
Constant	0.824*** (4.357)	0.553** (2.421)
Adjusted R^2	0.246	0.258
F Statistics	4.380	3.396
Number of Observations	125	125

***$p < 0.01$, **$p < 0.05$, *$p < 0.1$.

SSBGOV, Shariah governance strength score; SSBSIZE, the total number of Shariah; SSBEXP, the number of Shariah board members with financial expertise; SSBEDU, the number of Shariah board members with a PhD; SSBDD, dummy variable for having defined duties for the Shariah board; SSBMEET, the total number of Shariah board meetings during the year; ISAUD, dummy for the existence of internal Shariah audit unit; ESAUD, dummy for the performance of external Shariah audit; SIZE, natural logarithm of bank assets; ROAA, return on average assets; ROAE, return on average equity; EARQ, earnings quality ratio; C2INC, cost to income ratio; LEV, leverage; CAR, capital adequacy ratio; DBNDX, a World Bank index measuring the ease of doing business index; REGQ, an indicator of regulatory quality; PS, political stability indicator; GDP, GDP growth rate.

For the firm-level control variables, the results show that ROAA has a significant positive impact ($\beta = 0.416$, $t = 2.711$, $p < 0.01$) on the extent of disclosure. On the other hand, return on average equity (ROAE) has a significant negative impact ($\beta = -0.695$, $t = -4.138$, $p < 0.01$) on the extent of disclosure. Leverage (LEV) also has a statistically significant and positive association ($\beta = 0.310$, $t = 2.777$, $p < 0.01$) with the extent of disclosure.

For the macro-level control variables, the result indicates that the World Bank index for ease of doing business (DBNDX) has a significant negative impact ($\beta = -0.378$, $t = -2.757$, $p < 0.01$) on the extent of disclosure, while REGQ has a significant positive impact ($\beta = 0.391$, $t = 2.972$, $p < 0.01$) on the extent of disclosure. This seems to suggest that countries with easier and more efficient business requirements tend to have less disclosure. However, the result indicates that a stronger regulatory environment with robust and effective policies contributes to more transparency and higher disclosure. No significant impact on disclosure is detected for the remaining control variables.

Model (2) presents the results of the regression analysis for all the individual Shariah governance dimensions along with the control variables included in the regression analysis. As demonstrated in Table 7.2, the adjusted R^2 for the model is 0.258, which suggests that the individual variables related to the Shariah governance dimension, along with the control variables in the model, explain about 25.8% of the variance in the disclosure. The model for the individual Shariah governance variables is significant ($F = 3.396$, $p < 0.01$). The result indicates that the SSB duties defined (SSBDD) variable has a marginally significant and positive impact ($\beta = 0.245$, $t = 1.691$, $p < 0.10$) on the extent of disclosure. SSB meeting frequency (SSBMEET) has a marginally significant and positive effect ($\beta = 0.184$, $t = 1.768$, $p < 0.10$) on the extent of disclosure. Similarly, the result shows that the external Shariah audit (ESAUD) has a marginally significant positive impact ($\beta = 0.177$, $t = 1.907$, $p < 0.10$) on the extent of disclosure. This suggests that having an SSB with well-defined responsibilities that meets more frequently contributes to greater transparency. Moreover, the result supports the hypothesis that having an ESAUD, conducted by an independent third party, results in higher levels of disclosure by Islamic banks. The remaining individual Shariah governance dimensions do not have any significant effect on the extent of disclosure.

For the firm-level control variables, the results show that ROAA has a moderately significant positive impact ($\beta = 0.361$, $t = 2.711$, $p < 0.05$) on the extent of disclosure. On the other hand, ROAE has a significant negative impact ($\beta = -0.628$, $t = -3.424$, $p < 0.01$) on the extent of disclosure. LEV also has a moderately significant positive association ($\beta = 0.287$, $t = 2.253$, $p < 0.05$) with the extent of disclosure.

For the macro-level control variables, the result indicates that the World Bank index for ease of doing business (DBNDX) has a marginally significant negative impact ($\beta = -0.284$, $t = -1.910$, $p < 0.10$) on the extent of disclosure, while REGQ has a significant positive impact ($\beta = 0.450$, $t = 3.233$, $p < 0.01$) on the extent of disclosure. This seems to suggest that countries with easier and more efficient business requirements tend to have less disclosure. On the other hand, the result indicates that a stronger regulatory environment with robust and effective policies contributes to more transparency and higher disclosure. No significant impact on disclosure is detected for the remaining control variables.

7.3.3. OLS Regression Analysis with Robust Standard Errors for the Impact of Shariah Governance Dimensions on Disclosure for Islamic Banks

To further confirm the results of the main OLS regression analysis, this book undertakes an OLS regression analysis with robust standard errors. The result of the OLS analysis with robust standard error is presented in Table 7.3.

Table 7.3 presents the results of an OLS regression with robust standard errors on the impact of Shariah governance on the extent of disclosure by Islamic banks. As shown in Table 7.3, the OLS regression results with robust standard errors are generally consistent with the main OLS regression, thus confirming and further attesting to the robustness of the findings. A few insignificant differences were noted between the two analyses, as discussed below.

Model (1) results show that the findings are consistent with the main OLS regression analysis for all Shariah governance and control variables both in terms of the level of significance of the impact and its direction, except for the ease of doing business index (DBNDX) where the level of significance has decreased from a significant positive impact ($p < 0.01$) to a marginally significant positive impact

Table 7.3. OLS Regression Analysis with Robust Standard Error for Impact of Shariah Governance Dimensions on Disclosure for Islamic Banks.

Predictive Variables	**Model (1) Beta (*t*)**	**Model (2) Beta (*t*)**
SSBGOV	0.283*** (4.014)	
SSBSIZE		0.126 (0.883)
SSBEXP		−0.107 (−0.783)
SSBEDU		0.040 (0.538)
SSBDD		0.245*** (3.177)
SSBMEET		0.184* (1.876)
ISAUD		0.001 (0.019)
ESAUD		0.177*** (2.670)
SIZE	0.012 (0.088)	−0.115 (−0.743)
ROAA	0.416*** (2.874)	0.361** (2.399)
ROAE	−0.695*** (−3.279)	−0.628*** (−2.775)
EARQ	−0.031 (−0.334)	0.038 (0.377)
C2INC	0.046 (0.285)	0.031 (0.194)
LEV	0.310*** (4.168)	0.287** (2.628)
CAR	0.090 (1.329)	0.072 (1.084)
DBNDX	−0.378* (−1.921)	−0.284 (−1.406)
REGQ	0.391*** (2.462)	0.450*** (2.784)
PS	−0.038 (−0.389)	−0.010 (−0.107)

Table 7.3. (Continued)

Predictive Variables	Model (1) Beta (*t*)	Model (2) Beta (*t*)
GDP	−0.016	−0.011
	(−0.167)	(−0.114)
Constant	0.824***	0.553*
	(2.294)	(1.724)
Adjusted R^2	0.246	0.258
F Statistics	4.380	3.396
Number of observations	125	125

***$p < 0.01$, **$p < 0.05$, *$p < 0.1$.

SSBGOV, Shariah governance strength score; SSBSIZE, the total number of Shariah; SSBEXP, the number of Shariah board members with financial expertise; SSBEDU, the number of Shariah board members with a PhD; SSBDD, dummy variable for having defined duties for the Shariah board; SSBMEET, the total number of Shariah board meetings during the year; ISAUD, dummy for the existence of internal Shariah audit unit; ESAUD, dummy for the performance of external Shariah audit; SIZE, natural logarithm of bank assets; ROAA, return on average assets; ROAE, return on average equity; EARQ, earnings quality ratio; C2INC, cost to income ratio; LEV, leverage; CAR, capital adequacy ratio; DBNDX, a World Bank index measuring the ease of doing business index; REGQ, an indicator of regulatory quality; PS, political stability indicator; GDPG, GDP growth rate.

($p < 0.10$) on the extent of disclosure. Model (2), which has all the individual Shariah governance and control variables, shows a few differences from the main OLS regression analysis. SSBDD have changed from being a marginally significant positive impact ($p < 0.10$) to a significant positive impact ($p < 0.01$) after applying the robust standard errors. ESAUD has also changed, from having a marginally significant positive impact ($p < 0.10$) under the main OLS regression analysis to having a significant positive impact on the extent under the OLS regression analysis with robust standard errors. The impact for the ease of doing business index has decreased from a marginally significant impact ($p < 0.10$) to no impact because of the OLS regression analysis with robust standard errors. The remaining individual variables are all consistent with the main OLS regression analysis.

Based on the results of the OLS regression analysis with robust standard errors, it can be concluded that, other than the few insignificant differences discussed above, the results are consistent with the main OLS regression analysis. This confirms the robustness of the main regression analysis and validates the results of the analysis.

7.4. Partial Least Squares Structural Equation Modeling analysis

PLS-SEM analysis is performed to further validate and confirm the results of the main regression analysis and validate the hypotheses. As the purpose of

PLS-SEM analysis is to support and validate the main OLS regression analysis, the focus of the analysis is to test the structural model by using bootstrapping techniques to determine the relationship and its significance among the variables of interest (Hair et al., 2017; Sarstedt et al., 2021). Two models are constructed and analyzed to test the main Shariah governance hypothesis and sub-hypotheses. These models are run using SmartPLS software version # 3. Model (1) is concerned with testing the main Shariah governance hypothesis of this book, while Model (2) tests the individual Shariah governance dimensions along with the control variables. The results of the PLS-SEM analysis are summarized in Table 7.4. Moreover, Figs. 7.2–7.5 present the results of the PLS-SEM analysis in graphical form. The results of each model are discussed next.

Table 7.4. PLS-SEM Analysis for the Impact of Shariah Governance Dimensions on the Extent of Disclosure by Islamic Banks.

Predictive Variables	**Model (1) Beta (*t*)**	**Model (2) Beta (*t*)**
SSBGOV	0.283*** (3.245)	
SSBSIZE		0.071 (0.506)
SSBEXP		−0.030 (0.213)
SSBEDU		0.025 (0.374)
SSBMEET		0.185* (1.944)
ISAUD		0.199*** (2.709)
ESAUD		0.169** (2.256)
SIZE	0.012 (0.090)	−0.053 (0.346)
ROAA	0.416** (2.567)	0.398** (2.276)
ROAE	−0.695*** (−4.300)	−0.702*** (3.763)
EARQ	0.031 (0.354)	0.041 (0.431)
C2INC	0.046 (0.364)	0.049 (0.367)
LEV	0.310*** (3.970)	0.368*** (3.599)

Table 7.4. (Continued)

Predictive Variables	Model (1) Beta (*t*)	Model (2) Beta (*t*)
CAR	0.090 (1.399)	0.098 (1.528)
DBNDX	−0.378** (−2.174)	−0.288 (1.526)
REGQ	0.391*** (2.887)	0.446*** (3.205)
PS	−0.038 (0.410)	−0.009 (0.097)
GDP	−0.016 (0.181)	0.008 (0.087)
Adjusted R^2	0.246	0.245
Number of observations	125	125

***$p < 0.01$, **$p < 0.05$, *$p < 0.1$.

SSBGOV, Shariah governance strength score; SSBSIZE, the total number of Shariah; SSBEXP, the number of Shariah board members with financial expertise; SSBEDU, the number of Shariah board members with a PhD; SSBDD, dummy variable for having defined duties for the Shariah board; SSBMEET, the total number of Shariah board meetings during the year; ISAUD, dummy for the existence of internal Shariah audit unit; ESAUD, dummy for the performance of external Shariah audit; SIZE, natural logarithm of bank assets; ROAA, return on average assets; ROAE, return on average equity; EARQ, earnings quality ratio; C2INC, cost to income ratio; LEV, leverage; CAR, capital adequacy ratio; DBNDX, a World Bank index measuring the ease of doing business index; REGQ, an indicator of regulatory quality; PS, political stability indicator; GDPG, GDP growth rate.

Model (1) tests the impact of the Shariah governance strength score on the extent of disclosure, considering the control variables for this book. The Shariah governance strength score is a self-developed index which is comprised of several SSB and Shariah governance-related dimensions, such as SSB size, educational qualifications, financial expertise, and meeting frequency, as well as the existence of an internal Shariah review unit and an ESAUD. As demonstrated in Table 7.4, the adjusted R^2 is 0.246, which suggests that the overall Shariah governance strength dimension, along with the control variables in the model, explains about 24.6% of the variance in disclosure. The result indicates that SSBGOV has a significant positive impact ($\beta = 0.283$, $t = 3.245$, $p < 0.01$) on the dependent variable (disclosure score). The significant impact of SSBGOV indicates that SSBs with a higher level of effectiveness (i.e., a higher number of SSB members with a PhD, financial expertise, and more frequent meetings) contribute to greater transparency and disclosure in Islamic banks. The PLS-SEM findings confirm and are consistent with the results of the main regression analysis performed in this book.

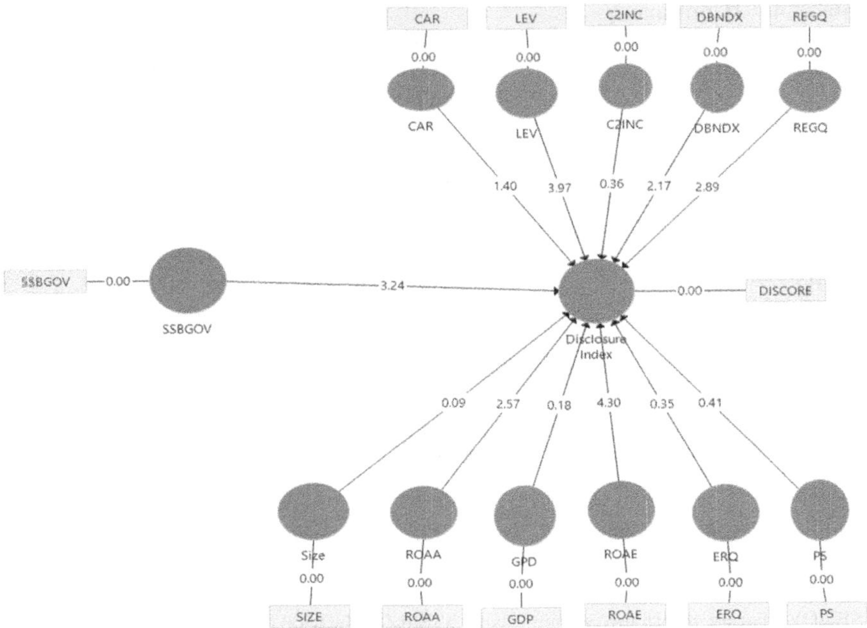

Fig. 7.2. Model 1 – Bootstrapping for the Impact of Shariah Governance Score on the Extent of Disclosure.

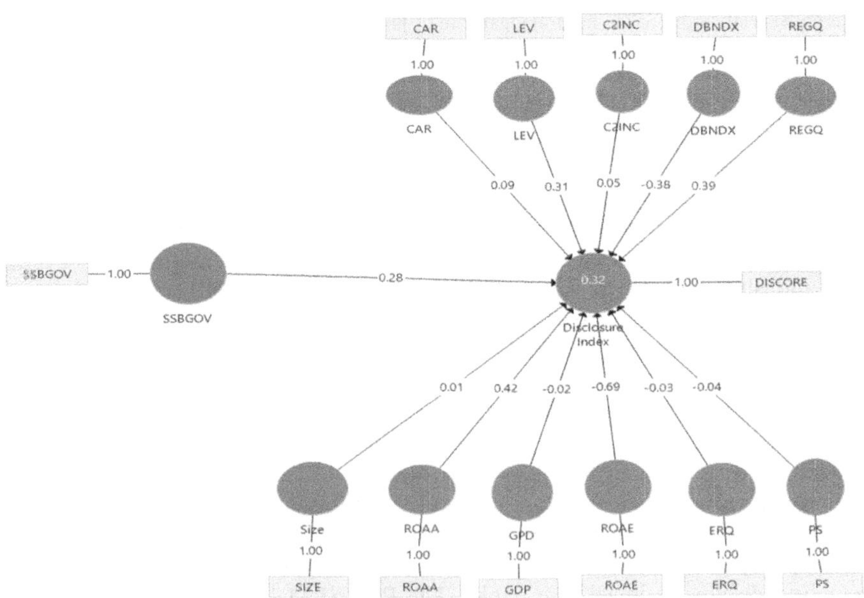

Fig. 7.3. Model 1 – Path for the Impact of Shariah Governance Score on the Extent of Disclosure.

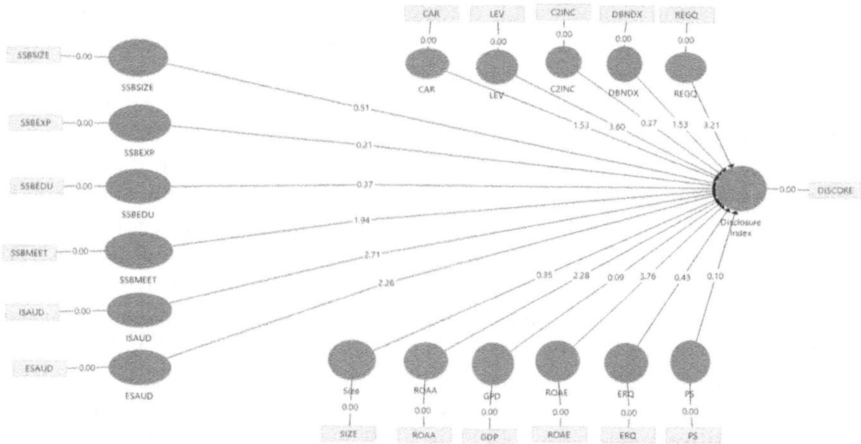

Fig. 7.4. Model 2 – Bootstrapping for the Impact of Shariah Governance Individual Dimensions on the Extent of Disclosure.

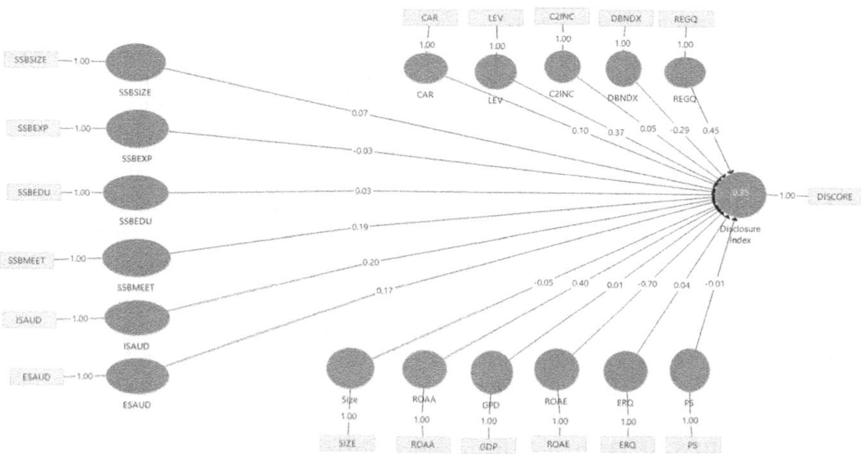

Fig. 7.5. Model 2 – Path for the Impact of Shariah Governance Individual Dimension on the Extent of Disclosure.

Several control variables show a significant impact on the extent of disclosure. With regards to the firm-level control variables, the results show ROAA also has a moderately significant positive impact ($\beta = 0.416$, $t = 2.567$, $p < 0.05$), while ROAE has a significant negative impact ($\beta = -0.695$, $t = -4.300$, $p < 0.01$) on the extent of disclosure. It is also noted that LEV has a statistically significant positive association ($\beta = 0.310$, $t = 3.970$, $p < 0.01$) with the extent of disclosure.

For the macro-level control variables, the result indicates that the ease of doing business index (DBNDX) has a moderately significant negative impact ($\beta = -0.387$, $t = -2.174$, $p < 0.01$) on the extent of disclosure, while REGQ has a significant positive impact ($\beta = 0.391$, $t = 2.887$, $p < 0.01$) on the extent of disclosure. No significant impact is detected for the remaining control variables. Overall, it can be observed that the Model (1) result of the PLS-SEM analysis for both the explanatory and control variables is generally consistent with the OLS regression and confirms the robustness of the findings for the main regression analysis.

Model (2) tests the impact of the individual Shariah governance dimensions along with the control variables on the extent of disclosure. These include SSB size, educational qualifications, financial expertise, meeting frequency, the existence of an internal Shariah audit (ISAUD), and the performance of an ESAUD. As shown in Table 7.4, the adjusted R^2 is 0.245, suggesting that the individual Shariah governance strength dimensions, along with the control variables in the model, explain about 24.5% of the variance in disclosure. The result indicates that SSBMEET has a marginally significant and positive impact ($\beta = 0.185$, $t = 1.944$, $p < 0.10$) on the extent of disclosure. The existence of an ISAUD function has a significant positive impact ($\beta = 0.199$, $t = 2.709$, $p < 0.01$) on the extent of disclosure. Additionally, the performance of an ESAUD is found to have a moderately significant positive association ($\beta = 0.169$, $t = 2.256$, $p < 0.05$) with the extent of disclosure. The remaining Shariah governance dimensions were found to have no impact on the extent of disclosure.

As for the firm-level control variables, the results show that bank size has a significant positive impact ($\beta = 0.221$, $t = 2.915$, $p < 0.01$) on the extent of disclosure. ROAE has a significant negative impact ($\beta = -0.339$, $t = -2.832$, $p < 0.01$) on the extent of disclosure. It is also noted that LEV has a statistically significant positive association ($\beta = 0.243$, $t = 3.292$, $p < 0.01$) with the extent of disclosure.

For the macro-level control variables, the result indicates that the ease of doing business index (BDNDX) has a significant negative impact ($\beta = -0.408$, $t = -4.252$, $p < 0.01$) on the extent of disclosure, while REGQ has a significant positive impact ($\beta = 0.390$, $t = 4.678$, $p < 0.01$) on the extent of disclosure. No significant impact is detected for the remaining control variables.

Overall, the Model (2) results of the PLS-SEM analysis for both the explanatory and control variables are mostly consistent with the OLS regression and confirm the robustness of the main regression analysis. Figs. 7.2–7.5 present the results of the PLS-SEM analysis in graphical form.

7.5. Conclusion

This chapter discusses in detail the inferential statistics pertaining to the tests and analysis performed to establish the relationship and impact of Shariah governance on the extent of disclosure by Islamic banks. Overall, the regression analysis shows that the Shariah governance strength score has a significant positive impact on the extent of disclosure, suggesting that stronger Shariah governance mechanisms lead to greater disclosure. Moreover, the study finds a significant positive association between some of the individual Shariah governance variables and the extent of disclosure, including SSBMEET, SSBDD, ISAUD unit, and ESAUD.

In summary, the chapter starts with an introduction and then presents the hypotheses, which are tested in line with the research questions. The chapter then presents the main OLS regression analysis performed to test the Shariah governance dimensions and discusses the findings. PLS-SEM analyses performed to support the main regression are then presented, along with the results. Finally, the chapter provides summaries of the data analysis performed and the findings that have been identified.

Chapter Eight

Discussion and Way Forward

Abstract

This book examines the impact of corporate governance on the extent of disclosure for Islamic and conventional banks in the GCC countries. This chapter discusses and synthesizes the results and provides an overall conclusion for this book. The chapter starts with an introduction and then thoroughly discusses the findings, synthesizing the results to answer the research questions and concluding on the hypotheses of this book. The chapter also presents the key research contributions as well as the limitations of the study. The chapter concludes with suggestions for future research areas and a summary of the main points discussed.

Keywords: Corporate governance; Shariah governance; disclosure; Board of Directors; Shariah Supervisory Board; Islamic banks

8.1. Introduction

Corporate governance has gained prominence during the last two decades largely due to accounting scandals in major corporations such as Enron and the 2008 financial crisis. These events have shaken the trust of investors and other stakeholders in financial markets and generated significant interest in corporate governance. In particular, there has been a growing demand to enhance the monitoring and oversight role of the board of directors and the audit committee and to adopt best practices in corporate governance in line with the requirements set forth by regulatory bodies and international standard setters. The BCBS issued guidelines on corporate governance in 2015 which called for the banking sector to promote sound corporate governance practices, including effective oversight and a strong internal control environment (BCBS, 2015). Moreover, in 2017, the CIBAFI conducted a major study on the corporate governance practices of Islamic banks, highlighting key governance aspects specific to Islamic banks (e.g., role of the SSB) and making

Corporate Governance and Disclosure in GCC Banks:
Islamic Perspectives, Empirical Insights and Policy Implications, 171–186

Published under exclusive licence by Emerald Publishing Limited
doi:10.1108/978-1-80686-279-520261008

important recommendations to strengthen the corporate governance practices of Islamic banks (CIBAFI, 2017).

8.2. Discussion of the Results

The main objective of this book is to examine the impact of corporate governance on the extent of disclosure by Islamic and conventional banks in the GCC countries. Three main dimensions of corporate governance as well as several sub-dimensions are used as explanatory variables along with bank- and country-level characteristics as control variables. Descriptive and inferential analyses are performed to examine the relationships as well as the impact of these explanatory and control variables on the extent of disclosure by Islamic and conventional banks in GCC countries. Chapter Six discussed the descriptive statistics and presented a detailed account of the disclosure index, examining it from cross-country and cross-dimensional perspectives. Chapter Six also presented the results of the correlation testing performed, highlighting the associations between the variables of interest and the disclosure index. Chapters Seven and Eight presented the empirical analysis for this book, where Chapter Seven presented the findings for the impact of corporate governance characteristics on the extent of disclosure for Islamic and conventional banks and Chapter Eight provided the result of the empirical analysis specific to Islamic banks. To perform the empirical analysis, this book used an OLS regression analysis. Further analysis was undertaken using OLS robust standard errors and PLS-SEM to attest the robustness of the regression results and ascertain the consistency of the findings. The findings are analyzed and discussed next.

8.2.1. Disclosure Index Analysis: Difference Between Islamic and Conventional Banks

Research question 1 is concerned with the extent of disclosure by Islamic and conventional banks and investigates whether there is a significant difference in disclosure between Islamic and conventional banks. The result of the disclosure index analysis performed in Chapter Six reveals that, overall, Islamic banks provide less disclosure than their conventional counterparts (mean disclosure score of 68% for Islamic banks and 72% for their conventional counterparts). Furthermore, the result of the independent samples *t*-test suggests that the difference in disclosure between Islamic and conventional banks is significant ($p = 0.002$). The result of the regression analysis also shows that the Islamic dummy variable has a significant negative coefficient, suggesting that Islamic banks provide less disclosure when compared to their conventional counterparts. The findings are consistent with those of Aribi and Gao (2010), who report significant differences in the disclosure of CSR information between Islamic and conventional banks for a sample of GCC banks. The finding answers one of the research questions concerning whether there is a difference between the disclosure practices of Islamic and conventional banks. The result confirms that there is a difference in disclosure practices between Islamic and conventional banks and that this difference is statistically significant. Given the recent establishment of the Islamic banks in Oman, further analysis is performed to determine if the difference in disclosure among the banks in GCC countries is due to the age of the bank. However, there was no significant difference found in disclosure practices between the recent (<25 years) and older banks (>25 years), indicating that the bank age has no significant impact on its disclosure practices. This result seems to support the argument that despite being recent entrants to the market, the Omani Islamic banks have been able to establish strong disclosure practices when compared to Islamic banks in other countries. The findings can be used by regulators and policymakers in other GCC countries to encourage the Islamic banks in their respective countries to adopt similar practices.

8.2.2. Impact of Board of Directors on the Extent of Disclosure

In line with prior studies (Al-Hadi et al., 2019; CIBAFI, 2017; Ishak & Al-Ebel, 2013), this book develops an index of board effectiveness to examine the impact of the board of directors on the extent of disclosure. The board effectiveness index is comprised of several board-related dimensions, such as board size, independence and meeting frequency, CEO role duality, and board diversity. In addition to examining the board characteristics at the aggregate level, this book examines the individual board characteristics to gain further insight and support the main findings. Table 8.1 provides summary of the result of the hypotheses testing for the board effectiveness dimensions.

Overall, the findings in Chapter Seven reveal that board effectiveness is significantly and positively associated with the extent of disclosure. Accordingly, hypothesis (*H1*) is accepted. The finding, which is significant at the 1% level ($p < 0.01$), suggests that more effective boards (larger in size, meet more frequently, have more independent board members, diverse, etc.) provide greater levels of disclosure. The findings are consistent with those of Ishak and Al-Ebel (2013) and Al-Hadi et al. (2019), who find that the corporate governance quality index (comprised of board characteristics) is significantly and positively associated with the extent of disclosure. This finding suggests that more effective boards enhance transparency and contribute to greater levels of disclosure. Furthermore, the findings provide important insight for regulators, governing bodies, and other stakeholders to strengthen the board of directors by ensuring appropriate board composition in terms of its size, independence, diversity, and CEO role duality, as well as board diligence (measured by number of board meetings per year).

The results of the individual characteristics of the board of directors show important findings which suggest that some of these individual variables have an impact on the extent of disclosure. While board size is found to be significantly and positively associated with the extent of disclosure in Model (3), however, in Model (6) where all the individual internal control variables along with the control variables are included, board size became insignificant. Similar results are found after running the additional robustness testing and PLS-SEM analysis. Therefore, hypothesis (*H2*) is rejected. The finding is in contrast with those of Akhtaruddin et al. (2009), Abeysekera (2010), Hidalgo et al. (2011), Allegrini

Table 8.1. Summary of the Hypotheses Results for the Board Effectiveness.

Hypothesis Number	Hypothesis Description	Expected Sign	Results	Conclusion
H1	*Board effectiveness is positively associated with the extent of disclosure*	Positive	Positive	Accepted
H2	*There is a positive association between the board size and the extent of disclosure*	Positive	None	Rejected
H3	*The proportion of independent board members is positively associated with the extent of disclosure*	Positive	Positive	Accepted
H4	*There is a positive relationship between the number of board meetings and the extent of disclosure*	Positive	None	Rejected
H5	*There is a negative relationship between CEO role duality and the extent of disclosure*	Negative	Positive	Rejected
H6	*There is a positive relationship between proportion of women on the board and the extent of disclosure*	Positive	None	Rejected

and Greco (2013), Jizi et al. (2014), Samaha et al. (2015), and Albassam and Ntim (2017), who report a significant and positive association with the extent of disclosure. However, the result is in line with those of Uyar et al. (2013), Ganesan et al. (2017), Nerantzidis and Tsamis (2017), and Khandelwal et al. (2020), who find that board size has no significant effect on the extent of disclosure. The findings seem to suggest that the number of board members does not represent an important indicator of board effectiveness and hence has no influence on the extent of disclosure. The results provide valuable insight to regulators and policymakers in the GCC region with regards to the size of boards. In their effort to enhance the corporate governance mechanism of banks, regulators and policymakers can focus on other measures of board effectiveness such as board independence instead of stipulating a specific number of board members.

Similarly, the research finds that board independence is significantly and positively associated with the extent of disclosure. The association is significant at the 1% level and, accordingly, hypothesis (*H3*) is accepted. The findings persist even after robustness testing and further PLS-SEM analysis. The findings are consistent with those of Chen and Jaggi (2000), Cheng and Courtenay (2006),

Huafang and Jianguo (2007), Uyar et al. (2013), Jizi et al. (2014), Grassa and Chakroun (2016), Nerantzidis and Tsamis (2017), Husted et al. (2019), and Salem et al. (2019), who find a positive association between board independence and the extent of disclosure. The findings provide evidence that independent board members strengthen the bank's corporate governance and play an important monitoring role. Furthermore, as suggested by agency and stakeholder theories, independent board members are in a better position to protect the interests of the owners by reducing information asymmetry between managers and owners while addressing the needs of stakeholders by providing greater disclosure. While the findings are consistent with the majority of studies, they are in contrast with those of Ganesan et al. (2017) and Bueno et al. (2018), who find that board independence has no significant impact on the extent of disclosure. The findings are also in contrast with those of Eng and Mak (2003), Barako et al. (2006), Alnabsha et al. (2018), and Tessema (2019), who report that board independence is negatively associated with the extent of disclosure.

Board meeting frequency is found to have no significant association with the extent of disclosure. Accordingly, the hypothesis (*H4*) is rejected. This result contrasts with those of Allegrini and Greco (2013), Nerantzidis and Tsamis (2017), and Alnabsha et al. (2018), who found a significant positive relationship between board meeting frequency and extent of disclosure. However, the result is consistent with numerous other studies, such as that of Allini et al. (2016), who find that board meeting frequency is not associated with the extent of risk disclosure for a sample of Italian-listed firms. This suggests that having a greater number of board meetings is not an important indicator of board diligence and has no influence on the disclosure levels of the banks.

CEO role duality is found to be positively associated with the extent of disclosure. Accordingly, hypothesis (*H5*) is rejected. The findings are inconsistent with those of Gul and Leung (2004), Allegrini and Greco (2013), Neifar and Jarboui (2018), and Husted and Sousa-Filho (2019), who find a significant negative association between CEO duality and extent of disclosure. However, the findings are in line with those of other studies, such as that of Jizi et al. (2014) who find that CEO role duality is positively and significantly associated with CSR disclosure for a sample of U.S. banks. Drawing from agency and stakeholder theories, the authors explain that the positive impact of CEO duality on disclosure indicates that powerful CEOs do encourage greater disclosure to protect their personal interests while also trying to appease their stakeholders. Based on prior studies and given the cultural context of the GCC countries, the findings from this book can be understood to suggest that CEO role duality can be considered an internal corporate governance mechanism for promoting greater transparency, thus providing more disclosure to meet stakeholder needs. Similarly, the result for CEO role duality is consistent with that of Grassa and Chokroun (2016), who document a positive association between CEO duality and the extent of corporate governance disclosure for a sample of banks in the GCC countries.

Regarding board diversity (measured by the number of women on the board), this book does not find any significant association between board diversity and the extent of disclosure. Hence, hypothesis (*H6*) is rejected. The findings are consistent with those of Shehata (2017), who find that board diversity is not associated with the extent of corporate governance disclosure for a sample of 270 GCC-listed firms. This suggests that board diversity is not an important determinant for disclosure in the GCC banking industry. Accordingly, it can be understood from the results that having more female board members does not lead to greater levels of disclosure by GCC Islamic and conventional banks. The finding is in contrast with that of Ghabayen et al. (2016), who find that board diversity has a negative impact on the extent of CSR disclosure for a sample of Jordanian listed banks. In a similar vein, the study contrasts with other studies, such as those of Uyar et al. (2015), Allini et al. (2016), and Salem et al. (2019), which find a positive association between board diversity and extent of disclosure.

8.2.3. Impact of Internal Controls on the Extent of Disclosure

This research developed an internal control strength score comprising the audit committee and the internal audit function (IAF) characteristics which are most examined in the literature, including audit committee size, independence, meeting frequency, and financial expertise, as well as the existence of an independent the IAF. Using OLS regression analysis and PLS-SEM analysis, the study examined the impact of the internal control strength score (ICSTRENGTH) on the extent of disclosure for Islamic and conventional banks. The results show several important findings for the impact of internal control strength on the extent of disclosure for Islamic and conventional banks. In addition to the overall internal control strength index results, the regression analysis documents the association between some of the individual internal control strength variables and the extent of disclosure. This book considers individual audit committee characteristics such as audit committee size, independence, meeting frequency, and financial expertise as part of the internal control environment of the bank. Moreover, the study considers the existence and independence of the IAF as part of the key individual variables of the internal control environment. Table 8.2 summarizes the result of the hypotheses testing for the internal control strength score and the related individual dimensions.

Overall, the results of the regression analysis show that the internal control strength score is significantly and positively associated with the extent of disclosure. The association is significant at the 1% level and is persistent even after running the robustness OLS regression analysis and PLS-SEM analysis. Therefore, hypothesis (*H7*) is accepted. This suggests that strong internal control (e.g., effective audit committee and independent IAF) contributes to greater transparency and results in more disclosure in GCC banks. These internal control systems strengthen the monitoring role of the board of directors and other governance mechanisms, thus helping reduce agency costs and contributing to meeting the information needs of stakeholders through increased disclosure. Additionally, the findings are consistent with the integrated theoretical framework adopted for this study, which posits that effective corporate governance mechanisms strengthen transparency and lead to greater disclosure because they provide owners the mechanism to minimize their agency costs (agency theory), strengthen the bank's

Table 8.2. Summary of the Hypotheses Results for the Internal Control Strength.

Hypothesis Number	Hypothesis Description	Expected Sign	Results	Conclusion
H7	*The internal control strength has positive association with the extent of disclosure*	Positive	Positive	Accepted
H8	*The size of the audit committee has a positive relationship with the extent of disclosure*	Positive	Positive	Accepted
H9	*The proportion of the independent members in the audit committee has a positive relationship with the extent of disclosure*	Positive	None	Rejected
H10	*The number of audit committee meetings held during the year is positively associated with the extent of disclosure*	Positive	None	Rejected
H11	*The proportion of audit committee members with financial expertise has a positive relationship with the extent of disclosure*	Positive	Positive	Accepted
H12	*The existence of an internal audit function has a positive association with the extent of disclosure*	Positive	None	Rejected
H13	*The independence of the internal audit function has a positive association with the extent of disclosure*	Positive	Positive	Accepted

ability to establish its legitimacy (legitimacy theory), signal positive news and good performance (signaling theory), and address stakeholder expectations and meet their needs (stakeholder theory).

Additionally, the results of the regression analysis reveal that some of the individual internal control strength variables have significant impact on the extent of disclosure. Among audit committee characteristics, the study finds that audit committee size is positively and significantly associated with the extent of disclosure. The association is significant at the 1% level. The significant association is persistent under all the models, including Model (6) which considers all corporate governance variables. Furthermore, the additional robustness testing and the PLS-SEM analysis confirm the significant positive impact between audit committee size and the extent of disclosure. Accordingly, hypothesis (*H8*) is accepted. The findings are consistent with those of Hidalgo et al. (2011), Akhtaruddin and Rouf (2012), Al-Moataz and Hussainey (2013), Madi et al. (2014), and Appuhami and Tashakor (2017), who find a significant positive association between audit committee size and the extent of disclosure. This suggests that having more audit committee members is likely to contribute to greater levels of disclosure by banks. Accordingly, the findings provide support for forming large audit committees and can be considered by regulators and bank boards of directors when nominating or establishing audit committees. In contrast, Mangena and Pike (2005) and Ridwan and Mayapada (2020) find that audit committee size is not associated with the extent of disclosure.

Audit committee independence is measured by the proportion of independent members to the total number of members. Model (5) of the OLS regression, which includes the individual internal control characteristics along with the control variables, shows that audit committee independence has a significant positive effect on the extent of disclosure at the 5% level. However, the result of Model (6), which includes board variables in addition to the internal control characteristics and control variables, finds that audit committee independence has no significant impact on the extent of disclosure. One explanation for the change in the level of impact is that it is moderated by individual board variables which cause the impact of audit committee independence to diminish. Consequently, the findings, when considered for all the models, do not support the hypothesis (*H9*). Hence, the hypothesis is rejected. This result is consistent with the findings of Kent and Stewart (2008), Hidalgo et al. (2011), Li et al. (2012), and Ridwan and Mayapada (2020), who report that audit committee independence has no significant association with the extent of disclosure. However, the result is in contrast with the findings of Barros et al. (2013), Madi et al. (2014), Appuhami and Tashakor (2017), Garas and ElMassah (2018), and Salem et al. (2019), who document that audit committee independence is significantly and positively associated with the extent of disclosure. Similarly, the findings contrast with those of Buallay and Al-Ajmi (2020), who report that audit committee independence is significantly and positively associated with the extent of disclosure for a sample of GCC firms.

The results of the OLS regression analysis for both Models (5) and (6) confirm that audit committee meeting frequency is not associated with the extent of disclosure. A similar result is found when the robustness testing and additional PLS-SEM analysis are performed. Thus, hypothesis (*H10*) is rejected. This result is consistent with the findings of Madi et al. (2014), who document that audit committee meeting frequency has no impact on the extent of disclosure in the Malaysian context. In contrast, Allegrini and Greco (2013), Appuhami and Tashakor (2017), and Buallay and Al-Ajmi (2020) find that audit committee meeting frequency has a significant positive association with the extent of disclosure. Nonetheless, the findings suggest that audit committee meeting frequency is not a significant measure of audit committee effectiveness in monitoring and influencing a bank's disclosure policy. Accordingly, it can be argued that having a larger audit committee meeting frequency does not contribute to a higher level of transparency or result in increased disclosure.

The results show that audit committee financial expertise has a significant positive impact with the extent of disclosure in both Models (5) and (6). The association is significant at the 1% level under Model (5) and at the 5% level under Model (6). The slight decrease in the significance of the association from the 1% level to the 5% level can be attributed to the inclusion of the board characteristics in Model (6). This result is unchanged even after the performance of robustness testing and additional PLS-SEM analysis. Consequently, hypothesis (*H11*) is accepted. The result is in line with those reported by Mangena and Pike (2005), Li et al. (2012), and Kusnadi et al. (2016), who document the significant positive impact of audit committee financial expertise on the extent of disclosure. In contrast, Akhtaruddin and Haron (2010) find that audit committee financial expertise has no significant effect on the extent of disclosure. Madi et al. (2014) also find that audit committee financial expertise is not associated with the extent of disclosure. Kusnadi et al. (2016) report that audit committee financial expertise results in higher financial reporting quality for a sample of 423 Singaporean-listed firms. Similarly, Appuhami and Tashakor (2017) document that AC financial expertise is not associated with the extent of disclosure for a sample of Australian-listed firms. The result also contrasts with findings by Kent and Stewart (2008) and Buallay and Al-Ajmi (2020), who document that audit committee financial expertise has a significant negative association with the extent of disclosure. The findings of this book support that having more audit committee members with financial expertise strengthens the monitoring role of the committee and enhances its ability to contribute to greater transparency and better disclosure policy by banks. As a result, the findings of the study provide important insight to regulators, governing bodies and stakeholders to ensure that audit committees have an adequate number of members with financial expertise so that they can strengthen the overall corporate governance quality of the bank.

The results of the regression analysis indicate that the existence of an IAF has no impact on the extent of disclosure. Accordingly, hypothesis (*H12*) is rejected. However, the independence of the IAF (i.e., reporting functionally to the audit committee or the board of directors) has a significant positive impact on the extent of disclosure. The impact is significant at the 1% level and remains at the 1% level after running the additional robustness analysis and PLS-SEM regression analysis. Therefore, hypothesis (*H13*) is accepted. The findings are consistent with those of Razek (2014), Alzeban (2019), Sulub et al. (2020), and Tumwebaze et al. (2022), who find that the quality of an IAF and its independence contributes to greater transparency and results in increased disclosure. However, the findings are in contrast with those of Lin et al. (2011), who report that IAF objectivity (measured by the communication of the chief audit executive with the audit committee of the board) has no significant impact on the extent of material weakness disclosure.

Overall, the significant impact of IAF independence on the extent of disclosure lends support to the postulation that the existence of an independent IAF plays an important role in the overall corporate governance of banks. Therefore, the result can be used by regulators and the oversight bodies of banks (e.g., board of directors) to enhance corporate governance quality by strengthening the independence of the IAF. It is worth noting that the role of the IAF has gained greater attention after the 2000 accounting scandals and the 2008 financial crisis, when many regulators, standard setters, and governing bodies began requiring the establishment of an in-house IAF with a sufficient level of independence from management to monitor management activities and internal control processes and report to the board and other governing parties.

8.2.4. Impact of Shariah Governance on the Extent of Disclosure (Specific to Islamic Banks)

In line with prior studies (Elamer et al., 2019; Farook et al., 2011; Rizkiningsih & Dewi, 2015), this study develops a Shariah governance strength score (SSB-GOV) comprising the Shariah governance characteristics most examined in the literature, including SSB size, meeting frequency, educational qualification and financial expertise, and the existence of internal and external Shariah audits. Drawing on an integrated theoretical framework and using OLS regression analysis and PLS-SEM analysis, this book examines the impact of the SSBGOV on the extent of disclosure for GCC Islamic banks. The results of the study show several important findings for the impact of Shariah governance on disclosure for Islamic banks. Table 8.3 summarizes the result of the hypothesis testing for the impact of Shariah governance strength on the extent of disclosure.

Overall, the study finds that the SSBGOV is significantly and positively associated with the extent of disclosure. The association is significant at the 1% level. Therefore, hypothesis (*H14*) is accepted. This suggests that stronger and more effective Shariah governance processes enhance the overall corporate governance function of Islamic banks and contribute to greater transparency and increased disclosure. It can be understood from the findings that the SSB plays an important monitoring and oversight role in Islamic banks and can be an effective mechanism for ensuring that Islamic banks discharge their responsibility to provide more disclosure. Drawing from the integrated theoretical framework adopted for this book, the results indicate that strong monitoring by an SSB helps reduce the bank's agency costs and addresses the information needs of Islamic bank stakeholders by providing increased disclosure. Furthermore, through increased disclosure, the SSB enhances the legitimacy of Islamic banks and signals to the community the Islamic banks' commitment to transparency, as emphasized by the Shariah. The result is consistent with those of Farook et al. (2011), Abdul Raman and Bukair (2013), and Elamer et al. (2019), who find that the Islamic governance

Table 8.3. Summary of the Hypotheses Results for the Impact of Shariah Governance Strength.

Hypothesis Number	Hypothesis Description	Expected Sign	Results	Conclusion
H14	*The Shariah governance strength has a positive association with the extent of disclosure*	Positive	Positive	Accepted

index is significantly and positively associated with the extent of various types of disclosures, such as risk governance and CSR, for a sample of Islamic banks in the MENA and Southeast Asian regions. The finding is in contrast with that of Rizkiningsih and Dewi (2015), who document that Shariah governance strength has no significant impact on the extent of disclosure.

As for the individual Shariah governance variables, this book finds no significant association between SSB size and the extent of disclosure. The result is consistent with those of Wan Abdullah et al. (2013), Sencal and Asutay (2020), as well as Ridwan and Mayapada (2020), who report that SSB size does not have any significant impact on disclosure. The result is in contrast with that of Grassa et al. (2018), who report that SSB size has a significant positive association with the extent of product and services disclosure. The research finds that SSB educational qualifications are also insignificant. The findings are consistent with those of Ridwan and Mayapada (2020), who find that educational qualifications of the SSB have no significant impact on disclosure. This book also finds that SSB financial expertise has no impact on the extent of disclosure. The result is in contrast with that of Wan Abdullah et al. (2013), who find that SSB financial expertise has a significant positive relationship with the extent of CSR disclosure. However, the result is consistent with that of Ridwan and Mayapada (2020), who report that SSB financial expertise is not related to extent of disclosure.

The study also finds that the SSB duties defined (SSBDD) variable has a significant positive impact on the extent of disclosure. This suggests that having well-defined roles and responsibilities for the SSB contributes to enhancing the overall effectiveness of the SSB, thus resulting in SSB members being able to discharge their duties more diligently, including the promotion of greater disclosures. Moreover, SSB meeting frequency has a weak positive association with the extent of disclosure. The association is significant at the 10% level. The findings lend support to the argument that having more SSB meetings strengthens the monitoring and oversight role of the SSB and results in greater levels of disclosure.

The results suggest that the existence of an internal Shariah audit unit has no significant impact on the extent of disclosure. The findings persist even after the additional robustness testing and PLS-SEM analysis are performed. The findings are somewhat in contrast with those of Sencal and Asutay (2020), who document that Islamic banks which have a dedicated internal Shariah audit function provide greater levels of disclosures in their annual Shariah reports. Finally, the results show that external Shariah audits have a significant positive association with the extent of disclosure. The association is significant at the 1% level. This suggests that an independent external Shariah audit is an important governance mechanism which helps strengthen the overall governance of Islamic banks and contributes to enhanced transparency and greater disclosure.

8.2.5. Association of Firm- and Country-level Characteristics with Extent of Disclosure

Regarding the control variables considered for this book, the results suggest that size is positively and significantly associated with the extent of disclosure. The significant association is persistent in all the OLS regression models (Models 1 through 6), including the model which contains all the individual corporate governance variables considered for this book (Model 6). The result is consistent with those of most prior studies (AlSaeed, 2006; Elamer et al., 2019; Hossain et al., 1995; Naser et al., 2002; Nerantzidis & Tsamis, 2017; Uyar et al., 2013), which find that company size is positively associated with the extent of disclosure. In line with the integrated theoretical framework adopted for this book, the findings suggest that larger banks are more inclined to provide higher levels of disclosure to reduce their agency costs, enhance their legitimacy, and meet stakeholder expectations.

Two profitability measures, namely ROAA and ROAE, are used to examine their association with the extent of disclosure. The results suggest that there is no significant relationship between ROAA and the extent of disclosure. However, unexpectedly, the results show that ROAE has a strong negative association with the extent of disclosure. This result is unexpected since prior literature supports the argument that when profit margins are high, management is more likely to disclose more information to signal the positive news to its stakeholders and communicate successes (AlSaeed, 2006; Mohamed & Basuony, 2015; Singhvi & Desai, 1971). This finding contradicts with most prior studies (Cheung et al., 2007; Gul & Leung, 2004; Jizi et al., 2014; Shehata, 2017), which find a positive association between ROAE and extent of disclosure. However, the findings are in line with some other studies which find a negative association between profitability and extent of disclosure. For instance, Rouf (2012) finds that profitability is negatively associated with the extent of voluntary disclosure for a sample of 120 listed firms in Bangladesh. Similarly, Allini et al. (2016) find that ROAE is negatively associated with the extent of disclosure for a sample of Italian companies. Garas and ElMassah (2018) report a significant negative association between profitability and extent of CSR disclosure for a sample of GCC firms.

Leverage is found to be positively associated with the extent of disclosure. The finding is consistent with several studies which find that leverage is positively associated with the extent of disclosure (Baldini et al., 2018; Hossain et al., 1995). These studies explain that in line with agency theory, firms that are highly leveraged try to provide more disclosure to reduce agency cost. This is in contrast with Uyar et al. (2013), who find that leverage is negatively associated with the extent of disclosure for a sample of Turkish-listed firms. The result also contradicts with that of Garas and ElMassah (2018), who find that leverage has no significant impact on CSR disclosure for a sample of GCC firms.

The index of doing business is found to be significantly and negatively associated with the extent of disclosure, while the regulatory quality ratio has a significant positive association with the extent of disclosure. This suggests that a highly efficient business environment may not support or require more disclosure of information. On the other hand, firms operating in countries with stronger regulatory environments may be required to provide greater disclosure to meet the information needs of stakeholders and the public.

The results of the study also indicate that Islamic bank dummy variable is negatively associated with the extent of disclosure. This suggests that Islamic banks provide less disclosure when compared to their conventional counterparts, and the difference is statistically significant. Similar results are found by Grassa and Chakroun (2016), who report that the nature of a bank being Islamic bank is negatively associated with the extent of disclosure.

8.3. Research Contributions

This research contributes to the literature in several ways. First, the study develops a comprehensive disclosure index comprising six categories, namely, (1) strategy and business profile; (2) corporate governance; (3) risk governance; (4) social responsibility, sustainability, and value creation; (5) Shariah governance; and (6) financial information. Most prior studies, especially those related to GCC countries, focus on specific aspects of disclosure (e.g., risk disclosure, intellectual property disclosure, or CSR-related disclosure). For further details on the self-developed disclosure index, see Table AI in the Appendix. Therefore, by developing a comprehensive disclosure index comprising 6 categories and 70 items, this book helps shed light on unexplored areas of disclosure and examines its determinants to better inform future research on the subject.

Second, the study extends the literature on corporate governance and disclosure by testing corporate governance literature at two levels: first at the thematic level, and second at the individual variables level. The three main thematic areas of corporate governance for Islamic and conventional banks are developed and considered to examine their impact on the extent of disclosure. These are board effectiveness, internal control strength, and Shariah governance strength (specific to Islamic banks). An index is developed for each of the three thematic areas, in line with prior studies (e.g., CIBAFI, 2017) which have used a board composite to analyze the effectiveness of the board of directors as a key corporate governance mechanism. Further regression testing is performed to examine the underlying individual corporate governance variables and determine their impact on the extent of disclosure, thus enabling the researcher to gain more insight and further validate the results.

Third, this book extends the literature on disclosure by analyzing certain corporate governance explanatory variables which are less explored in the literature, especially in studies related to the GCC countries. For instance, this study considers the impact of the IAF as a mechanism of corporate governance as part of the internal control strength of the bank. While the IAF as a corporate governance mechanism has been explored in developed countries, there is very limited research in developing countries, including the GCC, which examines the impact of the IAF on disclosure. By considering the IAF as a determinant of disclosure, this book sheds light on this corporate governance mechanism and informs policymakers and regulators considering ways to enhance the role of the IAF in the banking sector. On the other hand, for Islamic banks, this book considers less explored Shariah governance characteristics such as the internal Shariah audit function and the performance of an external Shariah audit.

Additionally, the study examines whether the age of the bank is associated with the extent of disclosure. While firm age has been considered as an explanatory variable in other studies (AlSaeed, 2006; Grassa & Chakroun, 2016; Harun et al., 2020), to the best of the researcher's knowledge, this has not been widely explored by prior studies of all GCC countries. Only a study by Harun et al. (2020) considers firm age as a control variable for all GCC countries. Other studies, such as those of AlSaeed (2006) and Grassa and Chakroun (2016), use bank age only for some of the GCC countries. In contrast, this study covers all GCC countries, including Oman, and examines the association of bank age with the extent of disclosure. The bank age variable is of particular importance to Oman because of the Islamic banking industry in Oman being a relatively new development compared to other GCC countries. Also, to-date, there is limited research on the Omani Islamic banking industry. By considering bank age as a control variable, this book is able to determine whether bank age has any impact on the extent of disclosure, thereby providing an insight to better understand the factors affecting the disclosure practices of the Omani Islamic banks.

Finally, this book performs a comparative analysis of the level of disclosure by Islamic and conventional banks in GCC countries, using aspects of corporate governance as explanatory variables. The study considers various categories of disclosure such as strategy, corporate governance, risk governance, CSR, Shariah, and financial information. While the extant literature has some prior studies which compare GCC Islamic and conventional banks, most of them examine bank performance. Even those which are related to disclosure only focus on specific categories of disclosure such as CSR, risk governance, or intellectual property disclosure. The result of the disclosure comparative analysis of GCC Islamic and conventional banks undertaken in this research shows that generally conventional banks provide greater disclosure. Moreover, the results indicate that there is a statistically significant difference in the level of disclosure between Islamic and conventional banks. The results of the comparative analysis provide insight to regulators and other stakeholders so that appropriate and more targeted steps can be taken to enhance transparency and disclosure among Islamic banks.

8.4. Research Limitations

This book has performed a comprehensive analysis of the impact of various corporate governance characteristics on the extent of disclosure by using a disclosure index comprising 6 categories and 70 items. Despite the insightful results gained from the study, it is the case that every study will have some limitations. This research is no exception and, therefore, has several limitations. For further details on the disclosure index, see Table AI in the Appendix.

First, the scope of this book is the GCC region, which plays crucial role in the global Islamic banking industry and has the highest share of Islamic finance assets globally. According to the Islamic Financial Services Board (IFSB), the total assets of the Islamic banks in the GCC countries constitute 52.4% of the total global Islamic finance assets (IFSB, 2022). While the study makes significant contributions in furthering the study of corporate governance related to the GCC countries and shedding light on the corporate governance mechanisms which play a crucial role in enhancing the level of transparency and disclosure for GCC banks, the result may not be generalized or applied to other regions such as Southeast Asia due to differences in culture, geography, and business practices. Therefore, further studies may be required to incorporate other regions such as Southeast Asia. Second, another limitation somewhat related to the first one is sample size and number of years. The sample size, which is 52 GCC Islamic and conventional banks, is based on banks which have annual reports available for the years of the study (i.e., 2015 through 2019) since the data are hand collected from annual reports. Moreover, although the study considers the annual reports for the sample banks for 5 years, it can be argued that more years of data would provide greater insight and more meaningful results.

Third, this research unexpectedly finds that CEO role duality is positively associated with the extent of disclosure. This suggests that powerful CEOs contribute to greater transparency and provide more disclosure. However, as this finding is inconsistent with the majority of prior studies which expect CEO duality to have a negative impact on disclosure, this book is unable to fully explain the reasons for the positive association. Fourth, this book considers gender (i.e., number of women on the board) as a proxy for board diversity and examines its impact on the extent of disclosure. While this is an important aspect of board diversity, there are other elements such as age and educational background which this book does not take into account. Accordingly, the study may not be fully capturing some important determinants related to board diversity.

8.5. Future Research Areas

Future research may consider expanding this book by adding other geographic locations such as Southeast Asia and by performing comparative studies for GCC and Southeast Asia banks. Moreover, future research can further examine the reasons why, in the GCC banking industry context, CEO duality is positively associated with the extent of disclosure. This can provide insightful analysis which may help the industry and/or regulators determine if combining the role of the CEO and board chairmanship leads to more effective corporate governance of banks and greater transparency.

The study considers the impact of board diversity, measured by the number of women on the board, on the extent of disclosure. The study finds no association between board diversity and the extent of disclosure. Given the fact that this book considers only gender as a proxy for board diversity, future studies can expand on considering multiple features of board diversity such as age and educational background.

8.6. Conclusion

The current research examines the impact of several corporate governance mechanisms on the extent of disclosure by Islamic and conventional banks in the GCC countries. To this end, the study develops a composite of the main thematic dimensions of corporate governance, namely, board effectiveness, internal control strength, and Shariah governance strength. Additionally, the study examines the effect of the individual corporate governance characteristics on the extent of disclosure along with several control variables which are most associated with disclosure. The study undertakes OLS regression analysis to measure the impact of corporate governance characteristics on the extent of disclosure. Further robustness testing and PLS-SEM analysis are performed to support and confirm the result of the main regression analysis.

The results of the regression analysis show that all three main indexes have a significant and positive impact on the extent of disclosure, providing support to the hypotheses and answering research questions regarding the impact of corporate governance mechanisms on the extent of disclosure. In addition, the results show that several individual corporate and Shariah governance characteristics have a significant impact on the extent of disclosure by Islamic banks. For instance, board independence, CEO role duality, audit committee size, audit committee financial expertise, and internal audit independence are found to have a significant impact on the extent of disclosure.

The overall result of this study provides support that corporate governance mechanisms such as the board of directors, the audit committee, and an IAF contribute to greater transparency and result in higher levels of disclosure. Moreover, the results confirm that effective Shariah governance plays an important role in enhancing the disclosure practices of Islamic banks. The results of the findings can be used by regulators, policymakers, Islamic and conventional bank management, and their stakeholders to strengthen corporate governance and empower boards and audit committees so that they can promote transparency and better disclosure policies.

Appendix

Table AI. Self-developed Disclosure Index.

Disclosure Category	Disclosure Item	References
(A) Bank profile and strategic information		
	1. Background and overview of the bank	Meek et al. (1995), Haniffa and Cooke (2002)
	2. Mission and vision statement	Barako et al. (2006)
	3. Mission statement reflects commitment to Shariah rules and principles	Haniffa and Hudaib (2007), Abdul Raman and Bukair (2013)
	4. Statement about the strategic goals and objectives of the bank	Lang and Ludholm (1993), Lan et al. (2013)
	5. Organizational structure	Barako et al. (2006)
	6. Major customers and markets	Gul and Leung (2004)
	7. Major product lines	Botosan (1997)
	8. Future prospects of the bank	Ho and Shun Wong (2001), Haniffa and Cooke (2002)
(B) Corporate governance		
	9. Board size	CIBAFI (2017)
	10. Separation of the roles of Board Chairperson and CEO	CIBAFI (2017)
	11. Number of independent board members	Barros et al. (2013), CIBAFI (2017)

(*Continued*)

Table AI. (Continued)

Disclosure Category	Disclosure Item	References
	12. Board of director names and titles	Akhtaruddin et al. (2009)
	13. Pictures of board of directors	Haniffa and Cooke (2002)
	14. Educational qualification of board members	CIBAFI (2017), Saha and Akter (2013)
	15. Board meetings and attendance information	Saha and Akter (2013), CIBAFI (2017)
	16. Compensation of board of directors	Akhtaruddin et al. (2009)
	17. Existence of audit committee	Haniffa and Hudaib (2007), Barros et al. (2013), CIBAFI (2017)
	18. Membership of the audit committee	CIBAFI (2017)
	19. Names and titles of the audit committee	Wan Abdullah et al. (2014)
(C) Risk governance		
	20. General risk information	Allegrini and Greco (2013), Abdallah et al. (2015)
	21. Bank's approach to risk management	Ariffin et al. (2007)
	22. Existence of risk governance committee	BCBS (2018), CIBAFI (2017)
	23. Chief Risk Officer position exists	CIBAFI (2017)
	24. Types of risks, including financial, operational, and other risks	Ariffin et al. (2007), Abdallah et al. (2015), BCBS (2018)
	25. Reserves, including statutory and legal reserves	Abdallah et al. (2015), BCBS (2018)

(D) Shariah governance[1]		
	26. Shariah supervisory board names and titles	AAOIFI (2012), Haniffa and Hudaib (2007)
	27. Educational background of the SSB members	Abdul Raman and Bukair (2013), Che Azmi et al. (2016)
	28. Cross-directorship in other Islamic banks	Hasan (2011)
	29. Compensation paid to members	Haniffa and Hudaib (2007)
	30. Structure and role of the Shariah Audit Unit	Wan Abdullah et al. (2015), Albassam and Ntim (2017)
	31. Information about the Shariah audits and the Shariah Audit department	Farook et al. (2011), Aribi et al. (2019)
	32. Detailed Shariah audit report, including findings, recommendations, and remedial actions	Farook (2011), Wan Abdullah et al. (2015)
	33. SSB fatwas and religious rulings and their basis	Abdul Raman and Bukair (2013), Aribi et al. (2019)
	34. Report on Shariah compliance and any violations occurred during the period	Che Azmi et al. (2016), CIBAFI (2017), Aribi et al. (2019)
	35. Nature and amount of prohibited (haram) income	Abdul Raman and Bukair (2013); Che Azmi et al. (2016)
	36. Information about how the prohibited income is disposed	Aribi et al. (2019)

[1]Disclosure items related to the Shariah governance category are specific to Islamic banks and are taken into account only when calculating the score for the Islamic banks.

(Continued)

Table AI. (Continued)

Disclosure Category	Disclosure Item	References
	37. Zakat calculation and distribution	Haniffa and Huddaib (2007), Ousama and Fatima (2010)
	38. Profit and loss distribution to investment account holders	CIBAFI (2017)
	39. Information about Qard Hassan	Ousama and Fatima (2010), Che Azmi et al. (2016)
	40. Policy on how to deal with late payments, insolvent customers, and defaults	Farook et al. (2011)
(E) Social responsibility, sustainability, and value creation		
	41. Approach and strategy toward value-based intermediation	Haniffa and Huddaib (2007)
	42. Commitment to value creation, positive impact, and community empowerment	Haniffa and Cooke (2002)
	43. Policy on sustainable business practices	Jizi et al. (2014)
	44. Commitment to good governance	Akhtaruddin et al. (2009)
	45. Information about product offerings aimed at achieved value-based intermediation	Jizi et al. (2014)
	46. Scorecard on measuring the outcome of the value-based intermediation initiative	Allegrini and Greco (2013)
	47. Sponsoring community programs and activities (education, sports)	Haniffa and Cooke (2002), Jizi et al. (2014)
	48. Supporting charitable community initiatives	Haniffa and Cooke (2002)

	49. Participation in government initiatives aimed at community development	Meek et al. (1995), Lan et al. (2013)
	50. Safety programs and information	Lang and Ludholm (1993), Meek et al. (1995)
	51. Policies on protection and concern for the environment	Wan Abdullah et al. (2015), Albassam and Ntim (2017)
	52. Environmental protection activities	Abdul Raman and Bukair (2013)
	53. Initiatives and campaigns for the environment such as recycling and energy preservation	Abdul Raman and Bukair (2013)
	54. Employee welfare	Abdul Raman and Bukair (2013)
	55. Training provided to employees	Allegrini and Greco (2013)
	56. Significant changes in personnel	Albassam and Ntim (2017)
	57. Employee code of conduct and ethics	Atan et al. (2016)
	58. Information about customer services	Mohammed et al. (2011)
	59. Commitment to customer satisfaction	Atan et al. (2016), Mohammed et al. (2011)
(F) Financial information		
	60. Revenue and market share information	Barros et al. (2013)
	61. Financial ratios	Gul and Leung (2004), Lan et al. (2013)
	62. Income and profitability	Gul and Leung (2004), Lan et al. (2013)
	63. Cash flow analysis	Ho and Shun Wong (2001), Barros et al. (2013)
	64. Details of expenditures (capital and operating)	Ho and Shun Wong (2001)

(Continued)

Table AI. (Continued)

Disclosure Category	Disclosure Item	References
	65. Comparison of previous financial performance to current year actuals	Gul and Leung (2004)
	66. Significant accounting policies and changes in policies during the period	Meek et al. (1995), Barako et al. (2006)
	67. Segment reporting	Barrett (1977), Haniffa and Cooke (2002)
	68. Stock price information and analysis	Meek et al. (1995), Ho and Shun Wong (2001), Gul and Leung (2004)
	69. Financial forecasting and future financial outlook	Ho and Shun Wong (2001), Lan et al. (2013)
	70. Shareholder equity	Barros et al. (2013)

Bibliography

Abbott, L. J., Parker, S., & Peters, G. F. (2004). Audit committee characteristics and restatements. *Auditing: A Journal of Practice & Theory*, *23*(1), 69–87.

Abdallah, A. A.-N., Hassan, M. K., & McClelland, P. L. (2015). Islamic financial institutions, corporate governance, and corporate risk disclosure in Gulf Cooperation Council countries. *Journal of Multinational Financial Management*, *31*, 63–82. http://dx.doi.org/10.1016/j.mulfin.2015.02.003

Abdel Karim, R. A. (1990). The independence of religious and external auditors: The case of Islamic banks. *Accounting, Auditing & Accountability Journal*, *3*(3), 34–44.

Abdel Karim, R. A. (1995). The nature and rationale of a conceptual framework for financial reporting by Islamic banks. *Accounting and Business Research*, *25*(100), 285–300.

Abdel Karim, R. A., & Archer, S. (2013). *Islamic finance: The new regulatory challenge*. John Wiley & Sons.

Abdelsalam, O., El-Masry, A., & Elsegini, S. (2008). Board composition, ownership structure and dividend policies in an emerging market: Further evidence from CASE 50. *Managerial Finance*, *34*(12), 953–964.

Abdul Raman, A., & Bukair, A. A. (2013). The influence of the Shariah supervision board on corporate social responsibility disclosure by Islamic banks of Gulf Co-operation Council countries. *Asian Journal of Business and Accounting*, *6*(2), 65–104.

Abeysekera, I. (2010). The influence of board size on intellectual capital disclosure by Kenyan listed firms. *Journal of Intellectual Capital*, *11*(4), 504–518.

Aboody, D., & Lev, B. (2000). Information asymmetry, R&D, and insider gains. *The Journal of Finance*, *55*(6), 2747–2766.

Abozaid, A., & Dusuki, A. W. (2007). *The challenges of realizing maqasid al-shariah in Islamic banking and finance*. IIUM international conference on Islamic banking and finance, IIUM Institute of Islamic Banking and Finance, pp. 23–25.

Abu Qa'dan, M. B., & Suwaidan, M. S. (2019). Board composition, ownership structure and corporate social responsibility disclosure: The case of Jordan. *Social Responsibility Journal*, *15*(1), 28–46. https://doi.org/10.1108/SRJ-11-2017-0225

Abu-Tapanjeh, A. M. (2009). Corporate governance from the Islamic perspective: A comparative analysis with OECD principles. *Critical Perspectives on Accounting*, *20*(5), 556–567. http://dx.doi.org/10.1016/j.cpa.2007.12.004

Accounting and Auditing Organization for Islamic Financial Institutions. (2012). *Governance standards*. AAOIFI.

Adams, R. B., Hermalin, B. E., & Weisbach, M. S. (2010). The role of boards of directors in corporate governance: A conceptual framework and survey. *Journal of Economic Literature*, *48*(1), 58–107.

Adawi, M., & Rwegasira, K. (2011). Corporate boards and voluntary implementation of best disclosure practices in emerging markets: Evidence from the UAE listed companies in the Middle East. *International Journal of Disclosure and Governance*, *8*(3), 272–293.

Agyei-Mensah, B. K. (2016). Internal control information disclosure and corporate governance: Evidence from an emerging market. *Corporate Governance: The International Journal of Business in Society*, *16*(1), 79–95.

Ahmed, H., & Chapra, M. U. (2002). *Corporate governance in Islamic financial institution* [Occasional Paper].

Ahmed, H., Mohieldin, M., Verbeek, J., & Aboulmagd, F. W. (2015). *On the sustainable development goals and the role of Islamic finance* (Policy Research Working Paper No. 7266, pp. 1–47). World Bank.

Ahmed, H., Tajul Ariffin, F. A., Karbhari, Y., & Shafii, Z. (2019) Diverse accounting standards on disclosures of Islamic financial transactions: Prospects and challenges of narrowing gaps. *Accounting, Auditing & Accountability Journal*, *32*(7), 1865–1894.

Ahmed, K., & Nicholls, D. (1994).The impact of non-financial company characteristics on mandatory disclosure compliance in developing countries: The case of Bangladesh. *The International Journal of Accounting*, *29*(1), 62–77.

Akerlof, G. (1995). The market for "lemons": Quality uncertainty and the market mechanism. In G. A. Akerlof, A. M. Spence, & J. E. Stiglitz (Eds.), *Essential readings in economics* (pp. 175–188). Springer.

Akhtaruddin, M., & Haron, H. (2010). Board ownership, audit committees' effectiveness and corporate voluntary disclosures. *Asian Review of Accounting*, *18*(1), 68–82.

Akhtaruddin, M., Hossain, M. A., Hossain, M., & Yao, L. (2009). Corporate governance and voluntary disclosure in corporate annual reports of Malaysian listed firms. *Journal of Applied Management Accounting Research*, *7*(1), 1.

Akhtaruddin, M., & Rouf, Md. A. (2012). Corporate governance, cultural factors and voluntary disclosure: Evidence from selected companies in Bangladesh. *Corporate Board: Role, Duties & Composition*, *8*(1), 46–58. https://ssrn.com/abstract=2565253

Al-Akra, M., Abdel-Qader, W., & Billah, M. (2016). Internal auditing in the Middle East and North Africa: A literature review. *Journal of International Accounting, Auditing and Taxation*, 2613–2627. https://doi.org/10.1016/j.intaccaudtax.2016.02.004

Alam, M. (2006). *Stakeholder theory. Methodological issues in accounting research: Theories and methods*, 207–222.

Alam, N., Gupta, L., & Shanmugam, B. (2017). Corporate governance in Islamic Banks. In *Islamic finance: A practical perspective* (pp. 359–396). Springer International Publishing. https://doi.org/10.1007/978-3-319-66559-7_9

Alam Choudhury, M., & Nurul Alam, M. (2013). Corporate governance in Islamic perspective. *International Journal of Islamic and Middle Eastern Finance and Management*, *6*(3), 180–199.

Al-Baluchi, A. E. (2006). *The impact of AAOIFI standards and other bank characteristics on the level of voluntary disclosure in the annual reports of Islamic banks*. University of Surrey (United Kingdom).

Albassam, W. M., & Ntim, C. G. (2017). The effect of Islamic values on voluntary corporate governance disclosure: The case of Saudi-listed firms. *Journal of Islamic Accounting and Business Research*, *8*(2), 182–202.

Alchian, A. A., & Demsetz, H. (1972). Production, information costs, and economic organization. *The American Economic Review*, *62*(5), 777–795.

Al-Hadi, A., Al-Yahyaee, K. H., Hussain, S. M., & Taylor, G. (2019). Market risk disclosures and corporate governance structure: Evidence from GCC financial firms. *The Quarterly Review of Economics and Finance*, 73136–73150. https://doi.org/10.1016/j.qref.2017.11.008

Alhammadi, S., Archer, S., Padgett, C., & Abdel Karim, R. A. (2018). Perspective of corporate governance and ethical issues with profit sharing investment accounts in Islamic banks. *Journal of Financial Regulation and Compliance*, *26*(3), 406–424.

Alhazaimeh, A., Palaniappan, R., & Almsafir, M. (2014). The impact of corporate governance and ownership structure on voluntary disclosure in annual reports among listed Jordanian companies. *Procedia – Social and Behavioral Sciences, 129*, 341–348. http://dx.doi.org/10.1016/j.sbspro.2014.03.686

Al-Hussain, A. H. (2009). *Corporate governance structure efficiency and bank performance in Saudi Arabia*. University of Phoenix.

Ali, A., Chen, T.-Y., & Radhakrishnan, S. (2007). Corporate disclosures by family firms. *Journal of Accounting and Economics, 44*(1–2), 238–286. http://dx.doi.org/10.1016/j.jacceco.2007.01.006

Al-Janadi, Y., Rahman, R. A., & Omar, N. H. (2012). The level of voluntary disclosure practices among public listed companies in Saudi Arabia and the UAE: Using a modified voluntary disclosure index. *International Journal of Disclosure and Governance, 9*(2), 181–201.

Alkhafaji, A. F. (1989). *A stakeholder approach to corporate governance: Managing in a dynamic environment*. Praeger Pub Text.

Allegrini, M., & Greco, G. (2013). Corporate boards, audit committees and voluntary disclosure: Evidence from Italian listed companies. *Journal of Management & Governance, 17*(1), 187–216.

Allini, A., Manes Rossi, F., & Hussainey, K. (2016). The board's role in risk disclosure: An exploratory study of Italian listed state-owned enterprises. *Public Money & Management, 36*(2), 113–120.

Al Mannai, M., & Ahmed, H. (2018). Exploring the workings of Shari'ah supervisory board in Islamic finance: A perspective of Shari'ah scholars from GCC. *The Quarterly Review of Economics and Finance*. https://doi.org/10.1016/j.qref.2018.05.017

Al-Moataz, E., & Hussainey, K. (2013). Determinants of corporate governance disclosure in Saudi corporations. *Journal of King Abdulaziz University: Economics & Administration, 27*(2), 411–430.

Al-Musalli, M. A. K., & Ismail, K. N. I. K. (2012). Corporate governance, bank specific characteristics, banking industry characteristics, and intellectual capital (IC) performance of banks in Arab Gulf Cooperation Council (GCC) countries. *Asian Academy of Management Journal of Accounting & Finance, 8*(Supplement 1), 115–135.

Alnabsha, A., Abdou, H. A., Ntim, C. G., & Elamer, A. A. (2018). Corporate boards, ownership structures and corporate disclosures: Evidence from a developing country. *Journal of Applied Accounting Research, 19*(1), 20–41.

Alnasser, A. S., & Muhammed, J. (2012). Introduction to corporate governance from Islamic perspective. *Humanomics, 28*(3), 220–231.

AlQassar, A. B., & Ahmed, H. (2021). Regulatory regimes for Sharīʿah governance: A framework of assessment and analysis. *Journal of Banking Regulation, 23*(2), 139–154.

AlSaeed, K. (2006). The association between firm-specific characteristics and disclosure: The case of Saudi Arabia. *Managerial Auditing Journal, 21*(5), 476–496.

Al-Shammari, B., & Al-Sultan, W. (2010). Corporate governance and voluntary disclosure in Kuwait. *International Journal of Disclosure and Governance, 7*(3), 262–280.

Al-Shetwi, M., Ramadili, S. M., Chowdury, T. H. S., & Sori, Z. M. (2011). Impact of internal audit function (IAF) on financial reporting quality (FRQ): Evidence from Saudi Arabia. *African Journal of Business Management, 5*(27), 11189.

Alzeban, A. (2019). Influence of internal audit reporting line and implementing internal audit recommendations on financial reporting quality. *Meditari Accountancy Research, 28*(1), 26–50.

Al-Zuhair, M. M. (2008). *Privatization programs, ownership structures, and market development: The role of country characteristics on defining corporate governance standards* [Doctoral dissertation]. The George Washington University.

Al-Zwyalif, I. M. (2015). The role of internal control in enhancing corporate governance: Evidence from Jordan. *International Journal of Business and Management, 10*(7), 57.

An, Y., Davey, H., & Eggleton, I. R. (2011). Towards a comprehensive theoretical framework for voluntary IC disclosure. *Journal of Intellectual Capital, 12*(4), 571–585.

Anderson, R. C., Mansi, S. A., & Reeb, D. M. (2004). Board characteristics, accounting report integrity, and the cost of debt. *Journal of Accounting and Economics*, *37*(3), 315–342. http://dx.doi.org/10.1016/j.jacceco.2004.01.004

Aoki, M. (2001). *Toward a comparative institutional analysis*. MIT Press.

Appuhami, R., & Tashakor, S. (2017). The impact of audit committee characteristics on CSR disclosure: An analysis of Australian firms. *Australian Accounting Review*, *27*(4), 400–420. https://doi.org/10.1111/auar.12170

Archer, S., Karim, R. A. A., & Al-Deehani, T. (1998). Financial contracting, governance structures and the accounting regulation of Islamic banks: An analysis in terms of agency theory and transaction cost economics. *Journal of Management and Governance*, *2*(2), 149–170.

Archer, S., Karim, R. A. A., & Nienhaus, V. (2009). Business models in Takaful and regulatory implications. In S. Archer, R. A. A. Karim, & V. Nienhaus (Eds.), *Takaful Islamic insurance: Concepts and regulatory issues* (pp. 7–30). John Wiley & Sons.

Aribi, Z. A., Arun, T., & Gao, S. (2019). Accountability in Islamic financial institution: The role of the Shari'ah supervisory board reports. *Journal of Islamic Accounting and Business Research*, *10*(1), 98–114.

Aribi, Z. A., & Gao, S. (2010). Corporate social responsibility disclosure: A comparison between Islamic and conventional financial institutions. *Journal of Financial Reporting and Accounting*, *8*(2), 72–91.

Ariffin, N. M., Archer, S., & Karim, R. A. A. (2007). Transparency and market discipline in Islamic banks. *Islamic Economics and Finance*, *5*, 49–73.

Armstrong, C. S., Core, J. E., & Guay, W. R. (2014). Do independent directors cause improvements in firm transparency? *Journal of Financial Economics*, *113*(3), 383–403.

Arnold, J., Boyle, P., Carey, A., Cooper, M., & Wallace, R. (1990). *The future of financial reports*. Institute of Chartered Accountants in England and Wales.

Arouri, H., Hossain, M., & Muttakin, M. B. (2011). Ownership structure, corporate governance and bank performance: Evidence from GCC countries. *Corporate Ownership and Control*, *8*(4D), 365–372.

Askari, H., Iqbal, Z., & Mirakhor, A. (2011). *New issues in Islamic finance and economics: Progress and challenges*. John Wiley & Sons.

Atan, R., Razali, F. A., Said, J., & Zainun, S. (2016). Environmental, social and governance (ESG) disclosure and its effect on firm's performance: A comparative study. *International Journal of Economics and Management*, *10*(2), 355–375.

Ayuso, S., Ariño, M. A., Garcia-Castro, R., & Rodriguez, M. A. (2007). *Maximizing stakeholders' interests: An empirical analysis of the stakeholder approach to corporate governance*.

Azid, T., & Alnodel, A. A. (2019). Determinants of Shari'ah governance disclosure in financial institutions: Evidence from Saudi Arabia. *International Journal of Ethics and Systems*, *35*(2), 207–226.

Azid, T., Asutay, M., & Burki, U. (2007). Theory of the firm, management and stakeholders: An Islamic perspective. *Islamic Economic Studies*, *15*(1), 1–30.

Bae, S. M., Masud, M., Kaium, A., & Kim, J. D. (2018). A cross-country investigation of corporate governance and corporate sustainability disclosure: A signaling theory perspective. *Sustainability*, *10*(8), 2611.

Baker, H. K., & Anderson, R. (Eds.). (2010). *Corporate governance: A synthesis of theory, research, and practice* (Vol. *8*). John Wiley & Sons.

Baldini, M., Maso, L. D., Liberatore, G., Mazzi, F., & Terzani, S. (2018). Role of country- and firm-level determinants in environmental, social, and governance disclosure. *Journal of Business Ethics*, *150*, 79–98.

Barako, D. G., Hancock, P., & Izan, H. Y. (2006). Factors influencing voluntary corporate disclosure by Kenyan companies. *Corporate Governance: An International Review*, *14*(2), 107–125.

Barrett, M. E. (1977). The extent of disclosure in annual reports of large companies in seven countries. *The International Journal of Accounting*, *12*(2), 1–25.

Barros, C. P., Boubaker, S., & Hamrouni, A. (2013). Corporate governance and voluntary disclosure in France. *Journal of Applied Business Research*, *29*(2), 561–578.

Basel Committee on Banking Supervision. (2018). *Basel III monitoring report*. Bank for International Settlements. https://www.bis.org/bcbs/publ/d438.html

Bassen, A., & Kovacs, A. M. M. (2008). Environmental, social and governance key performance indicators from a capital market perspective. *Zeitschrift für Wirtschafts- und Unternehmensethik*, *9*(2), 182–192.

Baydoun, N., Maguire, W., Ryan, N., & Willett, R. (2013) Corporate governance in five Arabian Gulf countries. *Managerial Auditing Journal*, *28*(1), 7–22.

Baydoun, N., Sulaiman, M., Willett, R. J., & Ibrahim, S. (2018). *Principles of Islamic accounting*. John Wiley & Sons.

Baydoun, N., & Willett, R. (1997). Islam ethical issues in the presentation of financial information accounting, commerce and finance. *The Islamic Perspective Journal*, *1*(1), 1–25.

Baydoun, N., & Willett, R. (2000). Islamic corporate reports. *Abacus*, *36*(1), 71–90. https://doi.org/10.1111/1467-6281.00054

BCBS. (2010). *Basel III: A global regulatory framework for more resilient banks and banking systems*. Basel Committee on Banking Supervision.

BCBS. (2015). *Corporate governance principles for banks*. Basel Committee on Banking Supervision.

Beasley, M. S. (1996). An empirical analysis of the relation between the board of director composition and financial statement fraud. *The Accounting Review*, *71*(4), 443–465.

Bebchuk, L. A., & Weisbach, M. S. (2010). The state of corporate governance research. *The Review of Financial Studies*, *23*(3), 939–961.

Beekes, W., & Brown, P. (2006). Do better-governed Australian firms make more informative disclosures? *Journal of Business Finance & Accounting*, *33*(3–4), 422–450.

Beekes, W., Brown, P., Zhan, W., & Zhang, Q. (2016). Corporate governance, companies' disclosure practices and market transparency: A cross country study. *Journal of Business Finance & Accounting*, *43*(3–4), 263–297.

Beji, R., Yousfi, O., Loukil, N., & Omri, A. (2021). Board diversity and corporate social responsibility: Empirical evidence from France. *Journal of Business Ethics*, *173*(1), 133–155. https://doi.org/10.1007/s10551-020-04522-4

Belal, A. R., Abdelsalam, O., & Nizamee, S. S. (2015). Ethical reporting in Islamic Bank Bangladesh Limited (1983–2010). *Journal of Business Ethics*, *129*(4), 769–784. www.jstor.org/stable/24702975

Belal, A. R., Mazumder, M. M. M., & Ali, M. (2019). Intellectual capital reporting practices in an Islamic bank: A case study. *Business Ethics*, *28*(2), 206–220. https://doi.org/10.1111/beer.12211

Belkaoui, A., & Kahl, A. (1978). *Corporate financial disclosure in Canada* (Research Monograph No. 1). Canadian Certified General Accountants Association.

Belkaoui, A., & Karpik, P. G. (1989). Determinants of the corporate decision to disclose social information. *Accounting, Auditing & Accountability Journal*, *2*(1), 36–51.

Bell, E., Bryman, A., & Harley, B. (2018). *Business research methods*. Oxford University Press.

Ben-Amar, W., Chang, M., & McIlkenny, P. (2017). Board gender diversity and corporate response to sustainability initiatives: Evidence from the carbon disclosure project. *Journal of Business Ethics*, *142*(2), 369–383. https://doi.org/10.1007/s10551-015-2759-1

Berg, B. L. (2001). *Qualitative research methods for the social sciences* (4th ed.). Allyn and Bacon.

Berle, A. A., & Means, G. G. C. (1991). *The modern corporation and private property*. Transaction Publishers.

Bhattacherjee, A. (2012). *Social science research: Principles, methods, and practices*. University of South Florida.

Bhatti, M., & Bhatti, M. I. (2010). Toward understanding Islamic corporate governance issues in Islamic finance. *Asian Politics & Policy*, *2*(1), 25–38.

Boesso, G., & Kumar, K. (2007). Drivers of corporate voluntary disclosure: A framework and empirical evidence from Italy and the United States. *Accounting, Auditing & Accountability Journal*, *20*(2), 269–296.

Bonazzi, L., & Islam, S. M. (2007). Agency theory and corporate governance: A study of the effectiveness of board in their monitoring of the CEO. *Journal of Modelling in Management*, *2*(1), 7–23.

Boone, A. L., Field, L. C., Karpoff, J. M., & Raheja, C. G. (2007). The determinants of corporate board size and composition: An empirical analysis. *Journal of Financial Economics*, *85*(1), 66–101.

Boonyawat, K. (2013). *The impact of ownership structure and other corporate governance mechanisms on firm performance, accounting discretions and investor perceptions: Evidence from Thailand before and after the corporate governance reforms* [Doctoral dissertation]. Durham University.

Botosan, C. A. (1997). Disclosure level and the cost of equity capital. *Accounting Review*, *72*(3), 323–349.

Bowen, G. A. (2009). Document analysis as a qualitative research method. *Qualitative Research Journal*, *9*(2), 27–40.

Brahim, N. B., & Arab, M. B. (2020). Social disclosure: Compliance of Islamic banks to governance standards No. 7 of AAOIFI (2010). *Journal of Islamic Accounting and Business Research*, *11*(7), 1427–1452. https://doi.org/10.1108/JIABR-12-2018-0199

Bravo, F. (2018). Does board diversity matter in the disclosure process? An analysis of the association between diversity and the disclosure of information on risks. *International Journal of Disclosure and Governance*, *15*(2), 104–114.

Brick, I. E., & Chidambaran, N. K. (2010). Board meetings, committee structure, and firm value. *Journal of Corporate Finance*, *16*(4), 533–553.

Brown, J. A., & Forster, W. R. (2013). CSR and stakeholder theory: A tale of Adam Smith. *Journal of Business Ethics*, *112*(2), 301–312.

Bryman, A. (2016). *Social research methods*. Oxford University Press.

Buallay, A., & Al-Ajmi, J. (2020). The role of audit committee attributes in corporate sustainability reporting evidence from banks in the Gulf Cooperation Council. *Journal of Applied Accounting Research*, *21*(2), 249–264. https://doi.org/10.1108/jaar-06-2018-0085

Bueno, G., Marcon, R., Pruner-da-Silva, A. L., & Ribeirete, F. (2018). The role of the board in voluntary disclosure. *Corporate Governance: The International Journal of Business in Society*, *18*(5), 886–910. https://doi.org/10.1108/CG-09-2017-0205

Burrell, G., & Morgan, G. (1979). *Sociological paradigms and organisational analysis: Elements of the sociology of corporate life* (1st ed.). Routledge. https://doi.org/10.4324/9781315242804

Bushman, R. M., Piotroski, J. D., & Smith, A. J. (2004). What determines corporate transparency? *Journal of Accounting Research*, *42*(2), 207–252.

Bushman, R. M., & Smith, A. J. (2001). Financial accounting information and corporate governance. *Journal of Accounting and Economics*, *32*(1–3), 237–333.

Buzby, S. L. (1975). Company size, listed versus unlisted stocks, and the extent of financial disclosure. *Journal of Accounting Research*, *13*(1), 16–37.

Cadbury Committee. (1992). *Report of the Committee on the Financial Aspects of Corporate Governance*. Gee & Co.

Calder, A. (2008). *Corporate governance: A practical guide to the legal frameworks and international codes of practice*. Kogan Page Publishers.

Camilleri, M. A. (2015). Environmental, social and governance disclosures in Europe. *Sustainability Accounting, Management and Policy Journal*, *6*(2), 224–242.

Campbell, D., Shrives, P., & Bohmbach-Saager, H. (2001). Voluntary disclosure of mission statements in corporate annual reports: Signaling what and to whom? *Business and Society Review*, *106*(1), 65–87.

Cerf, A. R. (1961). *Corporate reporting and investment decisions*. Public Accounting Research Program, Institute of Business and Economic Research, University of California.

Chalmers, K., Hay, D., & Khlif, H. (2019). Internal control in accounting research: A review. *Journal of Accounting Literature*, *42*(1), 80–103. https://doi.org/10.1016/j.acclit.2018.03.002

Chan, M. C., Watson, J., & Woodliff, D. (2014). Corporate governance quality and CSR disclosures. *Journal of Business Ethics*, *125*(1), 59–73.

Chatterjee, S., & Yilmaz, M. (1992). A review of regression diagnostics for behavioural research. *Applied Psychological Measurement*, *16*(3), 209–227.

Chau, G. K., & Gray, S. J. (2002). Ownership structure and corporate voluntary disclosure in Hong Kong and Singapore. *The International Journal of Accounting*, *37*(2), 247–265.

Che Azmi, A., Ab Aziz, N., Non, N., & Muhamad, R. (2016). Sharia disclosures: An exploratory study from the perspective of Sharia-compliant companies and professional users. *Journal of Islamic Accounting and Business Research*, *7*(3), 237–252.

Cheffins, B. R. (2013). *The history of corporate governance. The Oxford handbook of corporate governance* (pp. 46–64).

Chen, C. J. P., & Jaggi, B. (2000). Association between independent non-executive directors, family control and financial disclosures in Hong Kong. *Journal of Accounting and Public Policy*, *19*(4), 285–310.

Chen, W. P., Chung, H., Hsu, T. L., & Wu, S. (2010). External financing needs, corporate governance, and firm value. *Corporate Governance: An International Review*, *18*(3), 234–249.

Cheng, E. C. M., & Courtenay, S. M. (2006). Board composition, regulatory regime and voluntary disclosure. *The International Journal of Accounting*, *41*(3), 262–289. http://dx.doi.org/10.1016/j.intacc.2006.07.001

Cheung, S. Y.-L., Connelly, J. T., & Limpaphayom, P. (2007). Determinants of corporate disclosure and transparency: Evidence from Hong Kong and Thailand. *International Corporate Responsibility Series*, *3*, 3313–3342.

Cheynel, E. (2013). A theory of voluntary disclosure and cost of capital. *Review of Accounting Studies*, *18*(4), 987–1020.

Chin, W. W. (1998). The partial least squares approach to structural equation modeling. *Modern Methods for Business Research*, *295*(2), 295–336.

Ching, H. Y., & Gerab, F. (2017). Sustainability reports in Brazil through the lens of signaling, legitimacy and stakeholder theories. *Social Responsibility Journal*, *13*(1), 95–110.

Chiu, T.-K., & Wang, Y.-H. (2015). Determinants of social disclosure quality in Taiwan: An application of stakeholder theory. *Journal of Business Ethics*, *129*(2), 379–398. http://www.jstor.org.ezphost.dur.ac.uk/stable/24702920

Choudhury, M. Z., & Hoque, M.A.H. (2006). Corporate governance in Islamic perspective. *Corporate Governance: The International Journal of Business in Society*, *6*(2), 116–128.

Chow, C. W., & Wong-Boren, A. (1987). Voluntary financial disclosure by Mexican corporations. *Accounting Review*, *62*(3), 533–541.

CIBAFI. (2017). *Corporate governance practices in Islamic Banks 2017*. General Council for Islamic Banks and Financial Institutions (CIBAFI) and the World Bank.

Claessens, S., & Yurtoglu, B. (2012). *Corporate governance and development: An update*. Focus 10, Global Corporate Governance Network, International Finance Corporation. https://ssrn.com/abstract=2061562

Clarke, T. (1998). The stakeholder corporation: A business philosophy for the information age. *Long Range Planning, 31*(2), 182–194. http://dx.doi.org/10.1016/S0024-6301(98)00002-8

Clarke, T., & dela Rama, M. (2008). *Fundamentals of corporate governance*. Sage Publications.

Cohen, J. R., Krishnamoorthy, G., & Wright, A. (2004). The corporate governance mosaic and financial reporting quality. *Journal of Accounting Literature, 23*, 87–152.

Collis, J., & Hussey, R. (2013). *Business research: A practical guide for undergraduate and postgraduate students*. Macmillan International Higher Education.

Connelly, B. L., Certo, S. T., Ireland, R. D., & Reutzel, C. R. (2011). Signaling theory: A review and assessment. *Journal of Management, 37*(1), 39–67.

Cooke, T. E. (1989). Disclosure in the corporate annual reports of Swedish companies. *Accounting and Business Research, 19*(74), 113–124.

Copeland, R. M., & Fredericks, W. (1968). Extent of disclosure. *Journal of Accounting Research, 6*(2), 106–113.

Cotter, J., Lokman, N., & Najah, M. M. (2011). Voluntary disclosure research: Which theory is relevant? *Journal of Theoretical Accounting Research, 6*(2), 77–95.

Creswell, J. W. (2014). *Research design: Qualitative, quantitative, and mixed methods approaches* (4th ed.). SAGE Publications.

Daily, C. M., Dalton, D. R., & Cannella, A. A. (2003). Corporate governance: Decades of dialogue and data. *The Academy of Management Review, 28*(3), 371–382. https://doi.org/10.2307/30040727

Dalton, D. R., Daily, C. M., Ellstrand, A. E., & Johnson, J. L. (1998). Meta-analytic reviews of board composition, leadership structure, and financial performance. *Strategic Management Journal, 19*(3), 269–290.

Dalton, D. R., Daily, C. M., Johnson, J. L., & Ellstrand, A. E. (1999). Number of directors and financial performance: A meta-analysis. *Academy of Management Journal, 42*(6), 674–686.

Darmadi, S. (2013). Corporate governance disclosure in the annual report: An exploratory study on Indonesian Islamic banks. *Humanomics, 29*(1), 4–23.

Davies, A. (2012). *The globalisation of corporate governance: The challenge of clashing cultures*. Gower Publishing, Ltd.

Deegan, C. (2002). Introduction: The legitimising effect of social and environmental disclosures – A theoretical foundation. *Accounting, Auditing & Accountability Journal, 15*(3), 282–311.

Deegan, C. (2006). *Legitimacy theory. Methodological issues in accounting research: Theories and methods*, 161–182.

del Baldo, M. (2012). Corporate social responsibility and corporate governance in Italian SMEs: The experience of some "spirited businesses". *Journal of Management & Governance, 16*, 1–36.

del Baldo, M., Aureli, S., & Lombardi, R. (2021). The role of the internal audit function in fostering sustainability reporting. In S. Markovic, C. Sancha, & A. Lindgreen (Eds.), *Handbook of sustainability-driven business strategies in practice* (pp. 352–369). Edward Elgar Publishing.

Dey, A. (2005). *Corporate governance and financial reporting credibility*. Northwestern University.

DeZoort, F. T., Hermanson, D. R., Archambeault, D. S., & Reed, S. A. (2002). *Audit committee effectiveness: A synthesis of the empirical audit committee literature*, 2138.

DeZoort, F. T., & Salterio, S. E. (2001). The effects of corporate governance experience and financial-reporting and audit knowledge on audit committee members' judgments. *Auditing: A Journal of Practice & Theory, 20*(2), 31–47.

Diamond, D. W., & Verrecchia, R. E. (1991). Disclosure, liquidity, and the cost of capital. *The Journal of Finance, 46*(4), 1325–1359.

Dienes, D., Sassen, R., & Fischer, J. (2016). What are the drivers of sustainability reporting? A systematic review. *Sustainability Accounting, Management and Policy Journal, 7*(2), 154–189. https://doi.org/10.1108/SAMPJ-08-2014-0050

di Guida, C., Celentano, A., Mirone, F., & D'Amore, G. (2022). The role of board composition in CSR disclosure: An empirical analysis in four European countries. *Corporate Governance and Organizational Behavior Review, 6*(3), 74–86. https://doi.org/10.22495/cgobrv6i3p7

Donaldson, T., & Preston, L. E. (1995). The stakeholder theory of the corporation: Concepts, evidence, and implications. *Academy of Management Review, 20*(1), 65–91.

Donnelly, R., & Mulcahy, M. (2008). Board structure, ownership, and voluntary disclosure in Ireland. *Corporate Governance: An International Review, 16*(5), 416–429.

du Plessis, J. J., Hargovan, A., & Bagaric, M. (2010). *Principles of contemporary corporate governance*. Cambridge University Press.

Durnev, A. A. (2003). *Essays on corporate transparency and governance practices* [Doctoral thesis].

Dusuki, A. W. (2005). *Corporate social responsibility of Islamic banks in Malaysia: A synthesis of Islamic and stakeholders' perspectives*.

Dusuki, A. W. (2011). *Ethical and social responsibility models for Islamic finance*. ISRA.

Eccles, R. G., Serafeim, G., & Krzus, M. P. (2011). Market interest in nonfinancial information. *Journal of Applied Corporate Finance, 23*(4), 113–127.

Eisenhardt, K. M. (1989). Agency theory: An assessment and review. *Academy of Management Review, 14*(1), 57–74.

Elamer, A. A., Ntim, C. G., Abdou, H. A., & Pyke, C. (2019). Sharia supervisory boards, governance structures and operational risk disclosures: Evidence from Islamic banks in MENA countries. *Global Finance Journal*, 100488. https://doi.org/10.1016/j.gfj.2019.100488

Elfeky, M. I. (2017). The extent of voluntary disclosure and its determinants in emerging markets: Evidence from Egypt. *The Journal of Finance and Data Science, 3*(1), 45–59. https://doi.org/10.1016/j.jfds.2017.09.005

El-Halaby, S., & Hussainey, K. (2015). The determinants of social accountability disclosure: Evidence from Islamic banks around the world. *International Journal of Business, 20*(3), 202.

El-Halaby, S., & Hussainey, K. (2016). Determinants of compliance with AAOIFI standards by Islamic banks. *International Journal of Islamic and Middle Eastern Finance and Management, 9*(1), 143–168. https://search.proquest.com/docview/1826445518?accountid=49936

Elsayed, K. (2007). Does CEO duality really affect corporate performance? *Corporate Governance: An International Review, 15*(6), 1203–1214.

El-Tiby, A. M., & Grais, W. M. (2015). *Islamic finance and economic development: Risk management*. Regulation and Corporate Governance.

Eng, L. L., & Mak, Y. T. (2003). Corporate governance and voluntary disclosure. *Journal of Accounting and Public Policy, 22*(4), 325–345. http://www.sciencedirect.com/science/article/pii/S0278425403000371

Engelbrecht, L., Yasseen, Y., & Omarjee, I. (2018). The role of the internal audit function in integrated reporting: A developing economy perspective. *Meditari Accountancy Research, 26*(4), 657–674.

Engku Ali, E. R. A., & Oseni, U. A. (2017). Towards an effective legal and regulatory framework for Islamic financial transactions: Major initiatives of the Central Bank of Malaysia. *International Journal of Law and Management, 59*(5), 652–672.

Ernstberger, J., & Grüning, M. (2013). How do firm- and country-level governance mechanisms affect firms' disclosure? *Journal of Accounting and Public Policy, 32*(3), 50–67. http://dx.doi.org/10.1016/j.jaccpubpol.2013.02.003

Fama, E. F. (1980). Agency problems and the theory of the firm. *Journal of Political Economy, 88*(2), 288–307. http://www.jstor.org/action/showPublication?journalCode=jpoliecon

Fama, E. F., & Jensen, M. C. (1983). Agency problems and residual claims. *Journal of Law and Economics, 26*(2), 327–349. https://doi.org/10.2307/725105

Farinha, J. (2003). *Corporate governance: A survey of the literature*. Universidade do Porto Economia Discussion Paper.

Farook, S., Kabir Hassan, M., & Lanis, R. (2011). Determinants of corporate social responsibility disclosure: The case of Islamic banks. *Journal of Islamic Accounting and Business Research, 2*(2), 114–141.

Farook, S. Z., & Farooq, M. O. (2011). *Shariah governance for Islamic finance: Challenges and pragmatic solutions*, 1813483.

Fernando, S., & Lawrence, S. (2014). A theoretical framework for CSR practices: Integrating legitimacy theory, stakeholder theory and institutional theory. *Journal of Theoretical Accounting Research, 10*(1), 149–178.

Field, A. (2009). *Discovering statistics using IBM SPSS statistics*. Sage Publications.

Filatotchev, I. (2008). Developing an organizational theory of corporate governance: Comments on Henry L. Tosi, Jr. (2008) "Quo Vadis? Suggestions for future corporate governance research". *Journal of Management & Governance, 12*, 171–178.

Firth, M. (1979). The impact of size, stock market listing, and auditors on voluntary disclosure in corporate annual reports. *Accounting and Business Research, 9*(36), 273–280. https://doi.org/10.1080/00014788.1979.9729168

Florea, R., & Florea, R. (2013). Internal audit and corporate governance. *Economy Transdisciplinarity Cognition, 16*(1), 79.

Forker, J. J. (1992). Corporate governance and disclosure quality. *Accounting and Business Research, 22*(86), 111–124.

Freeman, R. E. (1984). *Strategic management: A stakeholder approach*. Pitman.

Freeman, R. E. (1997). A stakeholder theory of the modern corporation. In T. L. Beauchamp & N. E. Bowie (Eds.), *Ethical theory and business* (5th ed., pp. 66–76). Prentice Hall.

Freeman, R. E., Harrison, J. S., Wicks, A. C., Parmar, B. L., & de Colle, S. (2010). *Stakeholder theory: The state of the art*. Cambridge University Press.

Freeman, R. E. (2010). *Strategic management: A stakeholder approach*. Cambridge University Press.

Freeman, R. E., & McVea, J. (2001). A stakeholder approach to strategic management. In M. A. Hitt, R. E. Freeman, & J. S. Harrison (Eds.), *The Blackwell handbook of strategic management* (pp. 189–207). Blackwell Publishers.

Freeman, R. E., & Reed, D. L. (1983). Stockholders and stakeholders: A new perspective on corporate governance. *California Management Review, 25*(3), 88–106.

Fucci, M., & Cooper, T. (2019). The inclusion imperative for boards: Redefining board responsibilities to support organizational inclusion. *Deloitte Insights*. https://www2.deloitte.com/us/en/insights/topics/value-of-diversity-and-inclusion/redefining-board-responsibilities-to-support-organizational-inclusion.html

Ganesan, Y., Hwa, Y. W., Jaaffar, A. H., & Hashim, F. (2017). Corporate governance and sustainability reporting practices: The moderating role of internal audit function. *Global Business and Management Research, 9*(4s), 159–179.

Garas, S., & ElMassah, S. (2018). Corporate governance and corporate social responsibility disclosures: The case of GCC countries. *Critical Perspectives on International Business, 14*(1), 2–26.

Garcia-Meca, E., & Sanchez-Ballesta, J. P. (2010). The association of board independence and ownership concentration with voluntary disclosure: A meta-analysis. *European Accounting Review, 19*(3), 603–627.

Gelb, D. S. (2000). Managerial ownership and accounting disclosures: An empirical study. *Review of Quantitative Finance and Accounting, 15*(2), 169–185.

Ghabayen, M. A., Mohamad, N. R., & Ahmad, N. (2016). Board characteristics and corporate social responsibility disclosure in the Jordanian banks. *Corporate Board: Role, Duties and Composition*, *12*(1), 84–99.

Ghayad, R. (2008). Corporate governance and the global performance of Islamic banks. *Humanomics*.

Ghazali, N. A. M. (2008). Voluntary disclosure in Malaysian corporate annual reports: Views of stakeholders. *Social Responsibility Journal*, *4*(4), 504–516.

Ghosh, A., & Tang, C. Y. (2015). Assessing financial reporting quality of family firms: The auditors' perspective. *Journal of Accounting and Economics*, *60*(1), 95–116. http://dx.doi.org/10.1016/j.jacceco.2015.03.002

Ghosh, S. (2018). Governance reforms and performance of MENA banks: Are disclosures effective? *Global Finance Journal*, 3678–3695.

Giannarakis, G. (2014). Corporate governance and financial characteristic effects on the extent of corporate social responsibility disclosure. *Social Responsibility Journal*, *10*(4), 569–590.

Gibbins, M., Richardson, A., & Waterhouse, J. (1990). The management of corporate financial disclosure: Opportunism, ritualism, policies, and processes. *Journal of Accounting Research*, *28*(1), 121–143.

Gillan, S. L., Hartzell, J. C., & Starks, L. T. (2011). Tradeoffs in corporate governance: Evidence from board structures and charter provisions. *The Quarterly Journal of Finance*, *1*(04), 667–705.

Global Sustainable Investment Alliance. (2017). *Global sustainable investment review 2016*. https://www.gsi-alliance.org/

Gompers, P., Ishii, J., & Metrick, A. (2003). Corporate governance and equity prices. *The Quarterly Journal of Economics*, *118*(1), 107–156.

Graham, J. R., Harvey, C. R., & Rajgopal, S. (2005). The economic implications of corporate financial reporting. *Journal of Accounting and Economics*, *40*(1–3), 3–73. http://dx.doi.org/10.1016/j.jacceco.2005.01.002

Grais, W., & Pellegrini, M. (2006). *Corporate governance in institutions offering Islamic financial services: Issues and options: World Bank policy research working paper 4051*.

Gramling, A. A., Maletta, M. J., Schneider, A., & Church, B. K. (2004). The role of the internal audit function in corporate governance: A synthesis of the extant internal auditing literature and directions for future research. *Journal of Accounting Literature*, 23194.

Grassa, R. (2013). Shariah supervisory system in Islamic financial institutions: New issues and challenges: A comparative analysis between Southeast Asia models and GCC models. *Humanomics*, *29*(4), 333–348.

Grassa, R. (2015). Shariah supervisory systems in Islamic finance institutions across the OIC member countries: An investigation of regulatory frameworks. *Journal of Financial Regulation and Compliance*, *23*(2), 135–160.

Grassa, R., & Chakroun, R. (2016). Ownership structure, board's characteristics and corporate governance disclosure in GCC banks: What about Islamic banks? *International Journal of Accounting, Auditing and Performance Evaluation*, *12*(4), 360–395.

Grassa, R., Chakroun, R., & Hussainey, K. (2018). Corporate governance and Islamic banks' products and services disclosure. *Accounting Research Journal*, *31*(1), 75–89.

Grassa, R., & Matoussi, H. (2014). Corporate governance of Islamic banks. *International Journal of Islamic and Middle Eastern Finance and Management*, *7*(3), 346–362.

Gray, R., Javad, M., Power, D. M., & Sinclair, C. D. (2001). Social and environmental disclosure and corporate characteristics: A research note and extension. *Journal of Business Finance & Accounting*, *28*(3–4), 327–356.

Gray, R., Kouhy, R., & Lavers, S. (1995). Corporate social and environmental reporting: A review of the literature and a longitudinal study of UK disclosure. *Accounting, Auditing & Accountability Journal*, *8*(2), 47–77.

Gray, R., Owen, D., & Adams, C. (1996). *Accounting & accountability: Changes and challenges in corporate social and environmental reporting*. Prentice Hall.

Gray, S. J. (1988). Towards a theory of cultural influence on the development of accounting systems internationally. *Abacus*, *24*(1), 1–15.

Gray, S. J., & Vint, H. M. (1995). The impact of culture on accounting disclosures: Some international evidence. *Asia-Pacific Journal of Accounting*, *2*(1), 33–43.

Grossman, S. J. (1981). The informational role of warranties and private disclosure about product quality. *The Journal of Law & Economics*, *24*(3), 461–483.

Gul, F. A., & Leung, S. (2004). Board leadership, outside directors' expertise and voluntary corporate disclosures. *Journal of Accounting and Public Policy*, *23*(5), 351–379. http://dx.doi.org/10.1016/j.jaccpubpol.2004.07.001

Guthrie, J., & Parker, L. D. (1989). Corporate social reporting: A rebuttal of legitimacy theory. *Accounting and Business Research*, *19*(76), 343–352.

Habtoor, O., Hassan, W., & Aljaaidi, K. (2019). The relationship between board committees and corporate risk disclosure in Saudi listed companies. *International Journal of Advanced and Applied Sciences*, *6*(12), 41–57. https://doi.org/10.21833/ijaas.2019.12.005

Haddad, A. E., AlShattarat, W. K., AbuGhazaleh, N. M., & Nobanee, H. (2015). The impact of ownership structure and family board domination on voluntary disclosure for Jordanian listed companies. *Eurasian Business Review*, *5*(2), 203–234.

Hadi Zulkafli, A., & Abdul Samad, F. (2007). Corporate governance and performance of banking firms: Evidence from Asian emerging markets. In M. Hirschey, K. John, & A. K. Makhija (Eds.), *Issues in corporate governance and finance* (pp. 49–74). Emerald Group Publishing Limited.

Hail, L. (2003). The relationship between voluntary annual report disclosures and firm characteristics in Switzerland. *Die Unternehmung*, *57*(4), 273–290. http://www.jstor.org/stable/24185037

Hair Jr, J. F., Sarstedt, M., Ringle, C. M., & Gudergan, S. P. (2017). *Advanced issues in partial least squares structural equation modeling*. SAGE Publications.

Haji, A. A., & Ghazali, N. A. M. (2013). The quality and determinants of voluntary disclosures in annual reports of Shari'ah compliant companies in Malaysia. *Humanomics*, *29*(1), 24–42.

Hamid, F. Z. A. (2004). Corporate social disclosure by banks and finance companies: Malaysian evidence. *Corporate Ownership and Control*, *1*(4), 118–130.

Handajani, L., Subroto, B., Sutrisno, T., & Saraswati, E. (2014). Does board diversity matter on corporate social disclosure? An Indonesian evidence. *Journal of Economics and Sustainable Development*, *5*(12), 8–16.

Haniffa, R., & Hudaib, M. (2001). A conceptual framework for Islamic accounting: The Sharia paradigm. Paper presented at the *Accounting, Commerce & Finance: The Islamic Perspective International Conference IV*, New Zealand, pp. 12–14.

Haniffa, R., & Hudaib, M. (2006). Corporate governance structure and performance of Malaysian listed companies. *Journal of Business Finance & Accounting*, *33*(7–8), 1034–1062.

Haniffa, R., & Hudaib, M. (2007). Exploring the ethical identity of Islamic Banks via communication in annual reports. *Journal of Business Ethics*, *76*(1), 97–116. www.jstor.org/stable/25075497

Haniffa, R., & Hudaib, M. (2010). Islamic finance: From sacred intentions to secular goals? *Journal of Islamic Accounting and Business Research*, *1*(2), 85–91.

Haniffa, R. M., & Cooke, T. E. (2002). Culture, corporate governance and disclosure in Malaysian corporations. *Abacus*, *38*(3), 317–349.

Haniffa, R. M., & Cooke, T. E. (2005). The impact of culture and governance on corporate social reporting. *Journal of Accounting and Public Policy*, *24*(5), 391–430. http://dx.doi.org/10.1016/j.jaccpubpol.2005.06.001

Haque, F. (2017). The effects of board characteristics and sustainable compensation policy on carbon performance of UK firms. *British Accounting Review*, *49*(3), 347–364. https://doi.org/10.1016/j.bar.2017.01.001

Harahap, S. S. (2003). The disclosure of Islamic values – Annual report. The analysis of Bank Muamalat Indonesia's annual report. *Managerial Finance*, *29*(7), 70–89.

Harjoto, M., Laksmana, I., & Lee, R. (2015). Board diversity and corporate social responsibility. *Journal of Business Ethics*, *132*(4), 641–660.

Hart, O. (1995). Corporate governance: Some theory and implications. *The Economic Journal*, *105*(430), 678–689.

Hasan, Z. (2009a). Corporate governance: Western and Islamic perspectives. *International Review of Business Research Papers*, *5*(1), 277–293.

Hasan, Z. B. (2009b). Regulatory framework of Shari'ah governance system in Malaysia, GCC countries and the UK. *Kyoto Bulletin of Islamic Area Studies*, *3*(2), 82–115.

Hasan, Z. (2011). A survey on Shari'ah governance practices in Malaysia, GCC countries and the UK: Critical appraisal. *International Journal of Islamic and Middle Eastern Finance and Management*, *4*(1), 30–51.

Harun, M. S., Hussainey, K., Mohd Kharuddin, K. A., & Farooque, O. A. (2020). CSR disclosure, corporate governance and firm value: A study on GCC Islamic banks. *International Journal of Accounting & Information Management*, *28*(4), 607–638.

Hassan, A., & Harahap, S. S. (2010). Exploring corporate social responsibility disclosure: The case of Islamic banks. *International Journal of Islamic and Middle Eastern Finance and Management*, *3*(3), 203–227.

Hassan, E., & Rohayem, A. (2009). Transparency and financial reporting in Islamic insurance. *Takaful Islamic Insurance: Concepts and Regulatory Issues*, 265–284.

Hassan, M. (2013). *Corporate governance characteristics and voluntary disclosure: The case of UAE listed corporations*. International conference on business, economics, and accounting (2013 IBEA), Bangkok, Thailand.

Hassan, M. K., & Aliyu, S. (2018). A contemporary survey of Islamic banking literature. *Journal of Financial Stability*, 3412–3443. https://doi.org/10.1016/j.jfs.2017.11.006

Hassan, M. K., & Mollah, S. (2014). Corporate governance, risk-taking and firm performance of Islamic banks during global financial crisis. *Journal of Financial Services Research*, *51*(2), 195–219.

Hassan, O. A. G., & Marston, C. (2010). *Disclosure measurement in the empirical accounting literature – A review article*. 1640598.

Hassan, W. M. (2016). Corporate governance practices of Islamic Banks versus conventional banks: Evidence from the Middle East. *Journal of Finance and Bank Management*, *4*(1), 99–111.

Hassan Che Haat, M., Abdul Rahman, R., & Mahenthiran, S. (2008). Corporate governance, transparency and performance of Malaysian companies. *Managerial Auditing Journal*, *23*(8), 744–778.

Hawkamah. (2017). *Corporate governance forum: Independence, diversity and right mix of skills*. Hawkamah: The Institute for Corporate Governance. https://www.hawkamah.org/uploads/reports/2017%20Corporate%20Governance%20Forum.pdf

Hawkamah. (2019). *Board best practices in the Middle East*. Hawkamah: The Institute for Corporate Governance. https://www.hawkamah.org/news-publications/publications

Hayat, R., & Kabir Hassan, M. (2017). Does an Islamic label indicate good corporate governance? *Journal of Corporate Finance*, 43159–43174. https://doi.org/10.1016/j.jcorpfin.2016.12.012

Healy, P. M., & Palepu, K. G. (2001). Information asymmetry, corporate disclosure, and the capital markets: A review of the empirical disclosure literature. *Journal of Accounting and Economics*, *31*(1–3), 405–440.

Hemrit, W. (2020). Difference between the determinants of operational risk reporting in Islamic and conventional banks: Evidence from Saudi Arabia. *Journal of Operational Risk*, *15*(1), 1–38. https://doi.org/10.21314/JOP.2019.235

Hermalin, B. E., & Weisbach, M. S. (1998). Endogenously chosen boards of directors and their monitoring of the CEO. *The American Economic Review*, *88*(1), 96–118. http://www.jstor.org/stable/116820

Hermalin, B. E., & Weisbach, M. S. (2001). *Boards of directors as an endogenously determined institution: A survey of the economic literature.*

Hermalin, B. E., & Weisbach, M. S. (2012). Information disclosure and corporate governance. *Journal of Finance*, *67*(1), 195–234. https://doi.org/10.1111/j.1540-6261.2011.01710.x

Hermanson, D. R., & Rittenberg, L. E. (2003). Internal audit and organizational governance. *Research Opportunities in Internal Auditing*, *1*(1), 25–71.

Hidalgo, R. L., García-Meca, E., & Martínez, I. (2011). Corporate governance and intellectual capital disclosure. *Journal of Business Ethics*, *100*(3), 483–495. https://doi.org/10.2307/41475854

Hill, C. W. L., & Jones, T. M. (1992). Stakeholder-agency theory. *Journal of Management Studies*, *29*(2), 131–154.

Ho, S. S. M., & Shun Wong, K. (2001). A study of the relationship between corporate governance structures and the extent of voluntary disclosure. *Journal of International Accounting, Auditing and Taxation*, *10*(2), 139–156. http://dx.doi.org/10.1016/S1061-9518(01)00041-6

Hoang, T. C., Abeysekera, I., & Ma, S. (2018). Board diversity and corporate social disclosure: Evidence from Vietnam. *Journal of Business Ethics*, *151*(3), 833–852.

Hofstede, G. (1980). Culture and organizations. *International Studies of Management & Organization*, *10*(4), 15–41.

Hofstede, G. (1984). Cultural dimensions in management and planning. *Asia Pacific Journal of Management*, *1*(2), 81–99.

Hollindale, J., Kent, P., Routledge, J., & Chapple, L. (2019). Women on boards and greenhouse gas emission disclosures. *Accounting and Finance*, *59*(1), 277–308. https://doi.org/10.1111/acfi.12258

Holt, T. P., & DeZoort, T. (2009). The effects of internal audit report disclosure on investor confidence and investment decisions. *International Journal of Auditing*, *13*(1), 61–77.

Holt, T. P. (2012). The effects of internal audit role and reporting relationships on investor perceptions of disclosure credibility. *Managerial Auditing Journal*, *27*(9), 878–898.

Holthausen, R. W., & Leftwich, R. W. (1983). The economic consequences of accounting choice implications of costly contracting and monitoring. *Journal of Accounting and Economics*, *5*, 77–117.

Hopt, K. J., & Leyens, P. C. (2004). Board models in Europe – Recent developments of internal corporate governance structures in Germany, the United Kingdom, France, and Italy. *European Company & Financial Law Review*, *1*(2), 135–168.

Hossain, M., & Hammami, H. (2009). Voluntary disclosure in the annual reports of an emerging country: The case of Qatar. *Advances in Accounting*, *25*(2), 255–265.

Hossain, M., Perera, M. H. B., & Rahman, A. R. (1995). Voluntary disclosure in the annual reports of New Zealand companies. *Journal of International Financial Management & Accounting*, *6*(1), 69–87.

Htay, S. N. N., Rashid, H. M. A., Adnan, M. A., & Meera, A. K. M. (2012). Impact of corporate governance on social and environmental information disclosure of Malaysian listed banks: Panel data analysis. *Asian Journal of Finance & Accounting*, *4*(1), 1–24.

Htay, S. N. N., & Salman, S. A. (2013). Agency theory, stewardship theory and stakeholder theory: An Islamic perspective. *International Journal of Physical and Social Sciences*, *3*(9), 319.

Huafang, X., & Jianguo, Y. (2007). Ownership structure, board composition and corporate voluntary disclosure: Evidence from listed companies in China. *Managerial Auditing Journal, 22*(6), 604–619. https://doi.org/10.1108/02686900710759406

Huang, P., & Zhang, Y. (2011). Does enhanced disclosure really reduce agency costs? Evidence from the diversion of corporate resources. *Accounting Review, 87*(1), 199–229.

Hughes, P. J. (1986). Signalling by direct disclosure under asymmetric information. *Journal of Accounting and Economics, 8*(2), 119–142. http://dx.doi.org/10.1016/0165-4101(86)90014-5

Husted, B. W., & Sousa-Filho, J. M. D. (2019). Board structure and environmental, social, and governance disclosure in Latin America. *Journal of Business Research*, 102220–102227. https://doi.org/10.1016/j.jbusres.2018.01.017

Ibrahim, A. (2015). Accountability (Hisbah) in Islamic management: The philosophy and ethics behind its implementation. *International Journal of Humanities and Social Science, 5*(8), 184.

Ihantola, E.-M., & Kihn, L.-A. (2011). Threats to validity and reliability in mixed methods accounting research. *Qualitative Research in Accounting & Management, 8*(1), 39–58.

Ioannou, I., & Serafeim, G. (2016). The consequences of mandatory corporate sustainability reporting: Evidence from four countries. *Journal of Accounting and Public Policy, 35*(1), 1–29.

Iqbal, Z., & Mirakhor, A. (2004). Stakeholders model of governance in Islamic economic system. *Islamic Economic Studies, 11*(2), 43–63.

Ishak, A. H., & Osman, M. R. (2016). A systematic literature review on Islamic values applied in quality management context. *Journal of Business Ethics, 138*(1), 103–112.

Ishak, Z., & Al-Ebel, A. M. (2013). Board of directors, information asymmetry, and intellectual capital disclosure among Banks in Gulf Co-Operation Council. *Jurnal Pengurusan, 37*, 115–132.

Islahi, A. A. (1985). Ibn Taimiyah's concept of market mechanism. *Journal of Research in Islamic Economics, 2*(1), 53–63.

Islam, M. A., & Deegan, C. (2008). Motivations for an organisation within a developing country to report social responsibility information: Evidence from Bangladesh. *Accounting, Auditing & Accountability Journal, 21*(6), 850–874.

Islam, M. T., & Kokubu, K. (2018). Corporate social reporting and legitimacy in banking: A longitudinal study in the developing country. *Social Responsibility Journal, 14*(1), 159–179.

Islamic Financial Services Board (IFSB). (2022). *Islamic financial services industry stability report*. https://www.ifsb.org/

Issa, A., & Fang, H.-X. (2019). The impact of board gender diversity on corporate social responsibility in the Arab Gulf states. *Gender in Management, 34*(7), 577–605. https://doi.org/10.1108/GM-07-2018-0087

Istrefi, V. (2020). Corporate governance in Islamic financial institutions. *Journal of Governance and Regulation, 9*(2), 75–82. https://doi.org/10.22495/jgrv9i2art5

Jaggi, B., & Low, P. Y. (2000). Impact of culture, market forces, and legal system on financial disclosures. *The International Journal of Accounting, 35*(4), 495–519.

Jalbani, A. A., & Shaikh, S. A. A. (2009). Risk management in Islamic and conventional banks: A differential analysis. *Journal of Independent Studies and Research, 7*(2), 67–70.

Jati, K. W., Agustina, L., Muliasari, I., & Armeliza, D. (2020). Islamic social reporting disclosure as a form of social responsibility of Islamic banks in Indonesia. *Banks and Bank Systems, 15*(2), 47–55. https://doi.org/10.21511/bbs.15(2).2020.05

Jensen, M. C. (1993). The modern industrial revolution, exit, and the failure of internal control systems. *The Journal of Finance, 48*(3), 831–880. https://doi.org/10.2307/2329018

Jensen, M. C. (2010). Value maximization, stakeholder theory, and the corporate objective function. *Journal of Applied Corporate Finance, 22*(1), 32–42.

Jensen, M. C., & Meckling, W. H. (1976). Theory of the firm: Managerial behavior, agency costs and ownership structure. *Journal of Financial Economics*, *3*(4), 305–360. http://search.ebscohost.com/login.aspx?direct=true&db=bah&AN=12243301&site=ehost-live

Jiang, H., Habib, A., & Hu, B. (2011). Ownership concentration, voluntary disclosures and information asymmetry in New Zealand. *The British Accounting Review*, *43*(1), 39–53. http://dx.doi.org/10.1016/j.bar.2010.10.005

Jiang, L., André, P., & Richard, C. (2018) An international study of internal audit function quality. *Accounting and Business Research*, *48*(3), 264–298.

Jizi, M., Salama, A., Dixon, R., & Stratling, R. (2014). Corporate governance and corporate social responsibility disclosure: Evidence from the US banking sector. *Journal of Business Ethics*, 125601–125615. https://doi.org/10.1007/s10551-013-1929-2

Johl, S. K., Johl, S. K., Subramaniam, N., & Cooper, B. (2013). Internal audit function, board quality and financial reporting quality: Evidence from Malaysia. *Managerial Auditing Journal*, *28*(9), 780–814. https://doi.org/10.1108/MAJ-06-2013-0886

John, K., & Senbet, L. W. (1998). Corporate governance and board effectiveness. *Journal of Banking & Finance*, *22*(4), 371–403. http://dx.doi.org/10.1016/S0378-4266(98)00005-3

Johnson, R. B., & Onwuegbuzie, A. J. (2004). Mixed methods research: A research paradigm whose time has come. *Educational Researcher*, *33*(7), 14–26.

Kahl, A., & Belkaoui, A. (1981). Bank annual report disclosure adequacy internationally. *Accounting and Business Research*, *11*(43), 189–196.

Kahf, M. (2006). *Maqasid al Shari'ah in the prohibition of Riba and their implications for modern Islamic finance*. Presented paper at IIUM international conference on Maqasid Al-Shari'ah.

Kahf, M. (2013). *Islamic finance contracts*. Al Manhal. https://books.google.com.qa/books?id=xh6CoAEACAAJ

Kajola, S. O. (2008). Corporate governance and firm performance: The case of Nigerian listed firms. *European Journal of Economics, Finance and Administrative Sciences*, *14*(14), 16–28.

Kaler, J. (2006). Evaluating stakeholder theory. *Journal of Business Ethics*, *69*(3), 249–268.

Kanagaretnam, K., Lobo, G. J., & Whalen, D. J. (2007). Does good corporate governance reduce information asymmetry around quarterly earnings announcements? *Journal of Accounting and Public Policy*, *26*(4), 497–522. http://dx.doi.org/10.1016/j.jaccpubpol.2007.05.003

Karagiorgos, T., Drogalas, G., Gotzamanis, E., & Tampakoudis, I. (2010). Internal auditing as an effective tool for corporate governance. *Journal of Business Management*, *2*(1), 15–23.

Kasim, N. A. A. (2012). Disclosure of Shariah compliance by Malaysian takaful companies. *Journal of Islamic Accounting and Business Research*, *3*(1), 20–38.

Kasznik, R. (1999). On the association between voluntary disclosure and earnings management. *Journal of Accounting Research*, *37*(1), 57–81.

Katmon, N., Mohamad, Z. Z., Norwani, N. M., & Farooque, O. A. (2019). Comprehensive board diversity and quality of corporate social responsibility disclosure: Evidence from an emerging market. *Journal of Business Ethics*, *157*(2), 447–481. https://doi.org/10.1007/s10551-017-3672-6

Kent, P., & Stewart, J. (2008). Corporate governance and disclosures on the transition to international financial reporting standards. *Accounting & Finance*, *48*(4), 649–671.

Kent, P., & Zunker, T. (2013). Attaining legitimacy by employee information in annual reports. *Accounting, Auditing & Accountability Journal*, *26*(7), 1072–1106.

Khan, A., Muttakin, M. B., & Siddiqui, J. (2013). Corporate governance and corporate social responsibility disclosures: Evidence from an emerging economy. *Journal of Business Ethics*, *114*(2), 207–223.

Khan, M. A. (1985). Role of the auditor in an Islamic economy. *Journal of Research in Islamic Economics*, *3*(1), 31–42.

Khanchel El Mehdi, I. (2007). Empirical evidence on corporate governance and corporate performance in Tunisia. *Corporate Governance: An International Review*, *15*(6), 1429–1441.

Khandelwal, C., Kumar, S., Madhavan, V., & Pandey, N. (2020). Do board characteristics impact corporate risk disclosures? The Indian experience. *Journal of Business Research*, 121103–121111. https://doi.org/10.1016/j.jbusres.2020.08.004

Khatib, S. F. A., Abdullah, D. F., Elamer, A. A., & Abueid, R. (2021). Nudging toward diversity in the boardroom: A systematic literature review of board diversity of financial institutions. *Business Strategy and the Environment*, *30*(2), 985–1002. https://doi.org/10.1002/bse.2665

Kılıç, M., & Kuzey, C. (2019). The effect of corporate governance on carbon emission disclosures: Evidence from Turkey. *International Journal of Climate Change Strategies and Management*, *11*(1), 35–53. https://doi.org/10.1108/IJCCSM-07-2017-0144

Kiliç, M., Kuzey, C., & Uyar, A. (2015). The impact of ownership and board structure on Corporate Social Responsibility (CSR) reporting in the Turkish banking industry. *Corporate Governance*, *15*(3), 357–374. https://search.proquest.com/docview/1683339911?accountid=49936

King, J. (2018). The Banker's top Islamic financial institutions – 2018. *The Banker*. https://www.thebanker.com/content/075526d9-7cd6-5728-98b2-fd16c2214a8a

Klein, A. (2002). Audit committee, board of director characteristics, and earnings management. *Journal of Accounting and Economics*, *33*(3), 375–400. http://dx.doi.org/10.1016/S0165-4101(02)00059-9

Kolk, A., & Pinkse, J. (2010). The integration of corporate governance in corporate social responsibility disclosures. *Corporate Social Responsibility and Environmental Management*, *17*(1), 15–26. https://doi.org/10.1002/csr.196

Kothari, C. R. (2004). *Research methodology: Methods and techniques*. New Age International.

Kusnadi, Y., Leong, K. S., Suwardy, T., & Wang, J. (2016). Audit committees and financial reporting quality in Singapore: JBE. *Journal of Business Ethics*, *139*(1), 197–214. http://dx.doi.org/10.1007/s10551-015-2679-0

Lagasio, V., & Cucari, N. (2019). Corporate governance and environmental social governance disclosure: A meta-analytical review. *Corporate Social Responsibility and Environmental Management*, *26*(4), 701–711. https://doi.org/10.1002/csr.1716

Lahsasna, A. (2013). *Maqasid al-Shari'ah in Islamic Finance*. IBFIM.

Laksmana, I. (2008). Corporate board governance and voluntary disclosure of executive compensation practices. *Contemporary Accounting Research*, *25*(4), 1147–1182.

Lambert, R., Leuz, C., & Verrecchia, R. E. (2007). Accounting information, disclosure, and the cost of capital. *Journal of Accounting Research*, *45*(2), 385–420.

Lan, Y., Wang, L., & Zhang, X. (2013). Determinants and features of voluntary disclosure in the Chinese stock market. *China Journal of Accounting Research*, *6*(4), 265–285.

Landau, S., & Everitt, B. S. (2003). *A handbook of statistical analyses using SPSS*. Chapman and Hall/CRC.

Lang, M., & Lundholm, R. (1993). Cross-sectional determinants of analyst ratings of corporate disclosures. *Journal of Accounting Research*, *31*(2), 246–271.

Lang, M. H., & Lundholm, R. J. (1996). Corporate disclosure policy and analyst behavior. *Accounting Review*, *71*(4), 467–492.

la Porta, R., Florencio, L.-S., & Shleifer, A. (1999). Corporate ownership around the world. *The Journal of Finance*, *54*(2), 471–517. http://www.jstor.org/stable/2697717

la Porta, R., Lopez-de-Silanes, F., & Shleifer, A. (2002). Government ownership of banks. *The Journal of Finance*, *57*(1), 265–301.

la Porta, R., Lopez-de-Silanes, F., Shleifer, A., & Vishny, R. (2000). Investor protection and corporate governance. *Journal of Financial Economics*, *58*(1), 3–27.

Larcker, D. F., Richardson, S. A., & Tuna, A. (2007). How important is corporate governance? *The Accounting Review*, *82*(4), 963–1008.

Larcker, D. F., & Tayan, B. (2011). *Seven myths of corporate governance*. Rock center for corporate governance at Stanford University closer look series: Topics, issues and controversies in corporate governance no. CGRP-16.

Larmou, S., & Vafeas, N. (2010). The relation between board size and firm performance in firms with a history of poor operating performance. *Journal of Management & Governance*, *14*(1), 61.

Lazonick, W., & O'sullivan, M. (2000). Maximizing shareholder value: A new ideology for corporate governance. *Economy and Society*, *29*(1), 13–35.

Leftwich, R. W., Watts, R. L., & Zimmerman, J. L. (1981). Voluntary corporate disclosure: The case of interim reporting. *Journal of Accounting Research*, *19*(Suppl.), 50–77.

Lehn, K. M., Patro, S., & Zhao, M. (2009). Determinants of the size and composition of US corporate boards: 1935-2000. *Financial Management*, *38*(4), 747–780.

Leuz, C., & Wysocki, P. (2006). *Capital-market effects of corporate disclosures and disclosure regulation*. Research Study, Commissioned by the Task Force to Modernize Securities Legislation in Canada, 183–236.

Lev, B. (1992). Information disclosure strategy. *California Management Review*, *34*(4), 9–32.

Lewis, M. K. (2001). Islam and accounting. *Accounting Forum*, *25*(2), 103–127.

Lewis, M. K. (2005). Islamic corporate governance. *Review of Islamic Economics*, *9*(1), 5.

Li, D., Huang, M., Ren, S., Chen, X., & Ning, L. (2018). Environmental legitimacy, green innovation, and corporate carbon disclosure: Evidence from CDP China 100. *Journal of Business Ethics*, *150*(4), 1089–1104. https://doi.org/10.1007/s10551-016-3187-6

Li, J., Mangena, M., & Pike, R. (2012). The effect of audit committee characteristics on intellectual capital disclosure. *The British Accounting Review*, *44*(2), 98–110.

Li, Y., Armstrong, A., & Clarke, A. (2014). Relationships of corporate governance mechanisms and financial performance in Islamic banks: A meta-analysis. *Journal of Business Systems Governance and Ethics*, *9*(1), 50–63.

Liao, L., Luo, L., & Tang, Q. (2015). Gender diversity, board independence, environmental committee and greenhouse gas disclosure. *British Accounting Review*, *47*(4), 409–424. https://doi.org/10.1016/j.bar.2014.01.002

Licht, A. N., Goldschmidt, C., & Schwartz, S. H. (2005). Culture, law, and corporate governance. *International Review of Law and Economics*, *25*(2), 229–255. http://dx.doi.org/10.1016/j.irle.2005.06.005

Lim, S., Matolcsy, Z., & Chow, D. (2007). The association between board composition and different types of voluntary disclosure. *European Accounting Review*, *16*(3), 555–583. https://doi.org/10.1080/09638180701507155

Lin, S., Pizzini, M., Vargus, M., & Bardhan, I. R. (2011). The role of the internal audit function in the disclosure of material weaknesses. *The Accounting Review*, *86*(1), 287–323.

Lindblom, C. K. (1994, April). *The implications of organizational legitimacy for corporate social performance and disclosure*. Critical Perspectives on Accounting Conference, New York, NY, United States.

Love, I., & Klapper, L. F. (2002). *Corporate governance, investor protection, and performance in emerging markets*. The World Bank.

Maali, B., Casson, P., & Napier, C. (2006). Social reporting by Islamic banks. *Abacus*, *42*(2), 266–289.

Mace, M. L. (1971). *Directors: Myth and reality*. Harvard University Press.

Madi, H. K., Ishak, Z., & Manaf, N. A. A. (2014). The impact of audit committee characteristics on corporate voluntary disclosure. *Procedia – Social and Behavioral Sciences*, 164486–164492. https://doi.org/10.1016/j.sbspro.2014.11.106

Maher, M., & Andersson, T. (2002). Corporate governance: Effects on firm performance and economic growth. In *Convergence and diversity in corporate governance regimes and capital markets* (pp. 386–420). Oxford University Press.

Mak, Y. T., & Kusnadi, Y. (2005). Size really matters: Further evidence on the negative relationship between board size and firm value. *Pacific-Basin Finance Journal*, *13*(3), 301–318.

Makhija, A. K., & Patton, J. M. (2004). The impact of firm ownership structure on voluntary disclosure: Empirical evidence from Czech annual reports. *The Journal of Business*, *77*(3), 457–491. https://doi.org/10.1086/386526

Mallin, C., Farag, H., & Ow-Yong, K. (2014). Corporate social responsibility and financial performance in Islamic banks. *Journal of Economic Behavior & Organization*, *103*(Supplement), S21–S38.

Mamatzakis, E., & Bermpei, T. (2015). The effect of corporate governance on the performance of US investment banks. *Financial Markets, Institutions & Instruments*, *24*(2–3), 191–239.

Mangel, R., & Singh, H. (1993). Ownership structure, board relationships and CEO compensation in large US corporations. *Accounting and Business Research*, *23*(sup1), 339–350. https://doi.org/10.1080/00014788.1993.9729902

Mangena, M., & Pike, R. (2005). The effect of audit committee shareholding, financial expertise and size on interim financial disclosures. *Accounting and Business Research*, *35*(4), 327–349.

Manita, R., Bruna, M. G., Dang, R., & Houanti, L. (2018). Board gender diversity and ESG disclosure: Evidence from the USA. *Journal of Applied Accounting Research*, *19*(2), 206–224. https://doi.org/10.1108/JAAR-01-2017-0024

Mansell, S. F. (2013). An introduction to stakeholder theory. In *Capitalism, corporations and the social contract: A critique of stakeholder theory*. Cambridge University Press. https://doi.org/10.1017/CBO9781139058926.003

Mansour, W., & Bhatti, M. I. (2018). The new paradigm of Islamic corporate governance. *Managerial Finance*, *44*(5), 513–523.

Marshall, A. (1920). *Principles of economics* (8th ed.). Macmillan and Co.

Mason, C., & Simmons, J. (2014). Embedding corporate social responsibility in corporate governance: A stakeholder systems approach. *Journal of Business Ethics*, *119*(1), 77–86.

Matthews, B., & Ross, L. (2010). *Research method, Practical guide for social science*.

Md Zaini, S., Samkin, G., Sharma, U., & Davey, H. (2018). Voluntary disclosure in emerging countries: A literature review. *Journal of Accounting in Emerging Economies*, *8*(1), 29–65.

Meek, G. K., Roberts, C. B., & Gray, S. J. (1995). Factors influencing voluntary annual report disclosures by US, UK and continental European multinational corporations. *Journal of International Business Studies*, *26*(3), 555–572.

Meutia, I., & Devi, F. (2017). *Islamic social reporting in Islamic banking: Stakeholders theory perspective*. EDP Sciences. https://search.proquest.com/docview/1872790090?accountid=49936

Mihaela, D., & Iulian, S. (2012). Internal control and the impact on corporate governance, in Romanian listed companies. *Journal of Eastern Europe Research in Business & Economics*, *2012*, Article 676810, 1–11.

Milad, I. A. A., & Bicer, A. A. (2020). The association between board of directors characteristics and the level of voluntary disclosure: Evidence from listed banks in Borsa Istanbul. *Management & Economics Research Journal*, *2*(1), 166–185.

Millar, C. C. J. M., Eldomiaty, T. I., Choi, C. J., & Hilton, B. (2005). Corporate governance and institutional transparency in emerging markets. *Journal of Business Ethics*, *59*(1/2), 163–174. https://doi.org/10.2307/25123549

Mitchell, R. K., Agle, B. R., & Wood, D. J. (1997). Toward a theory of stakeholder identification and salience: Defining the principle of who and what really counts. *Academy of Management Review*, *22*(4), 853–886.

Mnif, Y., & Tahari, M. (2020). The effect of Islamic banks' specific corporate governance mechanisms on compliance with AAOIFI governance standards. *Journal of Islamic Accounting and Business Research*, *12*(1), 21–43.

Mohamed, E. K. A., & Basuony, M. A. K. (2015). Voluntary internet disclosure in four GCC countries: A study of attributes and determinants. *International Journal of Accounting and Finance*, *5*(2), 148–171.

Mohammed, A.-S., Shamsher, M. R., Taufiq, H. S. C., & Zulkarnain, M. S. (2011). Impact of internal audit function (IAF) on financial reporting quality (FRQ): Evidence from Saudi Arabia. *African Journal of Business Management*, *5*(27), 11189–11198.

Mollah, S., al Farooque, O., & Karim, W. (2012). Ownership structure, corporate governance and firm performance: Evidence from an African emerging market. *Studies in Economics and Finance*, *29*(4), 301–319.

Mollah, S., Hassan, M. K., al Farooque, O., & Mobarek, A. (2017). The governance, risk-taking, and performance of Islamic banks. *Journal of Financial Services Research*, *51*(2), 195–219.

Mollah, S., & Zaman, M. (2015). Shari'ah supervision, corporate governance and performance: Conventional vs. Islamic banks. *Journal of Banking & Finance*, 58418–58435. http://dx.doi.org/10.1016/j.jbankfin.2015.04.030

Morck, R., & Steier, L. (2005). The global history of corporate governance: An introduction. In R. K. Morck (Ed.), *A history of corporate governance around the world: Family business groups to professional managers* (pp. 1–64). University of Chicago Press.

Morris, R. D. (1987). Signalling, agency theory and accounting policy choice. *Accounting and Business Research*, *18*(69), 47–56.

Morrison, S. (2015). Oman's Islamic banking regulatory framework: The corporate governance of Shari'a compliance in a new jurisdiction. *Arab Law Quarterly*, *29*(2), 101–137. https://doi.org/10.1163/15730255-12341297

Mukhibad, H., Nurkhin, A., & Rohman, A. (2020). Corporate governance mechanism and risk disclosure by Islamic banks in Indonesia. *Banks and Bank Systems*, *15*(1), 1–11. https://doi.org/10.21511/bbs.15(1).2020.01

Mulyasari, W., & Mayangsari, S. (2020). Environmental management accounting, Islamic social reporting, and corporate governance mechanism on sharia-approved companies in Indonesia. *International Journal of Financial Research*, *11*(1), 284–292. https://doi.org/10.5430/IJFR.V11N1P284

Murphy, A., & Topyan, K. (2005). Corporate governance: A critical survey of key concepts, issues, and recent reforms in the US. *Employee Responsibilities and Rights Journal*, *17*, 75–89.

Musleh Al-Sartawi, A., & Reyad, S. (2018). Signaling theory and the determinants of online financial disclosure. *Journal of Economic and Administrative Sciences*, *34*(3), 237–247.

Muttakin, M. B., Khan, A., & Subramaniam, N. (2014). Do families shape corporate board structure in emerging economies? In *Corporate governance in emerging markets* (pp. 109–131). Springer.

Muttakin, M. B., Khan, A., & Subramaniam, N. (2015). Firm characteristics, board diversity and corporate social responsibility: Evidence from Bangladesh. *Pacific Accounting Review*, *27*(3), 353–372.

Naim, N. (2020). Islamic finance as a vehicle to promote improved intellectual property rights in the Gulf Cooperation Council. *Law and Development Review*, *13*(2), 407–442. https://doi.org/10.1515/ldr-2020-0050

Napier, C. (2009). Defining Islamic accounting: Current issues, past roots. *Accounting History*, *14*(1–2), 121–144.

Naser, K., Al-Khatib, K., & Karbhari, Y. (2002). Empirical evidence on the depth of corporate information disclosure in developing countries: The case of Jordan. *International Journal of Commerce and Management*, *12*(3/4), 122–155.

Natarajan, R. (2007). *Essays on disclosure and corporate governance*. Northwestern University.

Nathan, S. (2010). The performance of Shari'ah supervisory boards within Islamic financial institutions in the Gulf Cooperation Council countries. *Corporate Ownership & Control*, *8*(3), 124–136.

Nathan, S., & Ribière, V. (2007). From knowledge to wisdom: The case of corporate governance in Islamic banking. *Vine*, *37*(4), 471–483.

Nathan Garas, S. (2012). The conflicts of interest inside the Shari'a supervisory board. *International Journal of Islamic and Middle Eastern Finance and Management*, *5*(2), 88–105.

Nathan Garas, S., & Pierce, C. (2010). Shari'a supervision of Islamic financial institutions. *Journal of Financial Regulation and Compliance*, *18*(4), 386–407.

Neifar, S., & Jarboui, A. (2018). Corporate governance and operational risk voluntary disclosure: Evidence from Islamic banks. *Research in International Business and Finance*, 4643–4654.

Neifar, S., Salhi, B., & Jarboui, A. (2020). The moderating role of Shariah supervisory board on the relationship between board effectiveness, operational risk transparency and bank performance. *International Journal of Ethics and Systems*, *36*(3), 325–349. https://doi.org/10.1108/IJOES-09-2019-0155

Nerantzidis, M., & Tsamis, A. (2017). Going back to go forward: On studying the determinants of corporate governance disclosure. *Corporate Governance: The International Journal of Business in Society*, *17*(3), 365–402.

Neuman, W. L., & Robson, K. (2014). *Basics of social research*. Pearson Canada.

Nomran, N. M., Haron, R., & Hassan, R. (2018). Shari'ah supervisory board characteristics effects on Islamic banks' performance: Evidence from Malaysia. *International Journal of Bank Marketing*, *36*(2), 290–304.

Nugraheni, P., & Anuar, H. A. (2014). Implications of Shariah on the voluntary disclosure of Indonesian listed companies. *Journal of Financial Reporting and Accounting*, *12*(1), 76–98. https://search.proquest.com/docview/1660760371?accountid=49936

Nurkhin, A., Wahyudin, A., Mukhibad, H., Fachrurrozie, & Rohman, A. (2019). The determinants of Islamic governance disclosure: The case of Indonesian Islamic banks. *Banks and Bank Systems*, *14*(4), 143–152. https://doi.org/10.21511/bbs.14(4).2019.14

Obid, S. N. S., & Naysary, B. (2016). Toward a comprehensive theoretical framework for Shariah governance in Islamic financial institutions. In T. Harrison & E. Ibrahim (Eds.), *Islamic finance: Principles, performance and prospects* (pp. 10–31). Springer International Publishing. https://doi.org/10.1007/978-3-319-30918-7_2

O'Donovan, G. (1999). Managing legitimacy through increased corporate environmental reporting: An exploratory study. *Interdisciplinary Environmental Review*, *1*(1), 63–99.

O'Donovan, G. (2002). Environmental disclosures in the annual report: Extending the applicability and predictive power of legitimacy theory. *Accounting, Auditing & Accountability Journal*, *15*(3), 344–371.

Okaily, J. A., Dixon, R., & Salama, A. (2019). Corporate governance quality and premature revenue recognition: Evidence from the UK. *International Journal of Managerial Finance*, *15*(1), 79–99.

Omran, M. A., & El-Galfy, A. (2014). Theoretical perspectives on corporate disclosure: A critical evaluation and literature survey. *Asian Review of Accounting*, *22*(3), 257–286.

Organisation for Economic Cooperation and Development (OECD). (2004). The OECD principles of corporate governance. *Contaduría y Administración*, 1–66

Othman, R., & Ameer, R. (2015). Conceptualizing the duties and roles of auditors in Islamic financial institutions: What makes them different? *Humanomics*, *31*(2), 201–213.

Othman, R., Ishak, I. F., Arif, S. M. M., & Aris, N. A. (2014). Influence of audit committee characteristics on voluntary ethics disclosure. *Procedia – Social and Behavioral Sciences*, 145330–145342. https://doi.org/10.1016/j.sbspro.2014.06.042

Othman, R., Thani, A. M., & Ghani, E. K. (2009). Determinants of Islamic social reporting among top Shariah-approved companies in Bursa Malaysia. *Research Journal of International Studies*, *12*(10), 4–20.

Ousama, A. A., & Fatima, A. H. (2010). Voluntary disclosure by Shariah approved companies: An exploratory study. *Journal of Financial Reporting and Accounting*, *8*(1), 35–49.

Oussii, A. A., & Boulila Taktak, N. (2018). The impact of internal audit function characteristics on internal control quality. *Managerial Auditing Journal*, *33*(5), 450–469. https://doi.org/10.1108/MAJ-06-2017-1579

Owusu-Ansah, S. (1998). The impact of corporate attributes on the extent of mandatory disclosure and reporting by listed companies in Zimbabwe. *The International Journal of Accounting*, *33*(5), 605–631.

Park, J., & Kowal, S. (2013). Socially responsible investing 3.0: Understanding finance and environmental, social, and governance issues in emerging markets. *Georgetown Public Policy Review*, *18*(1), 17–18.

Patten, D. M. (1991). Exposure, legitimacy, and social disclosure. *Journal of Accounting and Public Policy*, *10*(4), 297–308.

Patton, M. Q. (1990a). *Qualitative evaluation and research methods*. SAGE Publications, Inc.

Phillips, R. (2003). *Stakeholder theory and organizational ethics*. Berrett-Koehler Publishers. http://site.ebrary.com/lib/qnl/docDetail.action?docID=10499936

Pigé, B. (2002). Stakeholder theory and corporate governance: The nature of the board information. *Management*, *7*(1), 1–17.

Platonova, E., Asutay, M., Dixon, R., & Mohammad, S. (2018). The impact of corporate social responsibility disclosure on financial performance: Evidence from the GCC Islamic banking sector. *Journal of Business Ethics*, *151*(2), 451–471.

Popa, A., Blidişel, R., & Bogdan, V. (2009). *Transparency and disclosure between theory and practice. A case study of Romania*. Proceedings of FIKUSZ'09 symposium for young researchers, pp. 173–183.

Presley, J. R., & Sessions, J. G. (1994). Islamic economics: The emergence of a new paradigm. *The Economic Journal*, *104*(424), 584–596.

Quttainah, M. A., Hasan, I., & Francis, B. (2012). *Four essays on the impact of Shari'ah (Islamic Law) as an institutional governance mechanism on organizational performance and managerial behavior*. Ann Arbor. https://search.proquest.com/docview/1082014064?accountid=49936

Rafay, A., & Farid, S. (2018). Shariah Supervisory Board Report (SSBR) in Islamic banks: An experimental study of investors' perception and behavior. *International Journal of Islamic and Middle Eastern Finance and Management*, *11*(2), 274–296.

Raffournier, B. (1995). The determinants of voluntary financial disclosure by Swiss listed companies. *European Accounting Review*, *4*(2), 261–280.

Rahman, A. R. A. (1998). Issues in corporate accountability and governance: An Islamic perspective. *American Journal of Islamic Social Sciences*, *15*(1), 55.

Rakiva, M. (2019). Firm-specific characteristics and voluntary disclosure reporting: An empirical research on listed companies of Bangladesh. *Journal of Accounting, Finance & Auditing Studies*, *5*(1), 298–317. https://doi.org/10.32602/jafas.2019.15

Rao, K., & Tilt, C. (2016). Board composition and corporate social responsibility: The role of diversity, gender, strategy and decision making. *Journal of Business Ethics*, *138*(2), 327–347. https://doi.org/10.1007/s10551-015-2613-5

Razek, M. A. (2014). The association between corporate social responsibility disclosure and corporate governance: A survey of Egypt. *Research Journal of Finance and Accounting*, *5*(1), 93–98.

Reuters. (2021). *Global Islamic finance forecast to grow as main markets recover – S&P*. Reuters. Retrieved September 24, 2022, from https://www.reuters.com/business/finance/global-islamic-finance-forecast-grow-main-markets-recover-sp-2021-05-03/

Ridwan, R., & Mayapada, A. G. (2020). Does sharia governance influence corporate social responsibility disclosure in Indonesia Islamic banks? *Journal of Sustainable Finance and Investment*. https://doi.org/10.1080/20430795.2020.1749819

Rini, R. (2014). The effect of audit committee role and sharia supervisory board role on financial reporting quality at Islamic banks in Indonesia. *Journal of Economics, Business & Accountancy Ventura*, *17*(1), 145–156.

Rizk, R., Dixon, R., & Woodhead, A. (2008). Corporate social and environmental reporting: A survey of disclosure practices in Egypt. *Social Responsibility Journal*, *4*(3), 306–323.

Rizk, R. R. (2006). *Corporate social and environmental disclosure practices: An international comparison of UK, Indian and Egyptian corporations*. Durham University.

Rizkiningsih, P., & Dewi, M. K. (2015). *Factors influencing Islamic social reporting (ISR) – An empirical study in Islamic Banks in Indonesia, Malaysia and the GCC countries*. Mehmet.

Ross, S. A. (1973). The economic theory of agency: The principal's problem. *The American Economic Review*, *63*(2), 134–139.

Ross, S. A. (1977). The determination of financial structure: The incentive-signalling approach. *The Bell Journal of Economics*, *8*(1), 23–40.

Rouf, M. A. (2012). The financial performance and corporate governance disclosure: A study in the annual reports of listed companies of Bangladesh. *Pakistan Journal of Commerce and Social Sciences*, *6*(1), 1–11. http://www.jespk.net/publications.php

Rouf, M. A. (2017). Firm-specific characteristics, corporate governance and voluntary disclosure in annual reports of listed companies in Bangladesh. *International Journal of Managerial and Financial Accounting*, *9*(3), 263–282.

Ruland, W., Tung, S., & George, N. E. (1990). Factors associated with the disclosure of managers' forecasts. *The Accounting Review*, *65*(3), 710–721.

Sacconi, L. (2012). *The economics of corporate social responsibility*. EconomEtica.

Sadiq, S., & Mushtaq, A. (2015). The role of Islamic finance in sustainable development. *Journal of Islamic Thought and Civilization*, *5*(1), 46–65.

Safieddine, A. (2009). Islamic financial institutions and corporate governance: New insights for agency theory. *Corporate Governance: An International Review*, *17*(2), 142–158.

Saha, A., & Akter, S. (2013). Corporate governance and voluntary disclosure practices of financial non-financial sector companies in Bangladesh. *Journal of Applied Management Accounting Research*, *11*(2), 45–61.

Said, R., Hj Zainuddin, Y., & Haron, H. (2009). The relationship between corporate social responsibility disclosure and corporate governance characteristics in Malaysian public listed companies. *Social Responsibility Journal*, *5*(2), 212–226.

Saidi, N., & Kumar, R. (2008). *Corporate Governance in the GCC*. Hawkamah Institute for Corporate Governance Paper, UAE.

Sakti, M. R. P., & Tareq, M. A. (2016). *Corporate governance from Islamic perspective: Review and synthesis from the literatures*. Innovation and management.

Salem, I. H., Ayadi, S. D., & Hussainey, K. (2019). Corporate governance and risk disclosure quality: Tunisian evidence. *Journal of Accounting in Emerging Economies*, *9*(4), 567–602. https://doi.org/10.1108/JAEE-01-2019-0005

Samaha, K., Dahawy, K., Hussainey, K., & Stapleton, P. (2012). The extent of corporate governance disclosure and its determinants in a developing market: The case of Egypt. *Advances in Accounting*, *28*(1), 168–178. http://dx.doi.org/10.1016/j.adiac.2011.12.001

Samaha, K., Khlif, H., & Hussainey, K. (2015). The impact of board and audit committee characteristics on voluntary disclosure: A meta-analysis. *Journal of International Accounting, Auditing and Taxation*, *24*, 13–28.

Sarens, G., Abdolmohammadi, M. J., & Lenz, R. (2012). Factors associated with the internal audit function's role in corporate governance. *Journal of Applied Accounting Research*, *13*(2), 191–204.

Sarker, M. A. A. (1999). Islamic banking in Bangladesh: Performance, problems, and prospects. *International Journal of Islamic Financial Services*, *1*(3), 15–36.
Sarstedt, M., Ringle, C. M., & Hair, J. F. (2021). Partial least squares structural equation modeling. In C. Homburg, M. Klarmann, & A. Vomberg (Eds.), *Handbook of market research* (pp. 587–632). Springer International Publishing.
Saunders, M., Lewis, P., & Thornhill, A. (2012). *Research methods for business students*. Pearson Education.
Schneider, A., & Scherer, A. G. (2015). Corporate governance in a risk society. *Journal of Business Ethics*, *126*(2), 309–323.
Sencal, H., & Asutay, M. (2020). Ethical disclosure in the Shari'ah annual reports of Islamic banks: Discourse on Shari'ah governance, quantitative empirics and qualitative analysis. *Corporate Governance: The International Journal of Business in Society*, *21*(1), 175–211.
Sengupta, P. (1998). Corporate disclosure quality and the cost of debt. *Accounting Review*, *73*(4), 459–474.
Shafii, Z., Salleh, S., & Shahwan, S. H. (2010). Management of Shariah non-compliance audit risk in the Islamic financial institutions via the development of Shariah compliance audit framework and Shariah audit programme. *Kyoto Bulletin of Islamic Area Studies*, *3*(2), 3–16.
Shafii, Z., Salleh, S., Zakaria, N., Hanefah, M. M., & Mokhtar, M. Z. (2014). Shariah audit certification contents: Views of regulators, Shariah committee, Shariah reviewers and undergraduate students. *International Journal of Economics and Finance*, *6*(5), 210–219.
Shahar, N. A., Nawawi, A., & Salin, A. S. A. P. (2020). Shari'a corporate governance disclosure of Malaysian IFIS. *Journal of Islamic Accounting and Business Research*, *11*(3), 845–868. https://doi.org/10.1108/JIABR-05-2016-0057
Shan, Y. G., Bhatti, M. I., & Tariq, A. R. (2015). The Islamic governance system and the institution of Hisbah. In M. I. Bhatti (Ed.), *Islamic corporate governance: An international perspective* (pp. 45–66). Routledge.
Shehata, N. (2014). Theories and determinants of voluntary disclosure. *Accounting and Finance Research (AFR)*, *3*(1), 38–47.
Shehata, N. F. (2013). How could board diversity influence corporate disclosure. *Corporate Board: Role, Duties & Composition*, *9*(3), 42–49.
Shehata, N. F. (2015). Development of corporate governance codes in the GCC: An overview. *Corporate Governance*, *15*(3), 315–338.
Shehata, N. F. (2017). The status and determinants of corporate governance disclosure: The case of the Gulf countries. *The Journal of Developing Areas*, *51*(4), 157–165.
Shi, Y., Magnan, M., & Kim, J.-B. (2012). Do countries matter for voluntary disclosure? Evidence from cross-listed firms in the US. *Journal of International Business Studies*, *43*(2), 143–165. http://www.jstor.org.ezphost.dur.ac.uk/stable/41408896
Shleifer, A., & Vishny, R. W. (1997). A survey of corporate governance. *The Journal of Finance*, *52*(2), 737–783.
Siddiqi, M. N. (2002). *The wisdom of prohibition of interest*. LaRiba annual meet at Los Angeles, CA, 192006.
Siddiqi, M. N. (2006a). Islamic banking and finance in theory and practice: A survey of state of the art. *Islamic Economic Studies*, *13*(2), 1–48.
Siddiqi, M. N. (2006b). *Shariah, economics and the progress of Islamic finance: The role of Shariah experts*. Concept paper presented at pre-forum workshop on select ethical and methodological issues in Shari'a-compliant finance, Cambridge, Massachusetts, USA.
Simpson, S. N. Y., Aboagye-Otchere, F., & Ahadzie, R. (2022). Assurance of environmental, social and governance disclosures in a developing country: Perspectives of regulators and quasi-regulators. *Accounting Forum*, *46*(2), 109–133.

Singhvi, S. S. (1967). *Corporate disclosure through annual reports in the USA and India* [Unpublished doctoral dissertation]. Graduate School of Business, Columbia University.

Singhvi, S. S., & Desai, H. B. (1971). An empirical analysis of the quality of corporate financial disclosure. *Accounting Review*, *46*(1), 129–138.

Skinner, D. J. (1994). Why firms voluntarily disclose bad news. *Journal of Accounting Research*, *32*(1), 38–60.

Smith, A. (1795). *Essays on philosophical subjects*. T. Cadell Jr. and W. Davies.

Smith, J., Haniffa, R., & Fairbrass, J. (2011). A conceptual framework for investigating 'capture' in corporate sustainability reporting assurance. *Journal of Business Ethics*, *99*(3), 425–439.

Smith, P. A. (2009). Gulf aims to take lead in corporate governance. *Middle East*, *396*, 52–56.

Solomons, D. (1989). *Guidelines for financial reporting standards*. Research Board of the Institute of Chartered Accountants in England and Wales.

Spence, M. (1973). Job market signaling. *The Quarterly Journal of Economics*, *87*(3), 355–374.

Spence, M. (2002). Signaling in retrospect and the informational structure of markets. *The American Economic Review*, *92*(3), 434–459.

Spitzeck, H., & Hansen, E. G. (2010). Stakeholder governance: How stakeholders influence corporate decision making. *Corporate Governance: The International Journal of Business in Society*, *10*(4), 378–391.

Srairi, S. (2015). Corporate governance disclosure practices and performance of Islamic banks in GCC countries. *Journal of Islamic Finance*, *4*(2), 1–17.

Srairi, S. (2019). Transparency and bank risk-taking in GCC Islamic banking. *Borsa Istanbul Review*, 19S64–19S74. https://doi.org/10.1016/j.bir.2019.02.001

Sridhar, V. R. (2022). An empirical study on the effectiveness of internal audit in corporate governance. *Management Accountant*, *57*(8), 89. https://www.proquest.com/scholarly-journals/empirical-study-on-effectiveness-internal-audit/docview/2700793365/se-2?accountid=49936

Ştefănescu, C. A. (2011). Disclosure and transparency in corporate governance codes – Comparative analysis with prior literature findings. *Procedia – Social and Behavioral Sciences*, *24*, 1302–1310. http://dx.doi.org/10.1016/j.sbspro.2011.09.056

Sternberg, E. (1997). The defects of stakeholder theory. *Corporate Governance: An International Review*, *5*(1), 3–10.

Stiglitz, J. E. (2000). The contributions of the economics of information to twentieth century economics. *The Quarterly Journal of Economics*, *115*(4), 1441–1478.

Suchman, M. C. (1995). Managing legitimacy: Strategic and institutional approaches. *Academy of Management Review*, *20*(3), 571–610.

Sudarma, M., Triyuwono, I., Ludigdo, U., & Meutia, I. (2010). *Qualitative approach to build the concept of social responsibility disclosures based on Shari'ah enterprise theory*. 1662860.

Sulaiman, M., & Willett, R. J. (2003). Using the Hofstede-Gray framework to argue normatively for an extension of Islamic corporate reports. *Malaysian Accounting Review*, *2*(1), 82–105.

Suleiman, N. M. (2000). Corporate governance in Islamic banks. *Társadalom és gazdaság Közép-és Kelet-Európában/Society and Economy in Central and Eastern Europe*, 98–116.

Sulub, S. A., Salleh, Z., & Hashim, H. A. (2020). Corporate governance, SSB strength and the use of internal audit function by Islamic banks: Evidence from Sudan. *Journal of Islamic Accounting and Business Research*, *11*(1), 152–167.

Ta, T. T., & Doan, T. N. (2022). Factors affecting internal audit effectiveness: Empirical evidence from Vietnam. *International Journal of Financial Studies*, *10*(2), 37. https://doi.org/10.3390/ijfs10020037

Tarraf, H. (2011). The role of corporate governance in the events leading up to the global financial crisis: Analysis of aggressive risk-taking. *Global Journal of Business Research*, *5*(4), 93–105.

Taymiyya, I. (1985). *Public Duties in Islam: The Institution of the Hisbah*, trans. *Mukhtar Holland*. Islamic Foundation.

Tessema, A. (2019). The impact of corporate governance and political connections on information asymmetry: International evidence from banks in the Gulf Cooperation Council member countries. *Journal of International Accounting, Auditing and Taxation*, 351–317. https://doi.org/10.1016/j.intaccaudtax.2019.05.001

Tilling, M. V. (2004). *Refinements in legitimacy theory in social and environmental accounting*. School of Commerce, Flinders University.

Tricker, B. (2015). *Corporate governance: Principles, policies, and practices*. Oxford University Press.

Trueman, B. (1986). Why do managers voluntarily release earnings forecasts? *Journal of Accounting and Economics*, *8*(1), 53–71.

Tumwebaze, Z., Bananuka, J., Kaawaase, T. K., Bonareri, C. T., & Mutesasira, F. (2022). Audit committee effectiveness, internal audit function and sustainability reporting practices. *Asian Journal of Accounting Research*, *7*(2), 163–181.

Turnbull, S. (1997). Corporate governance: Its scope, concerns and theories. *Corporate Governance: An International Review*, *5*(4), 180–205.

Ullah, H. (2014). Shari'ah compliance in Islamic banking: An empirical study on selected Islamic banks in Bangladesh. *International Journal of Islamic and Middle Eastern Finance and Management*, *7*(2), 182–199.

Ullah, S., Harwood, I. A., & Jamali, D. (2016). 'Fatwa Repositioning': The hidden struggle for Shari'a compliance within Islamic financial institutions. *Journal of Business Ethics*. https://doi.org/10.1007/s10551-016-3090-1

Umoren, A. O., Udo, E. J., & George, B. S. (2015). Environmental, social and governance disclosures: A call for integrated reporting in Nigeria. *Journal of Finance and Accounting*, *3*(6), 227–233.

Ungureanu, M. (2012). Models and practices of corporate governance worldwide. *CES Working Papers*, *4*(3a), 625–635.

Uyar, A., Kilic, M., & Bayyurt, N. (2013). Association between firm characteristics and corporate voluntary disclosure: Evidence from Turkish listed companies. *Intangible Capital*, *9*(4), 1080–1112.

Vadasi, C., Bekiaris, M., & Andrikopoulos, A. (2019a). Corporate governance and internal audit: An institutional theory perspective. *Corporate Governance: The International Journal of Business in Society*, *20*(1), 175–190.

Vafeas, N. (1999). Board meeting frequency and firm performance. *Journal of Financial Economics*, *53*(1), 113–142. http://dx.doi.org/10.1016/S0304-405X(99)00018-5

Vancil, R. F. (1987). *Passing the baton: Managing the process of CEO succession*. Harvard Business Review Press.

van Greuning, H., & Iqbal, Z. (2008). *Risk analysis for Islamic Banks*. The World Bank.

Verrecchia, R. E. (1983). Discretionary disclosure. *Journal of Accounting and Economics*, *5*, 179–194.

Verrecchia, R. E. (2001). Essays on disclosure. *Journal of Accounting and Economics*, *32*(1–3), 97–180.

Vitolla, F., Raimo, N., & Rubino, M. (2020). Board characteristics and integrated reporting quality: An agency theory perspective. *Corporate Social Responsibility and Environmental Management*, *27*(2), 1152–1163. https://doi.org/10.1002/csr.1879

Vural, D. (2018). Disclosure practices by family firms: Evidence from Swedish publicly listed firms. *Accounting in Europe*, 1–27.

Wahyuni, S., Pujiharto, & Rahayu, D. R. (2019). Islamic corporate governance index and Islamic social reporting disclosure index for enhancing firm value: An empirical study of Islamic banking in Indonesia. *International Journal of Innovation, Creativity and Change, 12*(1), 511–520. https://www.scopus.com/inward/record.uri?eid=2-s2.0-85086507986&partnerID=40&md5=cef65f78dd403936ae22f955f697504b

Wallace, R. S. O. (1987). *Disclosure of accounting information in developing countries: A case study of Nigeria.*

Wallace, R. S. O. (1988). Corporate financial reporting in Nigeria. *Accounting and Business Research, 18*(72), 352–362.

Wallace, R. S. O., & Naser, K. (1995). Firm-specific determinants of the comprehensiveness of mandatory disclosure in the corporate annual reports of firms listed on the stock exchange of Hong Kong. *Journal of Accounting and Public Policy, 14*(4), 311–368.

Wallace, R. S. O., Naser, K., & Mora, A. (1994). The relationship between the comprehensiveness of corporate annual reports and firm characteristics in Spain. *Accounting and Business Research, 25*(97), 41–53.

Wan Abdullah, W. A., Badak, K. G., & Stewart, J. (2014). *Corporate governance disclosure practices of Islamic banks: The case of Islamic banks in the Southeast Asian and the Gulf Cooperation Council region.* JIAR 2014.

Wan Abdullah, W. A., Percy, M., & Stewart, J. (2013). Shari'ah disclosures in Malaysian and Indonesian Islamic banks: The Shari'ah governance system. *Journal of Islamic Accounting and Business Research, 4*(2), 100–131.

Wan Abdullah, W. A., Percy, M., & Stewart, J. (2015). Determinants of voluntary corporate governance disclosure: Evidence from Islamic banks in the Southeast Asian and the Gulf Cooperation Council regions. *Journal of Contemporary Accounting & Economics, 11*(3), 262–279. http://dx.doi.org/10.1016/j.jcae.2015.10.001

Wang, M., & Hussainey, K. (2013). Voluntary forward-looking statements driven by corporate governance and their value relevance. *Journal of Accounting and Public Policy, 32*(3), 26–49. http://dx.doi.org/10.1016/j.jaccpubpol.2013.02.009

Wan-Hussin, W. N. (2009). The impact of family-firm structure and board composition on corporate transparency: Evidence based on segment disclosures in Malaysia. *The International Journal of Accounting, 44*(4), 313–333. http://dx.doi.org/10.1016/j.intacc.2009.09.003

Wardhany, N., & Arshad, S. (2012). *The role of Shariah board in Islamic banks: A case study of Malaysia, Indonesia, and Brunei Darussalam.* 2nd Isra Colloquium.

Watts, R. L., & Zimmerman, J. L. (1978). Towards a positive theory of the determination of accounting standards. *Accounting Review, 53*(1), 112–134.

Watts, R. L., & Zimmerman, J. L. (1983). Agency problems, auditing, and the theory of the firm: Some evidence. *The Journal of Law & Economics, 26*(3), 613–633.

Watts, R. L., & Zimmerman, J. L. (1986). *Positive accounting theory.* Prentice-Hall.

Weber, O. (2014). Environmental, social and governance reporting in China. *Business Strategy and the Environment, 23*(5), 303–317.

Wheeler, D., & Tiefelsdorf, M. (2005). Multicollinearity and correlation among local regression coefficients in geographically weighted regression. *Journal of Geographical Systems, 7*(2), 161–187.

Williamson, O. E. (1984). The economics of governance: Framework and implications. *Journal of Institutional and Theoretical Economics*, 195–223.

Williamson, O. E. (1988). Corporate finance and corporate governance. *The Journal of Finance, 43*(3), 567–591. http://www.jstor.org/stable/2328184

Wilmshurst, T. D., & Frost, G. R. (2000). Corporate environmental reporting: A test of legitimacy theory. *Accounting, Auditing & Accountability Journal, 13*(1), 10–26.

Wilson, R. (2006). Islam and business. *Thunderbird International Business Review, 48*(1), 109–123.

Wilson, R. (2012). *Legal, regulatory and governance issues in Islamic finance.* Edinburgh University Press.

Wiseman, J. (1982). An evaluation of environmental disclosures made in corporate annual reports. *Accounting, Organizations and Society*, *7*(1), 53–63.

Woertz, E. (2011). *Prospects of the banking and finance sector and the development of financial centers*. Gulf Research Center.

World Business Council for Sustainable Development. (1999). *Corporate social responsibility: Meeting changing expectations*. World Business Council for Sustainable Development.

Xu, F., & Akther, T. (2019). A partial least-squares structural equation modeling approach to investigate the audit expectation gap and its impact on investor confidence: Perspectives from a developing country. *Sustainability*, *11*(20), 5798.

Yaacob, H. (2012). *Issues and challenges of shari'ah audit in Islamic financial institutions: A contemporary view*. Proceedings of 3rd international conference on business and economics research.

Yermack, D. (1996). Higher market valuation of companies with a small board of directors. *Journal of Financial Economics*, *40*(2), 185–211. http://dx.doi.org/10.1016/0304-405X(95)00844-5

Young, M. N., Peng, M. W., Ahlstrom, D., Bruton, G. D., & Chen, G. (2008). Corporate governance in emerging economies: A review of the principal–principal perspective. *Journal of Management Studies*, *45*(1), 196–220.

Yussof, S. A. (2013). Prospects of a Shariah audit framework for Islamic financial institutions in Malaysia. *Islam and Civilisational Renewal (ICR)*, *4*(1), 97–108.

Yusoff, W. F. W., & Alhaji, I. A. (2012). Insight of corporate governance theories. *Journal of Business and Management*, *1*(1), 52–63.

Zaher, T. S., & Kabir Hassan, M. (2001). A comparative literature survey of Islamic finance and banking. *Financial Markets, Institutions & Instruments*, *10*(4), 155–199.

Zainuldin, M. H., Lui, T. K., & Yii, K. J. (2018). Principal-agent relationship issues in Islamic banks: A view of Islamic ethical system. *International Journal of Islamic and Middle Eastern Finance and Management*, *11*(2), 297–311.

Zeghal, D., Mouelhi, R., & Louati, H. (2007). An analysis of the determinants of research & development voluntary disclosure by Canadian firms. *Irish Accounting Review*, *14*(2), 49–76.

Zhang, Y., & Wiersema, M. F. (2009). Stock market reaction to CEO certification: The signaling role of CEO background. *Strategic Management Journal*, *30*(7), 693–710.

Zirman, Basri, Y. M., & Fitriasari, R. (2019). Shariah governance and its implication on Shariah bank performance. *International Journal of Scientific and Technology Research*, *8*(10), 3744–3757. https://www.scopus.com/inward/record.uri?eid=2-s2.0-85074714365&partnerID=40&md5=df65e8aea46c95c8aac30058485a2625

Zou, J. (2019). On the role of internal audit in corporate governance. *American Journal of Industrial and Business Management*, *9*(01), 63.

Zubairu, U. M., Sakariyau, O. B., & Dauda, C. K. (2011). Social reporting practices of Islamic banks in Saudi Arabia. *International Journal of Business and Social Science*, *2*(23), 110–118.

Index

Printed and bound by CPI Group (UK) Ltd, Croydon, CR0 4YY

05/10/2026

14975121-0001